Teaching and Researching Translation

Second edition

Basil Hatim

PEARSON

Harlow, England • London • New York • Boston • San Francisco • Toronto • Sydney
Auckland • Singapore • Hong Kong • Tokyo • Seoul • Taipei • New Delhi
Cape Town • São Paulo • Mexico City • Madrid • Amsterdam • Munich • Paris • Milan

Pearson Education Limited
Edinburgh Gate
Harlow
Essex CM20 2JE
United Kingdom
Tel: +44(0)1279 623623
Fax: +44(0)1279 431059
Website: www.pearson.com/uk

———————

First published in Great Britain in 2001
Second edition published 2013

Pearson Education is not responsible for the content of third-party internet sites.

ISBN 978-1-4082-9763-6

British Library Cataloguing-in-Publication Data
A CIP catalogue record for this book is available from the British Library

Library of Congress Cataloging-in-Publication Data
A CIP catalog record for this book is available from the Library of Congress

10 9 8 7 6 5 4 3 2 1
16 15 14 13 12

Set in 11/13pt Janson Text by 35
Printed in Malaysia (CTP-VVP)

Teaching and Researching Translation

APPLIED LINGUISTICS IN ACTION

General Editors:

Christopher N. Candlin and David R. Hall

Books published in this series include:

Contents

General Editors' Preface

Applied Linguistics in Action, as its name suggests, is a Series which focuses on the issues and challenges to teachers and researchers in a range of fields in Applied Linguistics and provides readers and users with the tools they need to carry out their own practice-related research.

The books in the Series provide the reader with clear, up-to-date, accessible and authoritative accounts of their chosen field within Applied Linguistics. Starting from a map of the landscape of the field, each book provides information on its main ideas and concepts, competing issues and unsolved questions. From there readers can explore a range of practical applications of research into those issues and questions, and then take up the challenge of undertaking their own research, guided by the detailed and explicit research guides provided. Finally, each book has a section which provides a rich array of resources, information sources and further reading, as well as a key to the principal concepts of the field.

Questions the books in this innovative Series ask are those familiar to all teachers and researchers, whether very experienced, or new to the fields of Applied Linguistics.

- What does research tell us, what doesn't it tell us, and what should it tell us about the field? How is the field mapped and landscaped? What is its geography?
- How has research been applied and what interesting research possibilities does practice raise? What are the issues we need to explore and explain?

- What are the key researchable topics that practitioners can undertake? How can the research be turned into practical action?
- Where are the important resources that teachers and researchers need? Who has the information? How can it be accessed?

Each book in the Series has been carefully designed to be as accessible as possible, with built-in features to enable readers to find what they want quickly and to home in on the key issues and themes that concern them. The structure is to move from practice to theory and back to practice in a cycle of development of understanding of the field in question.

Each of the authors of books in the Series is an acknowledged authority, able to bring broad knowledge and experience to engage teachers and researchers in following up their own ideas, working with them to build further on *their* own experience.

The first editions of books in this series have attracted widespread praise for their authorship, their design, and their content, and have been widely used to support practice and research. The success of the series, and the realization that it needs to stay relevant in a world where new research is being conducted and published at a rapid rate, have prompted the commissioning of his second edition. This new edition has been thoroughly updated, with accounts of research that has appeared since the first edition and with the addition of other relevant additional material. We trust that students, teachers and researchers will continue to discover inspiration in these pages to underpin their own investigations.

Chris Candlin & David Hall
General Editors

Author's acknowledgements

Writing a book of this kind inevitably involves the participation of many people. I should in particular like to thank Chris Candlin and David Hall for their insightful comments throughout the process of completing this work in its two editions.

A number of colleagues have my gratitude for commenting on individual chapters: Mona Baker, Ron Buckley, Ann Chebbo, John Cleary, Peter Crompton, Teresa Crompton, Charlene Constable, Ali Darwish, Peter Fallon, John Laffling, Margaret Lang, Ian Mason, Anthony Pym and Gavin Watterson.

The following institutions deserve a special mention for their support in providing me with the time and facilities which made this work possible: Heriot-Watt University, Edinburgh; King Fahd School of Translation, Tangiers; American University of Sharjah, United Arab Emirates, where I have been based since 1999.

Last but not least, I should like to express my heartfelt thanks to former and current editors at Pearson Education: Elizabeth Mann, Casey Mein, Verina Pettigrew, Alex Whyte, Jessica Harrison, Kate Ahl, Sarah Turpie and Kathy Auger, for seeing this work through the various stages of production.

About this book

Re-writing the research agenda

An interesting thread runs through the discourse found in many introductory books on translation studies. There is a tendency to use linguistics as a scapegoat – as something to blame for the ills that have befallen us in the study of translation. The argument usually lists the weaknesses of such paradigms as structural linguistics and trans-formational grammar (which admittedly leave a great deal to be desired as linguistic theories, let alone as translation models), only to conclude that linguistics has all but failed us.

This book suggests that the conceptual map of translation studies could be drawn differently and perhaps in more helpful ways. The script we will be working to is inspired by a simple yet telling coincidence. The year is 1955, and the place is Harvard. Noam Chomsky was lecturing on his theory of transformational generative grammar, and the linguists and psychologists – and a few translation theorists – were buzzing with excitement. In the same year, the British philosopher John Austin was also at Harvard to present the prestigious William James Lectures. In the course of these lectures, Austin outlined a programme for what was to have an enduring influence for generations to come – the study of language as **Action**, and language use as 'doing things with words'. Pragmatics has had a strong impact on a wide range of disciplines, including linguistics and translation.

The first question we must then ask of any linguistics-oriented model of translation is: What kind of linguistics is being applied? Yet, it is remarkable how all criticism of the role of linguistics in the study of translation seems to have focused on abstract and esoteric work divorced from practical considerations, and to ignore the contribution of those trends in linguistics which are anything but abstract and esoteric.

This book takes a close look at this inconsistency and asks: Would the conceptual map of translation studies have looked different, and linguistics perhaps less uninviting, had we been more discriminate of the kinds of 'linguistics' that were on offer? Would we have offered the translator more effective guidance had we paid more attention to such forward-looking models of linguistics description as pragmatics and to what these paradigms can do and have actually done for the translator? These are some of the questions that this book will attempt to answer.

Overview

Teaching and Researching Translation is divided into four major sections. Section I (Chapters 1–6) outlines the historical and conceptual background to translation studies, and highlights key issues in translation research. The various strands work together to provide answers for such questions as:

- *Which research is informed by which paradigm?*
- *What does research into the various paradigms tell us?*
- *What does it not tell us?*
- *What should it tell us?*

There seems to be a pattern to the way translation studies and research seem to have evolved. No matter which way the wind of fashion blows, translating or the study of translation has always and inescapably been seen in terms of the two extremes 'literal' vs 'free'. Thus, such requirements as whether it is the 'letter' or the 'spirit' of the original that can or needs to be reproduced in the translation have regularly been used as a basis for what have come to be well-known distinctions such as communicative vs semantic translation, or covert vs overt translation. In mainstream translation studies, distinctions such as the literal/free have also been influential in defining other aspects of translation method or strategy, and familiar categories such as 'interlinear' translation at one end, and 'imitation' at the other, are conceived within such frameworks. Distance from or adherence to the source text thus seems to be an important motif and one that has underpinned significant developments in the discipline. This metaphor is used as a main organising principle in this book.

Section II (Chapters 7–13) focuses on how the perspectives outlined in Section I have yielded operational frameworks for research. In this book, researching the practice is seen in terms of three major aspects of how texts function and how they get translated:

- Textual **register**, informed by a language use/user perspective.
- The **pragmatics** of intentionality, acceptability and related standards of textuality.
- Language as a social-**semiotic** impinging on micro- and macro-units of interaction and involving what users of language in social life actually do with **texts**, **genres** and **discourses**.

In this section, the questions asked are:

- *How has research on the ground been and how can research best be applied?*
- *What interesting research possibilities does practice raise?*

Section III (Chapters 14 and 15) presents current practical applications of translation research: How the areas represented by the three facets of translation research (register, pragmatics, semiotics) have shaped up in terms of practitioner action research projects (both carried out and yet to be carried out). With this, the question becomes:

- *What are the important researchable issues and topics that practitioners can research in an action research way?*

Section IV provides links and resources for translators and is supplemented by a glossary of basic terms. This will end a journey through a rather difficult terrain. Indeed, the case may not have been overstated when Ivor Richards (cited in Holmes, 1988: 73) once described translation as 'very probably the most complex type of event yet produced in the evolution of the cosmos'.

I Translation studies: History, basic concepts and key issues in research

Chapter 1

Translation studies and applied linguistics

This chapter will . . .

- describe how applied linguistics can contribute to the study of translating and translations;
- set the theory–practice debate against the background of pioneering work on educating reflective practitioners;
- propose the notion of practitioner/**action research** as an ideal methodology with which to study translation, and thus question the assumption that theory and practice are separate and distinct;
- introduce translation studies in terms of the way the subject has evolved as an interdisciplinary endeavour.

Translation studies, the discipline which concerns itself with the theory and practice of translation, has come of age and is maturing rapidly. Nevertheless, a number of obstacles remain and will have to be overcome if the discipline is to develop further.

To begin with, activities such as translating or translation teaching have, until fairly recently, been kept separate from 'research' into these and related issues. The polarisation is historical and is evidence of the misleading demarcation lines that are often too readily drawn between 'theoretician' and 'practitioner' in many disciplines. Theory and practice are ultimately complementary and, particularly in a field such as translation, the distinction needs to be re-examined.

Another obstacle in the development of translation studies has to do with a distinction also traditionally maintained between 'linguistics' and the range of disciplines within which translation is studied (e.g. cultural studies). Like the theory vs practice distinction, this division has militated against fostering an atmosphere of interdisciplinarity in the study of translation as an important form of intercultural communication.

To set the scene for this survey of how translation studies has evolved, the first question addressed is: *In what ways can applied linguistics, with its many and varied orientations, inform translation research?*

1.1   Applied linguistics and the translation analyst

> **Quote 1.1**
>
> Translation is characteristically purposeful as a profession; it has targets and goals. It is done on behalf of sponsors. It lacks (except in rare cases) the leisure of reflective consideration about the researchable questions of why like this, why here. Nonetheless, translators as applied linguists do have certain obligations to the furthering of our understanding of language and our ability to explain the acts of communicating in which we are continually engaged.
>
> Christopher Candlin (1991)

In applied linguistics, it is now generally accepted that what is applied in teaching or research is not so much knowledge about language as it is a way of investigating language. The identity of *what* exactly is being applied tends to be of secondary importance, compared with *how* the application might best be effected and *for what purpose*. There is still a great deal of uncertainty among linguists as to what the subject matter of their discipline is. Yet, this has not stood in the way of applied linguists using linguistics in the search for solutions to a wide range of practical problems in fields as varied as language teaching and speech pathology.

From an applied linguistic perspective, it is thus the *how* and, perhaps more important, the *why* of an application that should underpin any serious attempt to deal with translation. In this applied sense, a range of characteristics generally associated with sound scientific practice would be adhered to: objectivity, comprehensiveness, explicitness, precision.

Theoretical statements would also be valued, taking into account not only the 'facts' which one's methodology uncovers, but also how the facts may best be systematised and explained.

Applications conducted along these lines invariably seek to solve a problem. In practice, however, the notion of 'problem' is not so straightforward. In attempting to deal with a perceived problem, the first complication likely to arise relates to *responsibility*: Who decides whether there is a problem in the first place?

In this respect, reference to the practitioner or learner is standard practice in applied linguistics. In the first instance, these consumers of linguistic knowledge can reveal through tests, experiments and so on, what the problem is. The problem would then be viewed within a particular framework that 'linguistics' as the discipline applied makes available. Such procedures are being increasingly adopted in translation studies where traditionally armchair theoreticians have been the first to pronounce on problems of translation.

But no sooner is the issue of 'responsibility' resolved than another arises, this time relating to *constituency*. Language or translation analysts constantly come up against the question of whether groupings such as 'practitioners' or 'learners' are sufficiently homogeneous to yield meaningful generalisations about what the problem is. The issue at stake is complex and has a great deal to do with the varying degrees of *awareness* that members of a professional group bring to a task.

This 'awareness' factor influences the process of problem solving considerably. In terms of level of awareness regarding the nature of the problems encountered, two types of practitioner are generally recognised. Among trainees or in the workplace, for instance, there are those whose training has focused on such issues as the relevance of theoretical statements and the need for abstract models of description. However, there will also be those whose apprenticeship has all but excluded the benefits of a training that is theoretically oriented. The two groups will have different notions of what constitutes a 'problem', and this will make generalisations difficult to sustain.

In applied linguistics, one way of dealing with this disparity has been to use research techniques such as comparative data obtained from professional practitioners or experienced trainees vs novices and beginners (with one or the other grouping serving as a 'control group'). Recent work in the field of translation studies has adopted similar approaches. As a long-term solution and in order to overcome the difficulties inherent in dividing practitioners or learners into such neat categories as 'aware' and 'unaware', it is important to recognise that, prior to embarking on any analysis, more could be done through *awareness-raising* of entire population samples (with control groups deprived of such input). That is, there has to be a realisation that a problem is 'real' and that it is recognised as a problem by the majority of those affected by it. Unless such a consensus is reached, the purpose of the analysis will remain unclear. Thus, as a first step, the different parties concerned need to be alerted to the problem and sensitised to its side effects. Convincing explanations would have to be offered for why the problem exists in the first place, and only then might plausible descriptions of a problem be provided and effective solutions worked out.

At this point, the question of *how* the application should be effected becomes relevant. Several possible courses of action would be open to those involved. An *intellectual appeal* might be made to those professionals who are genuinely interested in placing what they do best on a more solid footing. *Self-criticism* should also be encouraged within the professional group through looking more systematically at the kind of difficulties encountered and the practices which engender them. This process of encouraging 'practitioner research' has come to be known as **action research**.

An intellectual appeal with the aim of raising critical awareness and thereby sensitising professionals to the nature of the problems encountered is thus one major course of action in any attempt to link up with those affected by the application of particular disciplines to the various domains of professional practice (e.g. linguistics applied to the study of literary translation, or **discourse** analysis to medical gate-keeping encounters). Such appeals can take many forms. An overriding consideration, however, is how best to communicate relevant research findings to practitioners largely unaware of what the problem is, and how far feedback received from these professionals, once engaged, can set the agenda for further research. In their discourse analytic work, for example, Roberts and Sarangi (2003: 338) were concerned with 'how discourse-based findings are fed back to practitioner professionals and the extent to which the feedback received from the latter can set the agenda for further discourse analytic work'. Drawing on their consultancy work with the Royal College of General Practitioners, the authors focused on those discourse-based findings relating to the specific context of medical gate-keeping encounters, and identified three interactionally grounded modes of talk: professional, institutional and personal experience. These theoretical, discourse analytic categories were then discussed with the practitioners concerned, and subsequently used as parameters with which to ascertain whether such distinctions were actually picked up and ultimately used as a heuristic for dealing with practical issues.

Concept 1.1 **Reflexivity**

Recognition of the dialectical relationship between 'research' and 'action', and a focus on the empowerment of practitioners to develop and execute their own research, are two of the ways in which unhelpful dichotomies such as 'theory' vs 'practice' may be reassessed. These tired clichés would be replaced by *reflexivity* as a more dynamic process and one in which theory and practice interact and mutually enrich one another. In adopting such a stance, however, we need to guard against inadvertently promoting yet another undesirable dichotomy, this time involving **action research** or research done by practitioners vs 'pure research' as the mainstay of **technical rationality**.

In this theory–practice dialectic of attempting to raise awareness and in the process engage practitioners in the identification and solution of problems, the mode is certainly both 'reflexive' and 'visionary' (i.e. professional groups tend to intellectualise what they do best and to develop a professional vision which will have its own discourses, practices and view of the world). But as Candlin and Sarangi (2001: 241) incisively point out, 'such a dialectic interprets reflexivity not merely as "reflection", nor simply as "action", [but also as a] critical appraisal of knowledge claims *and* an evaluation of effective action'. That is, reflexivity seen merely in terms of 'reflection' followed by 'action' would simply be too mechanical a process to capture the intricacies and dynamics of real-life problem solutions. To be purposeful, reflection must be honed with a healthy dose of criticalness, and action tempered with a much-needed evaluativeness. This echoes the general thrust of arguments developed in the 1970s and 1980s by American education theorist Donald Schön in his pioneering work on 'reflective practice'.

1.2 Reflective practice

Quote 1.2

Reflection is an important human activity in which people recapture their experience, think about it, mull it over and evaluate it. It is this working with experience that is important in learning.

Boud et al. (1985: 19)

Donald Schön was among the first to call into question such time-honoured distinctions as theory vs practice, and technical rationality vs craft knowledge. In his seminal book *The Reflective Practitioner* (1983), Schön argued that, in developing professional excellence, practitioners need to reconsider the role of traditionally highly valued 'technical knowledge' (the mainstay of 'technical rationality'), and to reinstate largely undervalued 'artistry' (knowledge as 'artful doing'). It is only then, Schön stressed, that the dilemma 'rigor' vs 'relevance' may be resolved, with the practitioner beginning to exhibit not only 'expertise' but also 'criticalness', as crucial elements of his or her professional portfolio. Reflective practice, then, is a process of reflecting on action as part of continuous, lifelong learning (Schön, 1983). In this way, reflective practice would entail 'paying critical attention to the practical values and theories which inform everyday actions, by examining practice reflectively and reflexively. This leads to developmental insight' (Bolton, 2010: xix).

In addition to the rationality and artistry issue, the concept of reflective practice is underpinned by another important distinction which Schön had earlier established – namely, between 'single loop' and 'double-loop' learning. Single-loop learning is the predominant mode among practitioners who, even after an error has been identified and corrected, continue uncritically to use current strategies and techniques. Double-loop learning, on the other hand, requires that current strategies and techniques be continuously reassessed for efficacy and that new problem-solution 'framings' be adopted even when seemingly similar situations arise (Argyris and Schön, 1978).

Another crucial set of concepts promoted by Schön relates to 'reflection-in-action' and 'reflection-on-action'. Reflection-in-action involves the ability of a practitioner to 'think on their feet', hence the label 'felt-knowing' (Walkerden, 2009). It is a form of intuitive knowledge which enables practitioners, when faced with a professional challenge, essentially to connect with their feelings, emotions and prior experiences, including attending to 'theories in use'. Reflection-on-action, on the other hand, is by definition post-experience, involving practitioners stepping back from the situation at hand and to analyse their reaction, explore the reasons for the way they reacted the way they did, and assess the consequences of their actions. This is usually carried out though a documented reflection of the situation.

Can the translator or interpreter be trained to become a reflective practitioner in this Schönian sense of reflective practice? This question will occupy us in Chapter 13 on the pedagogy of translation, and the answer is a resounding 'yes'. Like all practitioners, translators ought to be able to study their own 'translatory' behaviour and 'translational' practice (Koller, 1995), to determine what works best. True, translating is a complex phenomenon, and there is not one 'right' approach. But reflection is not about one-track choices of 'right' or 'wrong' – far from it. We could indeed reflect on different versions, different modes and different models, comparatively assessing the merits and demerits of a particular strategy, and in the process reshaping past and current experiences in a manner that could only lead to improved practices.

Schön's reflection-in-action assists practitioners in making professional knowledge systematically gained from experience a conscious part of decision making. But, to achieve this, we must make a leap from a knowledge base of discrete skills to a stage where skills are there only to be modified to suit specific contexts and situations, and eventually to give rise to newer and more effective strategies. In implementing a process of reflective practice, translators, for example, will be able to move themselves beyond existing models and theories, to a mode of practice that is open-ended, yet not entirely unpredictable or uncontrollable. That is, while translators should be encouraged to resist establishing a 'culture of control' and instead to become 'reflective practitioners', they should at the same time be empowered to deal in a disciplined and methodical manner with what is essentially a fluid and dynamic environment. In short, like all practitioners, translators can, through reflective practice, help themselves develop personally and professionally. It is surely not too much to ask oneself or one's trainees to keep a journal, solicit feedback, see experiences objectively, or take time at the end of each experience to reflect-on-actions taken or not taken.

1.3   Action research: The theory–practice cycle

Quote 1.3

If knowledge is tentative and contingent upon **context**, rather than absolute, then I believe that practitioners, rather than being consumers of other people's research, should adopt a research orientation to their own classrooms.

David Nunan (1992)

As indicated above, research in translation or interpreting and practical pursuits such as the teaching of these skills, have been pulling in somewhat different directions. Research has generally been seen as a matter of 'reflection', whereas activities such as teaching, translating or interpreting are taken to be the 'real action'.

From the perspective of practice-driven action research, however, it is advocated that an appreciation of what the problem is, why it needs to be solved, and how it may best be solved, can reverse the trend of treating practitioners as mere consumers of research. As work by Donald Schön and other writers on 'reflective practice' has made amply clear, the practitioner would be viewed as someone who is in fact heavily involved in the determination of the problem or 'puzzle'. Furthermore, such a practitioner/researcher would be seen as someone who possesses not only 'craft knowledge' but also **analytical knowledge**, and more. This would ensure that problems are properly identified and appropriate solutions proposed and duly explained. Solutions can never be definitive, but once action research is underway, the research cycle of practice–research–practice would have certainly been set in motion.

The kind of practitioner research proposed here and throughout this book couples the knowledge which practitioners have with their own immediate concerns, and yields:

> A form of self-reflective enquiry undertaken by participants in social situations in order to improve the rationality and justice of their own practices, and the situations in which the practices are carried out.
>
> (Carr and Kemmis, 1986: 162)

This is a standard definition of action research: an initial idea, followed by fact-finding, action plan, implementation, monitoring and revision, amended plan and so on (McDonough and McDonough, 1997). The cycle ensures that research is participant-driven, reflective, collaborative and of the type which leads to change. The change will impinge not only on how knowledge is acquired, but also on the **context** that motivates the enquiry in the first place. The basic premise underlying this new research focus on 'reflective practice' is that the practitioner may now be seen as someone with a portfolio of skills which includes, most notably, an enquiring mind.

Translation studies has been rather slow to interact with these developments, a situation that has been exacerbated by the polarisation of theory and practice cast in terms of two quite distinct and incompatible **universes of discourse**. Recently, however, such stark distinctions have been fast disappearing and the 'action' vs 'reflection' dichotomy is being increasingly called into question. Translation studies is genuinely seeking to promote the stance that research is not only something done *to* or *on* practitioners, but is also something done *by* practitioners. Nowadays, it is quite common to have practising or trainee translators, or indeed teachers of translation, engage in the identification of interesting problem areas, the choice of suitable investigative procedures, and the pursuit of research aimed at providing answers to a range of practical questions. There is a growing awareness that adopting a reflective attitude to the practical concerns of translators or translation teachers can only promote a healthy critical distance from the real-time process of the action itself.

1.4   Translation studies: A house of many rooms

Quote 1.4

It is our firm conviction that translation is 'a house of many rooms', and that these different rooms are often simply different discourses and perspectives on a common object of interest – translation.

Albrecht Neubert and Gregory Shreve (1992)

There remains a great deal of uncertainty over the status of translation studies as a discipline. From an applied linguistic perspective, this has had mainly to do with the extent to which translators are prepared to take an interest in theories of language and communication, and the extent to which linguists are willing to recognise that the translation process, not only the product, is worthy of attention.

This tension between linguists and translators has not completely disappeared, but the general picture can no longer be painted in such stark terms. To begin with, 'linguistics' has considerably broadened its scope. More and more linguists are embracing the challenge which the study of translation presents, and are using translation as a testing ground for their theories. Similarly, the majority of translation practitioners are now more and more conversant with theories and models of translation, and are particularly sensitive to issues raised not only in the science of language, but also further afield – in literary theory, the study of culture and society, and so on. For example, translation practitioners (and theorists of all persuasions) are becoming increasingly more interested in what linguistic knowledge about the nature and **function** of *texts* has to offer, and in the research methodology associated with the fairly new discipline of 'text linguistics'.

One obvious manifestation of the success of translation studies is the flourishing of translator and interpreter training as an academic pursuit in its own right. More and more graduate programmes are being set up around the world and international conferences on training issues are being organised regularly, with almost every country now having its own professional association.

Translation studies has also generated the intellectual excitement needed to attract the attention of scholars working in a variety of disparate fields. In many instances, the new discipline has come to play the larger role in this collaboration. For example, in the 'comparative' domain, it has even been suggested that 'comparative literature' or 'comparative linguistics' be considered branches of 'translation studies', and not the other way round.

Furthermore, with the help of a publishing industry interested in the new subject, translation theorists are publishing widely and interacting with each other much more than ever before. Research in translation studies has barely begun: hundreds of books have yet to be written, and hundreds of theoretical texts in a variety of disciplines have yet to be discovered and translated. Even so, the field is already booming, and new books and monographs are being produced at such a rate that it is becoming increasingly more difficult to keep abreast of the way thinking about translation is evolving (see Chapter 16 on 'resources').

In short, the study of translation is assuming a high profile, and what is remarkable is that this is happening not only in the traditional centres of learning in the West, but also worldwide. This has heightened awareness of cross-cultural issues and has thus enriched the debate: less individualistic Eurocentrism and more determination to look afresh at various translation traditions, spanning both East and West and centuries of translation practice (Baker and Saldanha, 2009). This is alongside an interdisciplinarity which has made it possible to see translation as a textual practice and translations as meaningful records of communicative and cultural events. Professional practice has followed suit and the old prescriptive discussions of translation have become a thing of the past, as has the tendency to devise arbitrary rules for the production of 'correct' translations.

Concomitant with this plurality of approach, a diversity of aims and objectives is also in evidence. These range from raising the profile of translators, to recognising the need to develop more powerful machine translation systems. The new focus is counterbalanced by research programmes actively pursuing purely theoretical issues relating to the product, process and **function** of translation.

Translating is thus a multi-faceted activity, and there is room for a variety of perspectives. This might conceivably be seen as the fragmentation of the discipline, but evidence points the other way. The discipline is consolidating and has all but forgotten its humble, slightly diffident beginnings. Consider how 'cultural studies' and 'text linguistics', each in its own way, have recently begun to address the issue of **ideology** in translation, to take but one example of a current, vigorous debate (Fawcett and Munday, 2009).

Concept 1.2   **Discourse and ideology**

Within **critical linguistics**, all use of language is seen as reflecting a set of users' assumptions which are closely bound up with individual and collective attitudes and perceptions. Consequently, *ideology* has been defined as the tacit assumptions, beliefs and value systems which are shared collectively by social groups (Simpson, 1993). Closely associated with this has been the use of the term *discourse* as institutionalised modes of speaking and writing which give expression to particular attitudes towards areas of socio-cultural activity (Kress, 1985).

In the theory and practice of translation, the 'cultural turn' has shifted the focus to the study of ideology as a shaping force (e.g. Bassnett and Lefevere, 1990a) and, within such trends as the **gendered** practices of feminist translation, to translation as 're-writing' (e.g. von Flotow, 1997). This widening of scope has run parallel with what may be labelled the 'contextual turn' in linguistics (e.g. Beaugrande, 1978). By the mid-1980s, linguists had already made inroads into the study of text in **context** and considered the implications which this orientation might have for the study of translation (e.g. Hatim and Mason, 1990).

Regarding the specific issue of ideological meaning in discourse, two complementary trends have emerged in translation studies:

- The 'ideology of translation', examined from the perspective of cultural studies, relates to how, in the context of a given translation tradition, the presence of the translator is linked either to a predominantly **domesticating** translation strategy or to a **foreignising** approach. That is, a transparent, fluent style is either favoured, thereby promoting an attitude which invariably works in favour of target, dominant cultures, or indeed shunned, thus ensuring that the voice of marginalised, dominated cultures is heard (e.g. the case of the Anglo-American translation tradition as examined in Venuti, 1995).

- The 'translation of **ideology**', seen from the perspective of **critical linguistics** and discourse analysis, focuses on how ideology is conveyed in and through the use of language (e.g. Hatim and Mason, 1997).

Further reading

For additional readings on the various key issues discussed in this chapter, the following basic references may be consulted:

- On the scope, methods and principles of applied linguistics, see Crystal (1981), Davies and Elder (2004).
- On action research and other relevant research methods, see McDonough and McDonough (1997), Nunan (1992), Burns (2009).
- On the notion of reflective practice, reflexivity and related concepts, see Schön (1983), Boud et al. (1985).
- On general introductions to translation studies' schools, trends and models, see Bassnett (1980, revised edition 1991), Chesterman (1989), Gentzler (1993), Munday (2001), Baker and Saldanha (2009).

Chapter 2

From linguistic systems to cultures in contact

This chapter will . . .

- describe how translation equivalence has been addressed within the linguistics paradigm;
- look in more detail at how two influential theories of translation view equivalence: Catford's **formal** linguistic model and Nida's socio- and psycho-linguistic model.

Concept 2.1   **Source-oriented translation studies**

The first set of issues to be dealt with in this survey of translation studies relates to the 'equivalence paradigm' and the contribution of linguistics. This and other translation trends may usefully be seen in terms of two dimensions – one covering the extent to which the source text is departed from or adhered to, the other, how wide or narrow the focus on language and translation happens to be.

One way of representing this is to use the shape of a triangle (Concept Map I). Adherence to the source text or alternatively pulling more in the direction of the target text is represented by the base line of the triangle, with various translation trends roughly lined up on either side: those on the left-hand side would display a predominantly source text orientation, those on the right-hand side a predominantly target text orientation.

The view of language and translation adopted within a particular trend is represented by the vertical line linking the base to the top angle. The upper end will reflect a predominantly narrower focus on language and translation, the lower end a predominantly wider focus.

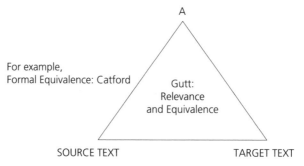

Concept Map 1   Map of TS
(source text orientation)

It should be noted that the extremes (ST for 'source text', TT for 'target text' and A for 'apex') represent ideal points on a scale and do not necessarily reflect what usually happens in practice. At the extreme ST angle, the source text would be so overemphasised that it would be difficult to distinguish between translation and such activities as transliteration. At the other extreme (the TT angle), the target text could theoretically become an end in itself, in which case translation would become indistinguishable from original text production. Finally, at the apex (A), translation would be so code-like and decontextualised that to talk of an orientation towards the source or the target text would simply be meaningless.

2.1   Formal equivalence

Quote 2.1

We can distinguish . . . between situational features which are linguistically relevant, and those which are functionally relevant in that they are relevant to the communicative function of the text in that situation. For translation equivalence to occur, then, both source language and target language texts must be relatable to the functionally relevant features of the situation. A decision, in any particular case, as to what is functionally relevant in this sense must in our present state of knowledge remain to some extent a matter of opinion.

J.C. Catford (1965: 94)

This survey of translation studies begins with the 1950s and 1960s, with linguistics as the predominant paradigm, and with 'equivalence' as the key concept in the study of translation. But to appreciate what the 'linguistics turn' in the theory and practice of translation actually involves, we must first inquire into the kind of linguistics that was current at the time and the extent to which it recognised, or was seen to be relevant to, the study of translation.

The vague and atomistic approach to how language works that was adopted by early models of linguistics (e.g. **structuralism**) stood in the way of any meaningful application of the subject to the study of translation. It was becoming increasingly clear to translation practitioners and theoreticians alike that the process of translating from one language to another could be captured only partly by precise, fixed rules.

An even greater impediment had to do with how the issue of 'meaning' was avoided by those early models of linguistics. The customary tools with which phonology and morphology were studied were simply insufficient for mapping such **cognitive** sites as human knowledge and experience that are crucial to any proper analysis of meaning relations.

The situation did not improve with the advent of such later models of linguistics as that represented by **transformational-generative grammar**. This particular paradigm had declared an interest in the creative and dynamic aspects of language use, but in practice would only deliver idealistic notions of **competence** and an illusory concept of meaning (Beaugrande, 1978).

2.1.1   Formal vs textual equivalence

Abstract notions of 'meaning' continued to prevail well into the 1960s, exercising considerable influence on how translation equivalence is conceived. In his linguistic theory of translation, the British linguist and translation theorist J.C. Catford (1965) argues that one of the central tasks of translation theory must be 'defining the nature and conditions of translation equivalence' (p. 21). Equivalence is here taken to be the basis on which source language (SL) textual material is 'replaced' by target language (TL) textual material. Translation is considered 'an operation performed on languages: a process of *substituting* a text in one language for a text in another' (Catford, 1965: 1; italics added). The reference to 'substitution' in this definition is important. According to Catford, we do not 'transfer' meaning between languages; we merely 'replace' a source language meaning by a target language meaning that can **function** in the same way in the situation at hand. This is achieved either through 'formal correspondence' or through what Catford calls 'textual equivalence'.

> ### Concept 2.2   Formal vs textual equivalence
>
> In Catford's theory of translation, *formal* correspondence involves adhering as closely as possible to the linguistic form of the source text. It covers **formal** relationships which exist when 'a TL category can be found which occupies the "same" place in the "economy" of the TL as the given SL category occupies in the SL' (1965: 27) – for example, translating an adjective by an adjective. Where this is not the case, *textual* equivalence will be aimed for. This obtains when any TL text or portion of text is 'observed on a particular occasion . . . to be the equivalent of a given SL text or portion of text' (p. 27) (e.g. translating an adjective by an adverbial phrase).

Thus, to be minimally adequate, any theory of translation needs to draw upon a theory of language and, for Catford, this prerequisite theory is envisioned specifically in terms of early Hallidayan **'scale and category grammar'** (or what is better known nowadays as Hallidayan **Systemic Functional Grammar**). Four 'levels' or 'planes' of language are recognised: the phonological, **graphological**, grammatical and lexical. In addition, four of the fundamental categories of linguistic theory are recognised: class (e.g. adjective, adverb), structure (e.g. subject–verb–complement), system (e.g. singular, plural) and unit or rank (e.g. morpheme, sentence).

2.1.2   Translation shifts

When translation cannot be carried out by adhering closely to the linguistic **form** of the source text, textual equivalence is achieved through 'translation shifts'. The concept of 'shift' is defined in terms of departures 'from **formal** correspondence in the process of going from the SL to the TL' (Catford, 1965: 73). Two major types of shift are identified: 'level shift' and 'category shift'.

> ### Concept 2.3   Level shift vs category shift
>
> *Level shift* occurs when an SL item has a TL translation equivalent at a different linguistic level from its own (grammatical, lexical, etc.). For example, source text **word play** achieved at the phonological level may be translated by exploiting the possibilities of the lexical level in the target language.
>
> *Category shift* is a generic term referring to shifts involving any of the four categories of class, structure, system and unit (e.g. ST adjectival phrase becomes an adverbial phrase in the TT).

> It has to be noted that the two kinds of shift are not mutually exclusive all the time. A translation through level shift could, on a different occasion or by a different translator, be achieved through category shift. Although Catford's model was not designed to account for phenomena such as translator preferences, there will always be cases (particularly regarding level shift) which will go beyond straightforward incompatibility between the SL and TL linguistic systems and which can be explained adequately only in such terms as the translator's own style. Further research is needed in this area of **motivated** decision making in translation (Wilss, 1994).

Category shifts are interesting and may involve:

- a 'class shift', when an SL item is translated by means of a TL item belonging to a different grammatical class – for example, the adjective in *medical student* becomes an adverbial phrase in the French or Arabic equivalent 'student in medicine';

- a 'structure shift' involving a change in grammatical structure between ST and target text TT – for example, *John loves Mary* becomes 'Is love at John on Mary' in Gaelic;

- a 'unit shift' where a strict rank-for-rank correspondence between SL and TL sentences, clauses, groups, words and morphemes is not observed – for example, the English definite article translated by a change in word order in Russian;

- an 'intra-system shift' which occurs when translation involves selection of a non-corresponding term in the TL system – this is regardless of whether the SL and TL possess systems which approximately correspond formally – for example, an SL 'singular' becomes a TL 'plural', although both number systems are available in both languages.

2.1.3   Catford's Formal and Textual Equivalence assessed

The reaction to Catford's approach has generally been lukewarm. According to his critics, Catford sees equivalence as being essentially quantifiable with translation merely a matter of 'replacing' each SL item with the most suitable 'TL equivalent' (Shuttleworth and Cowie, 1997: 50). Inevitably, the statistical bias characteristic of research within the framework proposed by Catford lends itself to such criticisms. In a sample of English texts, for example, the textual equivalents of the French item *dans* are found to be *in* with a probability of 73%, *into* (19%), *from* (1.5%) and *about/inside* (0.75%) (Catford, 1965: 30). Probabilities of this kind based on a sufficiently large corpus of data are used to form what Catford optimistically calls 'translation rules'. Such probability generalisations, which characterise Catford's whole approach and which appealed to machine translation advocates at the time, have been heavily theorising by many, including Delisle (1982) who finds the approach fundamentally flawed because of its static comparative-linguistic slant.

What the critics portray as an atomistic approach to language use is also said to be equally evident in the way Catford approaches 'textual equivalence'. For Catford, 'equivalence' obtains in cases where translation cannot be carried out by adhering closely to the linguistic **form** of the source text (e.g. when a preposition cannot be translated by a preposition). These shifts, as described by Catford, whether grammatical or lexical, are almost all purely linguistic and in most cases are opted for automatically by the translator, leading to minor structural differences between SL and TL. In this approach, crucial cultural, textual and other situational factors are ostensibly overlooked. Whereas in fact, as pointed out above, there will always be cases, particularly regarding 'level shift', which go beyond obvious incompatibilities between the SL and TL linguistic systems and which will necessarily involve translators' preferences.

These shortcomings notwithstanding, and although the entire analytical apparatus is self-evidently decontextualised and highly theoretical, Catford's contribution remains 'one of the very few original attempts to give a systematic description of translation from a linguistic point of view' (Fawcett, 1997: 121).

While Catford excludes contextual concerns from the remit he sets himself in the standard theory he proposes, noting in particular that deciding on what is 'functionally relevant' in a given situation is inevitably 'a matter of opinion' (p. 94), this exclusion or apparent lack of interest in matters contextual is, in fact, deliberate. In developing his scheme, Catford made a strategic choice: to provide an *account* of the nature and conditions of 'translation equivalence', a notion he deploys from the outset in its narrowest sense. Any assessment of Catford should, therefore, start from where Catford himself stands regarding what translation is and what the aims of his translation theory actually are.

It is often claimed with good reason that the intellectual climate prevalent at the time significantly influenced the narrow focus on translation and linguistics opted for by Catford. Indeed, this was a time when '**core**' linguistics was a dominant force. Yet this was also a time when numerous works on **context**-sensitive linguistics were becoming available, introducing the theories of Austin and Searle, Peirce and Grice, Firth and Halliday (e.g. Halliday et al., 1964; Enkvist et al., 1964; Widdowson, 1979; Leech, 1983). So, why did Catford not incorporate such new perspectives in his linguistic theory of translation, as his critics claim?

In fact, this wealth of material and the insights emanating from the new focus in linguistics did not go unnoticed by Catford: in his discussion of the concept of social–contextual **function** in his analysis of dialect translation, for example, he clearly shows that he was no stranger to contextual linguistics. Regarding dialect translation, Catford (1965: 87–8) incisively observes that 'the criterion . . . is the "human" or "social" geographical one . . . rather than a purely locational criterion'.

In re-assessing Catford's book some twenty years after publication, Henry (1984: 155) makes a special mention of Catford's final chapter, on the limits of translatability, and highlights Catford's assertion that translation equivalence, rather than being just a **formal** linguistic concept, tends to involve communicative features such as text and utterance **function** and relevance to the situation and culture.

In the same vein, it can be said that Catford uses the term 'textual equivalence' to refer to source and target items being more generally 'interchangeable in a given situation' (1965: 49) – that is, 'relatable to (at least some of) the same features of substance' (1965: 50), with 'substance' used in the **Firthian** sense as subsuming sound and script as well as extratextual factors and circumstances. This is a forward-looking and comprehensive notion that, even by today's standards, can adequately account for such intercultural issues as how users of different languages perceive and talk about reality from their own distinct cultural, historical and sociolinguistic vantage points.

2.2   Bridging cultural and linguistic differences

Quote 2.2

Translations which focus upon **cognitive** content in some instances or upon emotive response in others may be regarded as dynamic-equivalent translations. The way in which individual translations treat the underlying text may differ radically, and the legitimacy of each translation must depend upon both the nature of the original text and the type of receptor for which the translation is prepared.

Eugene Nida (1979: 52)

Based largely on a sociolinguistic theory of translation, the work of the American scholar and Bible translator Eugene Nida represents another landmark in translation studies. The emphasis here is on the relationships between language, culture and society and on how some of the more practical insights yielded by linguistic analysis may be functionally applied to the study of translation. This has meant that the narrow focus on linguistic meaning and structure widens considerably to take in a variety of contextual factors.

A number of basic assumptions have underpinned this research activity. First, a 'universalist' rather than a 'particularist' view is adopted, succinctly expressed in statements like 'anything which can be said in one language can be said in another, unless the **form** is an essential element of the message' (Nida and Taber, 1969: 4). Second, a 'communicative' view of the translation process is promoted whereby, without losing sight of the original message producer, the focus is shifted to the role of the receptor. According to Nida and Taber (1969: 1),

> What one must determine is the response of the receptor to the translated message. This response must then be compared with the way in which the original receptors presumably reacted to the message when it was given in its original setting.

2.2.1   Dynamic equivalence

Concept 2.4   **Dynamic vs formal equivalence**

Nida's model of translation has come to be inextricably linked to the notion of *dynamic equivalence*. Particularly in the context of Bible translation, equivalence of this type refers to the set of procedures by means of which 'the message of the original text [will be] so transported into the receptor language that the response of the receptor is essentially like that of the original receptors' (Nida and Taber, 1969: 200). This may be compared with what Nida calls *formal equivalence*: an orientation to translation which 'focuses attention on the message itself, in both form and **content**' (1964: 159).

Dynamic equivalence procedures thus include:

- Substituting more **appropriate** target-language cultural material for less accessible source-language items.
- Making references which are implicit in the source text linguistically explicit in the target language.

- Exploiting the possibilities of **redundancy** in order to facilitate comprehension.

Well-known examples such as the Bible's *Lamb of God* rendered as *Seal of God* in an Eskimo language graphically illustrate the **socio-cultural** aspect of this translation method at work. But the process is also in evidence at deeper levels of meaning. As Nida (1964: 159) puts it, the translator working within the framework of dynamic equivalence will be more interested in trying to 'relate the receptor to modes of behaviour relevant within the **context** of his own culture'. That is, these translators will be much less concerned with matching the receptor-language message with the source-language message than with preserving the intended effect.

2.2.2 Adjustment

In Nida's scheme, the distinction 'formal' vs 'dynamic' equivalence is seen in a slightly different light from that of traditional dichotomies such as **'free'** vs **'literal'**. The equivalence relations involved are described in terms of a number of procedures, including 'adjustment'. Formal equivalents represent the source text on its own terms, with little or no adjustment by way of bringing the text nearer to target-language linguistic or cultural mores. Because of the numerous incompatibilities which inevitably exist between source and target languages and cultures, this method of translation can be a cause for concern. For example, formal equivalence often 'distorts the grammatical and stylistic patterns of the receptor language' (Nida and Taber, 1969: 201).

Adjustment includes a set of modification techniques aimed at upholding translation equivalence and, in the process, ensuring that the target language version is accessible. Adjustment may involve ironing out structural differences, establishing semantic harmony, achieving stylistic appropriateness and taking care of problems associated with what communication theorists call the 'information load' (Nida, 1964). In dynamically equivalent translations, recourse may also be made to certain adjustment techniques which together aim at modifying the source text by removing any element likely to be perceived as alien, if not totally incomprehensible, to the target audience. These techniques include adding or taking away information, altering the material, and providing footnotes. This is to ensure that translations are dynamically equivalent and that the communicative channel is not blocked or over-loaded (1964: 131).

2.2.3   The intertemporal gap

A situation common in Bible translation is the translation between two languages, both of which the translator has acquired (e.g. a German translator rendering biblical Greek into one of the Ethio-Semitic languages). In such a context, translation is a particularly complex process, a situation that may be exacerbated by the difficulty inherent in the languages and cultures involved exhibiting a significant intertemporal gap. There is frequently the problem of the mediating language and culture of the translator possibly exerting an influence on the way in which the target text takes shape. More serious perhaps is the problem of the translated work losing its original contextual significance (e.g. the **genre** in which the ST is written becoming defunct in the TL at the time of translating – Bassnett, 1980: 83).

While such contingencies are virtually unavoidable, Nida argues, the ultimate criterion for the success of translation in this kind of situation is the extent to which an appropriate target audience response is elicited, and a dynamic form of equivalence secured.

2.2.4   Nida's Formal and Dynamic Equivalence assessed

The equivalence framework proposed by Nida has had a considerable influence on research in translation studies, but has in equal measure attracted a great deal of criticism. In a series of papers published in 1992 and 1993 in *Meta*, Qian Hu, for example, demonstrates the implausibility of what Nida calls 'equivalence response'. In addition to the difficulty of achieving equivalent effect when meaning is bound up in **form** (e.g. the effect of word order in Chinese and English), Qian Hu raises the issue of 'natural equivalents' often standing in a contradictory relation with 'dynamic equivalents' (e.g. Chinese 'overtranslations' of English words such as *animal, vegetable* and *mineral*). This echoes Larose (1989: 78) and van den Broeck (1978: 40) who doubt whether equivalent effect or response can ever be achieved (how can 'effect' be measured, and on whom, particularly if the texts are separated by considerable cultural or temporal gaps?).

To assess these and similar criticisms, it might be useful to highlight some of the more important points which Nida and his colleagues have made and which have in a sense anticipated and to an extent preemptively responded to some the criticisms that were subsequently made.

Nida states in no uncertain terms that 'there can be no absolute correspondence between languages' (1964: 156). The same is also said of the kind of response that dynamically equivalent translations are supposed to generate, and of how this can never be identical with what the original elicits from its readers (Nida and Taber, 1969: 24). Dynamic vs formal equivalence (or dynamic vs structural correspondence) are thus taken by Nida to represent points on a cline. They are more-or-less, not either–or dichotomies. Given this built-in variability, there are no absolute techniques, but rather general tendencies. Often, we are up against varying and not absolute degrees of dynamism or formality (1964: 160).

Thus, despite its apparent limitations, formal equivalence can sometimes be the most appropriate strategy to follow. As Nida observes, besides being frequently selected for the translation of biblical and other sacred texts, formal equivalence is also useful in situations where the translator or interpreter may for some reason be unwilling to accept responsibility for changing the wording of the target text (e.g. diplomatic correspondence).

In terms of general relevance, the categories and techniques proposed by Nida have stood the test of time and proved to be applicable not only to Bible translation (for which they might have been primarily intended) but also to other **text types**. The religious message is no different from any other message. Literary translation is an obvious area to which the scheme outlined above may be usefully applied, but research into other **genres** can also benefit from the wealth of insights which Nida's work has provided for us over the years. In Nida's work, the likely response of the receiver is no doubt emphasised. However, Nida harbours no illusions regarding the nature of response and the unattainability of absolute communication: 'for no two people ever . . . understand words in exactly the same manner' (Nida and Taber, 1969: 4).

2.2.5 The process of translation

Alongside the sociolinguistic focus explained above, the seeds of what is now more commonly known as the 'psycholinguistics of translation' can also be seen clearly in Nida's simple, yet insightful three-stage model of the translation process and of the constraints at work. It is within the ambit of this approach, generally believed to be directly influenced by **transformational-generative linguistics** (e.g. Chomsky, 1965), that Nida's central thesis concerning equivalence and text-receiver response may best be appreciated and appraised.

Nida's process model is practice-driven. It is specifically intended to provide Bible translators with analytical tools appropriate for the situation of working with an ancient text and rendering it effectively into a diverse range of modern tongues. A linguistic orientation is apparent and translation is seen as a process in which

> the translator first analyses the message of the source language into its simplest and structurally clearest forms, transfers it at this level, and then restructures it to the level in the receptor language which is most appropriate for the audience which he intends to reach.
>
> (Nida, 1969: 484)

Analysis

Analysis begins with a set of procedures which are employed in 'discovering the **kernels** underlying the source text and the clearest understanding of the meaning, in preparation for the transfer' (Nida and Taber, 1969: 197).

Concept 2.5   Kernel sentences

Kernels are the basic structural elements to which syntactically more elaborate surface structures of a language can be reduced. Underlying the procedure of kernel analysis is a theory of **semantics**: kernels are realised by sequences of items belonging to four basic categories (Nida, 1969: 485):

- Object words (nouns referring to physical objects including human beings) – O.
- Event words (including actions represented by verbs) – E.
- Abstracts (words relaying features of objects, events, other abstracts) – A.
- Relationals (linguistic items functioning as linking devices) – R.

Kernel sentences are derived from **actual** sentences by means of a variety of techniques, including **back-transformation** and **componential analysis**. In explicating grammatical relationships, source text surface structures are 'paraphrased' into formulae capturing how elements from the various categories listed in Concept 2.5 are combined. Referential meaning, on the other hand, is handled by means of an analysis which isolates shared and contrastive features exhibited by the semantic range of given items in the original message (i.e. meaning 'components', hence 'componential analysis').

An example of 'back-transformation' may make some of these concepts clearer (Nida, 1964a: 64). The phrase *will of God* may be analysed as:

B (object, *God*) performs A (event, *wills*)

Compare this with *creation of the world*, with the preposition *of* now yielding

B (object, *the world*) is the goal of A (event, *creates*).

Note that, in this kind of analysis, what is traditionally designated as a 'thing-word' (a noun), for example, may turn out to **function** as an 'event'.

Transfer

Transfer is the stage 'in which the analysed material is transferred in the mind of the translator from language A to language B' (Nida and Taber, 1969: 33). The translator has the **kernels** to work with and, in the light of his or her knowledge of target-language structure, these are modified until a form is settled on which 'will be optimal for transfer into the receptor language' (1969: 51). But, kernel elements (e.g. 'event' words and the way they combine with other elements) do not occur in a conceptual vacuum. They will somehow be marked temporally, spatially and logically. Transfer imbues initial kernel analysis with context and dictates the necessary adjustments: semantic elements may be redistributed through such processes as expansion and synthesis and structural differences between source and target languages may have to be compensated for. These interventions involve the entire range of linguistic expression, syntactic and semantic: from discourse to the sentence, to the word, and even to the level of the sound.

Restructuring

In addition to analysis and transfer, the third and final stage in the process of translation is 'restructuring' the transferred material, which until now exists only in the form of **kernel** sentences. What is needed is a mechanism by which the input that has accrued so far may be transformed into a 'stylistic form **appropriate** to the receptor language and to the intended receptors' (Nida and Taber, 1969: 206). Another important aim of the restructuring process is to ensure that the impact which the translation is to have on its intended receptors is in line with what the source-text producer has intended: 'any message which does not communicate is useless' (Nida, 1969: 494–5). Thus it is only when a translation produces in the receiver a response which is essentially the same as that of the original audience that the translation can be considered dynamically equivalent to its source text.

2.2.6   Nida's process model assessed

In the 'analysis' stage (which could occur before or after the other two as the three stages do not necessarily have to come strictly in that order), grammar and lexis are handled first by means of appropriate techniques such as **componential analysis**. But this leaves us with the troubling question of what to do with stylistic or with **connotative** meanings. Nida does not propose any specific techniques to deal with this level of meaning, However, he strongly recommends that features of style (including word **connotations**) should somehow be accounted for and, despite the rather open-ended nature of this kind of meaning, particularly in the area of style, Nida's emphasis on '**appropriateness**' throughout the discussion of the restructuring stage is worth noting. Emphasised are features such as the choice of oral or written mode and the role of sociolinguistic and situational factors, such as

- the selection of appropriate **genre** and type of **discourse**;
- the adoption of appropriate language varieties or styles;
- the choice of formal features and lexical items.

These elements would be borne in mind and assessed in terms of whether or not they are intended to produce special effects worth preserving.

In the 'transfer' stage, which ideally flows from 'analysis' and precedes 'restructuring', it has to be noted that what is involved is a meaningful act of reworking a text and not simply an exercise in mixing and matching. What is entailed by the process is more than the straightforward replacement of source-language elements with their most **literal** target-language equivalents. To illustrate this level of complexity, Nida and Taber (1969: 199) insist on an important analytic distinction between what they call 'contextual' consistency and 'verbal' consistency. Contextual consistency is 'the quality which results from translating a source language word by that expression in the receptor language which best fits each context rather than by the same expression in all contexts'. That is, in haphazardly adopting 'verbal consistency' as a procedure, translators would simply be failing to recognise that any text is an organic whole and not simply a concatenation of words and sentences.

Further reading

- On linguistics and translation, see Jakobson (1959/2000), Beaugrande (1978/1980), Snell-Hornby (1988).

- On Catford and formal equivalence in general, see Larose (1989) and Qian Hu (1993), Snell-Hornby (1988).

- On Nida and dynamic equivalence in general, see Fawcett (1997), Vinay and Darbelnet (1958, 2nd edition 1977), Qian Hu (1993), Gentzler (1993), Venuti (1995).

Chapter 3

Equivalence: Pragmatic and textual criteria

This chapter will . . .

- describe how linguistic models of translation equivalence have accommodated insights from pragmatics (e.g. Koller's 'relational' model, Gutt's 'relevance' model);
- look in more detail at how a concern with text and textuality has featured prominently in recent work on translation equivalence (e.g. Beaugrande's text-linguistic approach).

3.1 Opening up to pragmatics

Quote 3.1

A translation 'has to stand in some kind of *equivalence relation* to the original. . . . Equivalence in translation is not an isolated, quasi-objective quality; it is a *functional concept* that can be attributed to a particular *translational situation*'.

Albrecht Neubert (1994)

3.1.1 Translation vs non-translation

Within the burgeoning field of translation studies, an important issue to come to the fore in the 1970s and early 1980s related to the distinction between *translation* and *non-translation*, and the need to define the 'object' of translation research. This debate was particularly important since, as the German linguist and translation theorist Werner Koller (1995) put it, the contours of what did or did not constitute translation were being drawn and redrawn in so many different ways, and were becoming vaguer and more difficult to pinpoint.

This uncertainty may be illustrated by two sets of extreme views held at the time regarding what translation is. To German **functionalists** like Margaret Amman (1990), for example, a strict distinction between translation and non-translation is simply untenable:

> On the basis of modern translation theory, we can talk of 'translation' when a source text (of oral or written nature) has, for a particular purpose, been used as a model for the production of a text in the target culture. As a translator, I am also in a position to judge when a source text is unsuitable as model for a target culture, and to propose to the client the production of a new text for the target culture.
>
> (cited in Koller, 1995: 194)

This growing tendency to view the translator as cultural interpreter-cum-PR agent disturbed ardent proponents of equivalence. Koller (1995) asks: What does the term 'translatory' imply, if it also includes advising a client or even original text production? This kind of question, which has consistently coloured the debate in translation studies ever since, prompts Koller (1995: 196) to warn that

> If translation theory is to regard original text production as belonging to its field of concern as well, or rather, if it doesn't strive to differentiate between (original) text production and translatory text reproduction, then it falls into [a] methodological trap.

Note the particular use of 'translatory' in this and similar kinds of statement by Koller and others upholding strict notions of what 'translation' should be, to signify slightly more than simply 'belonging to the field of translation'. The use of 'translatory' is to highlight that which is 'symptomatic' (i.e. characteristic, typical) of good translator behaviour (adherence to source text, strict equivalence, etc.) as opposed to activities which masquerade as 'translation' but which take liberty with the source text to fulfill target text receiver expectations, **commission** requirements, and so on.

Concept 3.1   **What is translation?**

While *translation* no doubt shares significant features with a range of other text-processing activities, all of which proceed from a source text to a derived, secondary text (e.g. summarising, explaining), fundamental differences remain between the two kinds of output. Koller (1995: 196) puts forward the following working definition of what he takes 'translation' to be:

> The result of a text-processing activity, by means of which a source language text is transposed into a target-language text. Between the resultant text in L2 (the target-language text) and the source text in L1 (the source-language text) there exists a relationship, which can be designated as a translational, or equivalence relation.

3.1.2   Equivalence relations

Within this view of translation equivalence which subscribes to 'pragmatics' (the study of the purposes for which utterances are used), the scope of what constitutes an 'equivalence relation' is constrained in a number of ways. Equivalence is taken to be a relative concept in that it is subject, on the one hand, to the historical–cultural conditions under which texts and their translations are produced and received, and, on the other hand, to a variety of potentially conflicting linguistic–textual and extratextual factors and circumstances. More specifically, the process of transfer is influenced by such factors as:

- SL/TL code properties, possibilities and limitations;
- how reality is perceived and talked about in source and target languages and cultures;
- linguistic, stylistic and aesthetic **norms**;
- translation norms and traditions;
- client or commission specifications.

Clearly emphasised here is the role of the source text as a fundamental element in the translation process (and in the study of translation). However, the link which exists between the translation and certain conditions relevant to the production of the target text is not overlooked. In translation, there is what Koller (1979) sees as a 'double-linkage' to the source text and to the communicative circumstances on the receiver's side. Equivalence relations are differentiated in the light of this double bind, and a number of what Koller highlights as 'frameworks of equivalence' emerge as a result (1979: 187–91).

Concept 3.2   **Equivalence frameworks**

Translation equivalence may be achieved at any or all of the following levels:

- SL and TL words having similar orthographic or phonological features (*formal equivalence*);
- SL and TL words referring to the same thing in the real world (*referential* or *denotative equivalence*);
- SL and TL words triggering the same or similar associations in the minds of speakers of the two languages (*connotative equivalence*);
- SL and TL words being used in the same or similar contexts in their respective languages (*text-normative equivalence*);
- SL and TL words having the same effect on their respective readers (*pragmatic* or *dynamic equivalence*).

The scheme of equivalence relations given under Concept 3.2 may usefully be compared with those proposed by various trends which have either pulled in the direction of 'quantitative' criteria or, alternatively, extended the process outward to incorporate 'textual' criteria. On the quantative side, the Leipzig translation scholar Otto Kade puts forward a quasi-mathematical equivalence typology along the following lines (Kade, 1968):

- One-to-one equivalence, when there is a single expression in the TL for a single SL expression.
- One-to-many equivalence, when more than one TL expression is available for a single SL expression.
- One-to-part-of-one equivalence, when a TL expression that covers part of a concept is designated by a single SL expression.
- Nil equivalence, when no TL expression exists for an SL expression.

Such predominantly quantitative approaches have been found useful in applied translation **domains** such as terminology and technical translation. As equivalence typologies, however, they have been called into question for being too restricted to the word level and overly **system-oriented** (Snell-Hornby, 1988: 20). This has paved the way for what is seen by some translation scholars (e.g. Newmark, 1984/5) as yet another extreme position to adopt – namely, the discourse or text analysis approaches. Within such frameworks, it is suggested that similarity between ST and TT may be sought more productively in terms of discursive and textual parameters such as serving a particular ideo-logical stance at the level of **discourse** or thematic progression and cohesive ties at the level of **text** (Hatim and Mason, 1990; Baker, 1992).

3.1.3   The equivalence relations model assessed

A fact little appreciated by critics of Koller and his equivalence model is that, in working out his scheme of 'equivalence relations', pragmatics-advocate Koller was most careful not to overlook the complex network of relations at work between a source text producer and a source text and a target text receiver and a target text, with the translator performing a crucial mediating role. In his *Einführung in die Übersetzungswissenschaft* (1979), Koller discusses the various 'textual', 'formal' and what he advisedly calls 'translational' criteria which must be invoked in the determination of any kind of equivalence. These may be seen from the vantage-point of what he terms *Korrespondenz*, catering for formal similarity between virtual language systems at the level of *langue* (i.e. at the level of the linguistic system). True equivalence, however, is best determined from the more helpful perspective of what he terms *Äquivalenz*, which covers those equivalence relations that obtain between real texts and utterances at the level of *parole* (i.e. at the level of lan-guage use). It is this latter text-mediated kind of equivalence which is thus taken to be the real object of inquiry in translation studies.

Koller's five types of equivalence have the further advantage of turn-ing equivalence into a relative and not an either–or concept. Equivalence now has inscribed in it the notion of difference (minimum equivalence), as well as identity (maximum equivalence). Certainly, the point made by Hermans (1991: 157) that such a formulation lacks precision is valid:

> How much of each? If total or maximum equivalence was plainly unattain-able, what was the minimum equivalence required for a given text to be regarded as a translation of another text?

However, as Koller himself has argued, these frameworks are not the last word on the matter. They

> can and must be expanded upon, differentiated, refined and modified and in particular examined against concrete translational phenomena. A number of meaning components can be accommodated in this model of equivalence frameworks only with difficulty, or not at all: interlinguistic, intra-textual and **socio-cultural** meanings (a headache for literary translators).
>
> (Koller, 1995: 198)

Thus, formal uniformity is no longer so much emphasised and '**form**' no longer so highly rated over 'meaning', nor the language 'system' over communicative 'context' (Beaugrande, 1978). To capture this, translation studies needed, and in the main found, models of language and translation which were more radically text-oriented.

3.2   Textuality and equivalence

> **Quote 3.2**
>
> No adequate general theory of translation can be developed before scholars have turned from a sentence-restricted linguistics to produce a full theory of the nature of texts. Such a theory will devote extensive attention to the form of texts – how their parts work together to constitute an entity, to the way texts convey often very complex patterns of meaning, and to the manner in which they function communicatively in a given socio-cultural setting.
>
> James Holmes (1978b: 100)

After many decades of formal linguistics, translation studies turned to discourse analysis and text linguistics which became major sources of influence on translation research in the 1980s and subsequently. The neat split of language into 'form' and 'meaning', operative until then, was all but abandoned, as was the notion that communicative contexts were essentially diffuse, accidental and therefore unmanageable. By no means restricted to 'poetry', the approach to 'poetic translating' developed by Austrian text linguist and translation scholar Robert de Beaugrande (1978) demonstrates the resourcefulness of contextual information. The proposed model is firmly grounded in the belief that contexts possess a 'psychological reality' (i.e. are not only abstract blueprints) and that contextual factors are constantly invoked by language users as parameters in the light of which meanings are constructed and negotiated.

Concept 3.3   Textual 'meaning'

It is worth pointing out that 'meaning' itself is a theory (or a set of theories) language users agree to share whenever they engage in meaningful interaction. Even though we can never physically prove we know 'what we mean', let alone what anyone else means, being meaningful *of* and *in* itself carries forward its own quotidian evidence. For example, the phrase *wide-ranging* does not necessarily mean 'unsystematic, chaotic'. However, this is what the phrase presumably means in the sentence *and their examples were vague and wide-ranging*. Meaning is such an amazingly successful theory because it drives and is driven by practice in such rich profusion that we can hardly manage to be amazed at all – until, that is, we are pressed to explain or account for it (Beaugrande, 1978: 23).

3.2.1   Equivalence in texts

Beaugrande (1978: 13) defines equivalence incisively in terms of the translation being 'a valid representative of the original in the communicative act in question'. Approached in this way, equivalence would be partly subject to criteria that are rule-governed, and partly to factors surrounding the use of language in a given text at a given historical moment. This general framework rests on a number of basic assumptions, which have collectively informed research into the status of textuality in translating and in the assessment of translations. It is postulated that:

- the relevant unit of translation is the text, not the individual word or the single sentence;
- translating should be studied not only in terms of the similarities and differences between a source and a target text, but also as a process of interaction between author, translator, and reader of the translation;
- the interesting factors are not text features in themselves, but underlying strategies of language use, usually manifested by text features;
- these strategies must be seen in relation to the context of communication;
- the act of translating is guided by several sets of strategies signalled within the text. (Beaugrande, 1978: 13)

These basic assumptions have underpinned a text-linguistic approach to translation that seeks to account for such aspects of texts and translation as:

- the systemic differences between the two languages involved (e.g. in terms of the **lexico-grammar**);

- the type of language use found in individual texts (e.g. in terms of **register, genre**);
- the selection of equivalent items within their relevant contexts (in terms of such meaning relationships as denotation and **connotation**, and the equivalence relations involved).

3.2.2   The notion of textual dynamism

Concept 3.4   Dynamism

Dynamism subsumes various aspects of what Beaugrande and Dressler (1981) call **'informativity'** in the use of texts. Informativity is a standard of textuality which concerns the extent to which utterances happen to be expected or unexpected (i.e. 'given' in the sense of 'expected and ordinary', or 'new', that is, 'creative and interesting'). As a textual variable, dynamism is thus not totally unconstrained and is best seen on a continuum which covers the extent to which an instance of language use exhibits linguistic **markedness** *and* textual **evaluativeness**. Thus, linguistic markedness is not the only variable at work. **Defamiliarising** effects which dynamic uses of language convey are more pervasive and can set in whenever certain devices of linguistic expression (e.g. word order) are used in such a way that, in a particular context and **text type** (and not all contexts or types of texts), the use itself attracts attention and is perceived as somewhat 'non-ordinary'. **Text**, **genre** and **discourse** considerations (subsuming the mobilisation of a vast range of **ideational**, **interpersonal** and **textual** choices) are brought to bear on the way such acts of **defamiliarisation** or **foregrounding** are perceived (e.g. the remarkable incidence of short 'active' 'material clauses' as a textual feature of Hemingway's fictional style, as an important element of what has become a genre in its own right, and as an effective carrier of sexist discourse). (See also Chapter 15 on the translation of **'mind style'**).

Features of dynamic uses of language and the way they are dealt with in translation have always been contentious issues in the theory or practice of translation. In the majority of cases, the general practice has been that non-ordinary constructions in the source language (parallelism, emotive vocabulary, etc.) are translated by non-ordinary usage in the target language. However, a number of factors tend to complicate this seemingly straightforward equation, and only notions of equivalence which view translations as textual practice can account adequately for such relations.

Context-sensitive models of translation are well placed to deal with problems of this kind. Within this framework, non-ordinariness is no longer seen in static terms: what is linguistically marked (which, as explained in Concept 3.4, may or may not always be defamiliarising) is not simply reconstructed, with the forms of the original transferred intact. Rather, a process is set in motion in which the **communicative** status of the feature in question is 'negotiated' to establish what precisely is intended by the source (i.e. to ascertain whether the form in question is functionally defamiliarising), and only then to determine how the target reader is to be made aware of the implications. The communicative resources of the target language may have to be stretched, but this has always to be interpretable. That is, the target reader must be in a position to assess and appreciate more or less fully how he or she is supposed to react to what is conveyed in the translation (see Concept 3.3 and reflect on how to preserve in another language the textual meaning of *wide-ranging* – which in some contexts can denote 'chaotic').

An example from modern standard Arabic may make this point clearer. In this part of the world, political and religious discourse tends to exhibit masterful use of rhetoric which can at times be overpowering. Leaders (the late PLO Chairman Yasser Arafat is a prime example) often rely heavily on a set of concepts which, while deep-rooted in Arab–Islamic heritage and are thus very effective for an Arab audience, do not translate well. What is at issue in this 'untranslatability' has to do with the fact that some of these concepts have all but lost their original meaning, a semantic shift which baffles translators not well versed or fully immersed in the Arab–Islamic culture, or not sufficiently sensitive to the expectations of target audiences from a variety of cultural and linguistic backgrounds.

An example of such problematical concepts is *jihad* (literally 'holy war'), and part of the problem lies in the very effect it has on an Arab audience. Unless used in the context of talking, say, about Islamic history or culture, this term is virtually meaningless for a non-Arab/Islamic audience and should be used with extreme caution. The concept has evolved and its original meaning is now practically defunct in modern standard Arabic and in current political or religious Arabic discourse. In fact, it is invariably not the intention of those who use the term nowadays to allude to the older meaning. In current contexts, the word *jihad* simply means 'concerted effort'. Even after it was hijacked by the *jihadists* in recent times and in the process became almost synonymous with 'extremism' or, worse, 'suicide bombing', the term certainly does not denote 'holy war'. Translators seem to overlook these **connotations**, with misrenderings so serious that diplomatic incidents of all kinds have become the order of the day as a result.

3.2.3   Text as a unit of translation

From a text-linguistic perspective, then, the word or the sentence is no longer seen as an adequate unit of translation (Concept 3.5). The parameters for a proper transfer of meaning across linguistic and cultural divides must instead be texts in communication, with words and sentences yielding not simply one definite meaning but rather an array of possible meanings.

Concept 3.5   **The genre–text–discourse triad**

The unit *text* may be seen in relation to 'rhetorical purpose' and in terms of the way sequences of sentences are formally organised to serve such purposes (e.g. narrating, counter-arguing). What the 'text analyst' is primarily concerned with would be the analysis of such textual phenomena as sequential relationships, intersentential structure, and text organisation.

Texts acquire **efficiency**, **effectiveness** and **appropriateness** when they occur within a variety of **genres** (e.g. Letter to the editor, cooking recipes). A *genre* is defined as a mode of using language conventionally and in a manner **appropriate** to given **communicative** occasions and to the goals of the participants in them (Kress, 1985). What the 'genre analyst' would be interested in is how **norms** regulating the conventional use of language are upheld within well-defined communicative events or activity types (Bhatia, 2002). In translation theories which use the text model, the units 'text' and 'genre' have been seen to perform an 'enabling' function, that is, to facilitate the expression of attitudinal meanings within discursive practices (e.g. a racist or sexist attitude) (Hatim, 1997a). *Discourse* is defined (after Kress, 1985) as institutionalised modes of speaking and writing which give expression to particular attitudes towards areas of **socio-cultural** activity. In other words, discourse involves the way a text's formal organisation becomes contextually **motivated**. What the 'discourse analyst' is interested in would thus be processing activities such as negotiating and interpreting sequences and structures, and examining the social relationships which emanate from interaction (Bhatia et al., 2008).

These **semiotic macro-structures** are established, promoted and disseminated through the mechanism of **intertextuality**, a standard of textuality which taps our knowledge of previously encountered texts and regulates how **text types**, genre conventions and ultimately discursive formations evolve. (The genre–text–discourse triad will be dealt with in greater detail in Chapter 9.)

In this approach, it is no longer possible to entertain such blanket, all-purpose translation dichotomies as 'formal' vs 'pragmatic' resemblance. Instead, a number of criteria should be systematically invoked to determine which types of 'resemblance' are most crucial for a given text or part of a text in a particular situation of language use, and with a specific communicative goal in mind.

One way of establishing such a basis is to recognise that form and **content** are not independent variables and that neither aspect may be emphasised to the exclusion of the other. Since formal manifestations of texts are themselves always functional in arranging and interpreting meanings, the question of whether their outward form is preserved in translation becomes of secondary importance.

Source-text interpretability may be enhanced by exploiting the target user's language and cultural experience. Referring to the *jihad* example cited above, a rendering such as 'make concerted efforts' or, or even 'bend over backwards' or 'leave no stone unturned', for jihad when used in modern political discourse may thus be a more appropriate solution.

3.2.4   The textuality model of translation assessed

Mainstream translation theory has reacted strongly and somewhat unfavourably to new developments in text-linguistics and translation. This harsh, critical attitude, prevalent even today, dates as far back as the 1980s. Newmark (1984: 11), for example, resented in the strongest terms

> The present excessive emphasis in linguistics on discourse analysis, which is resulting in the corresponding idea in translation theory that the only unit of translation is the text, and that almost any deviation from **literal** translation can be justified in any place by appealing to the text as an overriding authority.

However, a wider perspective on equivalence is urgently needed and the textual model responds to this need most adequately. The new focus has had important implications not only for the practice of translation but also for the analysis of the process. The translation analyst is no longer exclusively concerned with confronting text with text but, more crucially, with assessing how texts are produced and how readers are affected by them. Within this more comprehensive view of translation, incidental incompatibilities between languages are seen to carry far less weight than systematic communicative factors shared by all languages (Beaugrande, 1978: 13). These methods cast light on such perennial issues as equivalence and the success or otherwise of certain translation methods and procedures (e.g. free vs literal, **compensation**). **Cognitive** linguistics and the pragmatics of **relevance** to be tackled next are welcome additions to the variety of approaches recognised as ground-breaking in current translation studies.

3.3   Translation and relevance

The translation theories presented so far have been mostly concerned with texts or text fragments as the objects of translation research. In the more recent literature on translation, the process has also been accounted for in terms of the psychology of communication. Key **cognitive**–linguistic terms such as **frames**, **schemata** and **relevance** are found useful in dealing with the process of translation, and in explaining aspects of language and cognition not properly understood before in translation theory.

Quote 3.3

If we ask in what respects the intended interpretation of the translation should resemble the original, the answer is: in respects that make it adequately relevant to the audience, that is, that offer adequate contextual effects; if we ask how the translation should be expressed, the answer is: it should be expressed in such a manner that it yields the intended interpretation without putting the audience to unnecessary processing effort.

Ernst-August Gutt (1991: 101–2)

3.3.1   The notion of relevance

Relevance theory views translation as a special instance of the wider concept of 'communication', and seeks to account for deeper relationships underlying complex processes like decision making and evaluation. The ability to draw **inferences** is an example of such relationships. According to Bible translator and relevance theoretician Ernst-August Gutt (1991, 1998), inference relationships, such as 'cause-and-effect', are central in the negotiation of meanings. Consider the following short exchange:

A: Will Sarah be long?
B: She is with Frank at the moment.

The **semantic** content of B's utterance is certainly important, but interpreting speaker-intended meaning will depend on various contextual factors, including A's ability to reach such conclusions as 'knowing how talkative Frank can be, Sarah will be there for hours'. Thus, speakers usually use a 'stimulus' (verbal or otherwise). This is to guide hearers towards an 'informative intention' of some kind (i.e. what is meant). In language, the stimulus is usually a 'linguistic' formula (i.e. a linguistic artefact, a phrase, a sentence, etc.), turned into a 'mental' formula which yields 'semantic representations' (i.e. 'meanings'). Further processing dresses up these representations with proper thoughts that describe the world. These **propositions** may be true or false, but meaningful communication will have got underway once these propositions are properly processed.

Whether 'being with Frank' means that 'Sarah will be there for hours' or that 'she will be back in two seconds' is a matter that can be settled only through 'context'. But to the relevance analyst, 'context' does not merely subsume the various elements of the 'external environment' (the situation), but also, and much more importantly, all the significant 'assumptions' which language users entertain vis-à-vis the world ('context' proper). Thus, what we know about Frank's talkativeness, together with the assumption that had this particular factor not been 'relevant', the speaker would probably not have mentioned or highlighted it, are some of the situational and contextual factors which collectively facilitate the interpretation 'Sarah could be there for hours'.

Concept 3.6   **Context in relevance theory**

An important characteristic of context in relevance theory is the variable degree of accessibility that various contextual assumptions tend to exhibit. By 'accessibility' is meant 'utilisability' (i.e. the use to which a given assumption may be put and become worth entertaining, in processing terms). Not all assumptions speakers or hearers make are equally accessible all the time. Factors such as the **function** of the utterance and the occasion of use may have to be invoked for meaning to be properly negotiated. For example, if A in the above exchange is unaware of what Frank is like, B's intended meaning would be highly inaccessible, whereas those who do know what Frank is like will immediately get the point.

3.3.2   Effort and reward

By making certain contextual assumptions less accessible than others, different acts of communication impose different demands on those involved in the communicative transaction. That is, whether or not a given contextual assumption is within reach affects the amount of effort required for its retrieval. Obviously, the less accessible a contextual assumption, the more demanding its retrieval will be. In practice, however,

> it seems that communication, no doubt like many other human activities, is determined by the desire for optimization of resources, and one aspect of optimization is to keep the effort to a minimum.
>
> (Gutt, 1991: 26)

To put this postulate in terms of cost and benefit, language users tend to choose those contextual assumptions that will

- have the largest benefits ('contextual effects');
- cost least in terms of processing effort.

This works smoothly as long as people say what they mean and mean what they say, as the saying goes. However, as the above exchange shows, communication is not always so straightforward: we exaggerate, we use metaphors, we respond indirectly and so on. In such cases, to keep effort to a minimum would only yield minimal benefits (e.g. banal, pointless communication). In order to maximise benefits, more effort would have to be expended, but more reward would be expected and would have to be provided. This is the kind of equilibrium which 'relevance' safeguards and which is the goal of all successful communication. How do co-communicants achieve this linguistic feat?

Benefits are assessed in terms of one basic communicative requirement – namely, that the receiver of a given act of communication (e.g. A in the above exchange) should ultimately be able to:

- derive contextual implications (e.g. Sarah will be there for hours or for seconds);
- strengthen or confirm assumptions previously held (knowing Frank, this does or doesn't surprise A); or
- eliminate certain assumptions which turn out to be contradictory (e.g. A believed Frank was on an overseas trip).

3.3.3   Translation and relevance

The discrepancy between what people have in mind and what they actually say or how they say it may also be seen in cross-cultural terms within a relevance framework. Consider the following text-initial sentence:

> *Certainly, tomorrow's meeting of OPEC is formally about prices and about the decision of Saudi Arabia to lower them (Time editorial).*

In English, an argumentative text could start in this way and the implication would be:

> 'There are those who suggest that tomorrow's meeting of OPEC is about prices, but this is not the point.'

To see this sentence in this way is to see it, at one level, not as a statement of what the speaker actually believes, but more as a representation of what someone else believed, thought or said, cited to be opposed on this occasion. At this level (so-called **straw man gambit** in the rhetoric of argumentation), the reason why the speaker makes this statement is to use the citation for his or her own ends. In this context, the speaker's goal is to prepare for a rebuttal of the statement: the text would go on to assert that the real purpose of OPEC meeting is to discuss the 'cohesion' of the organisation which is in tatters.

In Farsi or Arabic, on the other hand, starting an argument in what to a Western reader would be a 'straw man gambit' way conveys the opposite effect. The utterance would be about what the speaker actually holds to be true, a proposition that would normally be followed by further assertion:

> 'I wholeheartedly believe this to be the case, and it *is* the point, because. . . .'

To see the sentence in this way is to see it not so much as what someone may 'cite in order to oppose', but as what someone holds to be a true representation of a state of affairs. The reason why the speaker makes this statement is to express conviction, which is an end in itself (in this context to prepare for a position argument, to argue a point through).

Concept 3.7   **Descriptive vs interpretive use**

In relevance theory, these two modes of language use are recognised as two ways of representing thoughts in the same language or across languages.

- An utterance is said to be *descriptive* if the words are intended to be taken as an accurate representation of what the speaker holds to be true and desires to convey as a statement of belief (e.g. the way the above sentence is processed in Arabic or Farsi).

- An utterance is said to be *interpretive* if the words are intended to be what someone else believed, thought or said (e.g. the way the sentence in the above example is processed in English).

Applied to translation, the distinction between descriptive and interpretive use may be stretched slightly to mean that:

- if a translation is seen only in terms of a relationship it has in some way with a source text, then this will be a case of interpretive use (i.e. there is an air of 'tentativeness' about translations of this kind);
- if a translation is intended to survive on its own, without the receiver ever being aware of the existence of a source text, then this will be a case of descriptive use (i.e. there is an air of 'finality' about translations of this kind).

Thus, an interpretive translation is always crucially dependent on a source language original. The result of a descriptive translation, on the other hand, could conceivably be a text composed with little or no reference to an 'original'. To see the implications of the distinction more clearly, it might be helpful to reflect on two translation situations involving the production in English of a French perfume advertisement. The translation of the advert could be done within a normal translation **brief** (i.e. translate as an advert), or it could conceivably be done with the instruction that the translation is to be used by senior marketing strategists who want to find out 'what' the original advertisement actually said or 'how' it said it. The advert-to-advert translation would most probably be fairly '**free**' and is thus a case of 'descriptive' language use, whereas the more **literal** non-operative version would definitely be a case of 'interpretive' language use.

From the perspective of translation and relevance, a 'true' translation is always a case of interpretive use. That is, translation proper involves the representation of what someone else believed, thought or said, presented with all the 'tentativeness' which translations are naturally conceived to be. In this sense, translations are intended to achieve relevance, not alone as communication in their own right, but by standing in for some original. In fact, Gutt insists that renderings of the kind which involve descriptive use are 'not really translations'. These have been called translations, Gutt maintains, only through loose usage of the term, or where it has been more economical to modify an existing translation than to start a new text from scratch.

3.3.4   The urge to communicate

Concept 3.8   Direct vs indirect translation

Relevance theoreticians have sensed that the concept of interpretive use as applied to translation is so restrictive that it is not operationally useful for many translation purposes, applied or theoretical. To extend the scope of the term, Gutt (1991) invokes the distinction between 'direct' and 'indirect' speech and, having dispensed with the 'descriptive use' side of the argument as 'not really translation', focuses on two kinds of interpretive translation:

- *Direct translation* is a translation in which the translator 'has to some-how stick to the explicit contents of the original' (p. 122). A translation is considered to be direct 'if and only if it purports to interpretively resemble the original completely in the context envisaged for the original' (p. 163).

- *Indirect translation* is a translation in which the translator 'is free to elaborate or summarize' (p. 122). This heeds 'the urge to communicate as clearly as possible' rather than 'the need to give the receptor language audience access to the authentic meaning of the original' (p. 177).

In indirect translation, then, the decision is in favour of communicating more naturally. The implicit information of the source text is explicated and cultural material which is retrievable only by the source language audience is explained. The context envisaged by the ST writer will, as far as possible, be made equally available to the TL audience, hence the generous amount of explanatory information.

These procedures (the 'indirect' mode of which, according to the critics of relevance theory, is reminiscent of 'descriptive' translation before it was abandoned) are carried out in accordance with a basic assumption which communicators entertain and seek to make manifest to the addressee – namely, that what is offered . . . must be 'relevant enough to make it worth the addressee's while to process' (Sperber and Wilson, 1986: 158).

These issues have been researched extensively in the last two decades or so. In the appropriate section under research models (p. 224), this topic is re-visited in the analysis of **communicative clues** in Chapter 8, section 8.3, and in Chapter 15. The research question addressed will be:

Should the outward form of textual manifestations be preserved in translation?

3.3.5   Relevance in translation assessed

The translation model of relevance insists that the **cognitive** feat of inferencing and related mechanisms described above can be 'achieved without recourse to typologies of texts, communicative acts and the like' (Gutt, 1991: 128). Furthermore, notions such as effort and reward are seen solely in terms of categories such as descriptive vs interpretive, which are by and large too sharply **binary**. To be meaningful for the translator, however, 'relevance' must allow for some correlation, even if fairly weak, between orientation (e.g. interpretive use), translation strategy (e.g. semantic) and the constraints of **text type** and rhetorical purpose (e.g. translating counter-arguments). Similarly, values related to such inferencing mechanisms as 'effort' and 'reward' can be more helpfully seen on a sliding scale and not in binary terms: the relationships involved are at best probabilistic.

Regarding direct translation, dealing with translation as a case of interpretive use entails that an interpretation resembles that of the original 'closely enough in relevant respects'. This feels intuitively right as part of general human psychology, and ensures that what the translator intends to communicate tallies with what the original text intended to communicate. The question that Gutt begs, however, is: If maximising relevance for a different audience is held to be the ideal in translation, why exclude from the theory those translation practices defined as descriptive, whose very purpose is to maximise relevance? (Fawcett, 1997: 138).

Further reading

- On pragmatics and translation seen from the vantage point of Koller's relational model of translation equivalence, see Koller in Chesterman (1989), Koller (1995), Munday (2001), Pym (1995, 1997).

- On textuality and translation see Beaugrande (1978, 1980), Beaugrande and Dressler (1981), Hatim and Mason (1990), Munday (2001), Baker (1992), Newmark (1988).

- On relevance theory and translation, see Gutt (1991), Fawcett (1997), Malmkjaer (1992).

Chapter 4

Cultural studies and translator invisibility

This chapter will . . .

- explore how the concept of translation equivalence has become broader and more flexible under the banner of 'cultural studies';
- look more closely at the gradual emergence of a target text orientation (in the theory and practice of feminist translators and under the influence of such trends as **deconstruction**).

Concept 4.1 **Source or target, but wider focus**

At this stage in the evolution of translation studies, the process of translation could be seen to lean equally forcibly towards the source text within some trends, or towards the target text within others. In terms of our schematic triangle, the focus on language and translation should in theory continue to be narrower for those subscribing to a source text orientation, and wider for those subscribing to a target orientation. In practice, however, what seems to be happening at this juncture is a general dismantling of this source-target narrow-broad edifice. There seems to be a gradual shift towards a focus on language and translation that will widen considerably as we move along, regardless of whether a given trend happens to be ideologically source or target oriented. This is represented in Concept Map II.

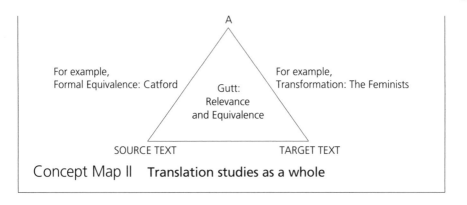

Concept Map II   Translation studies as a whole

Quote 4.1

Other . . . writers . . . redirected their energies to conform to thematics and styles that might meet a more favourable reception – but at certain costs. By re-writing texts to 'appeal' to Western audiences, certain themes, styles, modes of reference, and referents themselves were elided from the texts translated. Those 'silences' in the text, often known only to the translator, were often not only the most interesting in terms of creativity, but also the most revealing with regard to cultural differences.

Edwin Gentzler (1993: xii)

This is an appropriate point at which to introduce another influential trend in recent translation studies: the cultural model. This paradigm, which falls within what has been dubbed 'the cultural turn', addresses some of the issues raised thus far in the discussion of 'equivalence' both under text linguistics and within relevance theory. For example, in the discussion of the various theoretical trends covered so far, one important question remains outstanding: Particularly in the translation of sacred and sensitive texts, should outward form be preserved, and what are the wider implications of such decisions?

We will have more to say on this and related issues as this volume unfolds (see Chapter 15 for example). By way of background, however, it is perhaps useful to note how the cultural model has been pitted against the linguistic model, a demarcation which needs to be looked at more closely before moving on to full-fledged target-oriented approaches. Writing specifically about the American translation tradition, cultural theorist, translator and translation scholar Lawrence Venuti (1998: 315) concludes with the following portrayal of the current scene:

In the 1990s, as translation begins to emerge as a scholarly discipline in its own right, two rather different paradigms appear to be driving research. On the one hand is an approach that can generally be called text linguistics, in which notions of equivalence are grounded on the classification of **text types** and **functions**. On the other hand is an approach that can generally be called cultural studies, which is concerned with how values, ideologies, and institutions shape practices differently in different historical periods.

What are the distinctive features of the cultural studies approach to translation? Does work on issues such as 'translation strategy' within this paradigm represent any real advance on what has already been done within the established models of translation? Does the cultural model substantially differ from recent trends within linguistics in dealing with such issues as **ideology** in translation? These are some of the concerns that will be addressed in the following discussion.

4.1   Translator invisibility

The key issue in recent work on translation within cultural studies simply relates to whether the translator should remain invisible. The term **invisibility** describes the extent to which certain translation traditions do not tolerate the often intrusive presence of the translator in the translation. According to Venuti (1992, 1995), 'invisibility' has thus come to involve two distinct yet related phenomena:

- The 'effect of discourse', that is, the translator's use of language.
- A 'practice of reading', or the way source texts and their translations are received and evaluated.

Within the Anglo-American translation tradition, for example, prevailing attitudes to translations among the reading public or the critics are said especially to value 'fluency' and 'transparency' in translated works. Cultural studies commentators argue that these qualities are usually acquired at a price (Venuti 1995; Gentzler 1993). They relay an illusory effect which overshadows not only essential aspects of source text meaning but also how the translation actually comes to be (i.e. the multifarious conditions under which translators work and translations are produced).

Positions which advocate that translators should remain invisible are thus criticised for promoting values such as easy readability and a perception that the translation is not in fact a translation but an/the 'original'. These practices are said to obscure how translators interact with the process. Specifically in the Anglo-American translation tradition, translators are by and large discouraged from engaging with the source text in an attempt to capture source cultural nuances and re-introduce them at crucial points in the translation. It is firmly believed that the continuity of target text syntax must not be impeded and that the mores of current usage in the target language must not be tampered with. In short, translation is generally thought to be a matter of undisturbed communication and the best translations are those which convey 'meaning' best and with maximal accessibility.

An influential trend within cultural studies (well represented by theorists such as Venuti) sees all of this in terms of a political agenda (Baker, 1996). English is the most translated language and the least translated into, and the trickle of foreign language works which find their way into English is rigorously vetted. Venuti (1995) documents in great detail how foreign texts (and English-language translations when available) would be ignored if they failed the 'fluency' test, that is, if they proved too resistant to easy readability. The conclusion drawn from this is that an entire translation tradition has evolved in the West to serve imperialistic goals abroad and xenophobic values at home.

Concept 4.2   **Foreignisation vs domestication**

The subject of 'translation strategy' is perhaps the single most important issue around which the contribution of research into translator **invisibility** has revolved. *Domestication*, said to be the hallmark of dominant translation traditions such as the Anglo-American, is seen as an approach to translation which, in order to combat some of the 'alienating' effects of the foreign text, tends to promote a transparent, fluent translating style. This is contrasted with *foreignisation*, a translation strategy which deliberately breaks target linguistic and cultural conventions by retaining some of the 'foreignness' of the source text. The distinction is traced back to German theologian and translator Friedrich Schleiermacher, who glosses foreignisation and domestication in the following terms:

> The translator can either leave the writer in peace as much as possible and bring the reader to him, or he can leave the reader in peace as much as possible and bring the writer to him.
>
> (Schleiermacher, 1838, cited in Wilss, 1982: 33)

Within cultural studies, a domesticating translation is fiercely attacked for the exclusionary impact it can have on source culture values. Stereotypes of national identities are invariably constructed and particular perceptions are formed as a result. Furthermore, it is through such translation methods that literary **canons** in the target language are usually maintained and more prestigious poetic forms or narrative structures are ensured a place at the expense of weaker discourses. In the process, translation strategies which are more resistant to cultural hegemony are eliminated, closing off any thinking about cultural, literary or ideological alternatives.

4.1.1   Freud in translation: A case in point

In his critique of the way Sigmund Freud was translated into English, Bruno Bettelheim draws attention to how these translations 'appear to readers of English as abstract, depersonalized, highly theoretical, erudite and mechanized – in short "scientific" – statements about the strange and very complex workings of our mind' (1983: 5). For example, excessively precise scientific terms such as 'parapraxis' are used for the straightforward German *Fehlleistung* (which Bettelheim unassumingly renders as 'faulty achievement'). Such obfuscation cumulatively contributes to an overall effect which permeates the entire fabric of the text. **Diction**, which in the source text is so unpretentious (German words which could have been simply rendered as 'forgetting' or 'go out of my head'), gives way to a scientism that stands out noticeably.

To explain this methodical distortion, Bettelheim first turns to the intellectual climate that prevailed at the time in Anglo-American psychology and philosophy, and took its inspiration from eighteenth-century **positivism**. The translator would invariably jettison anything which betrayed **hermeneutism** and spiritualism. Such an attitude was propped up by a range of social institutions, with which psychoanalysis had to align itself in order to gain acceptance in the years following the Second World War. Bettelheim (1983: 32) explains some of the decisions which translators made in dealing with Freud's material:

> When Freud appears to be either more abstruse or more dogmatic in English translation than in the original German, to speak about abstract concepts rather than about the reader himself, and about man's mind rather than about his soul, the probable explanation isn't mischievousness or carelessness on the translator's part but a deliberate wish to perceive Freud strictly within the framework of medicine.

It is important in connection with this to allude to a major influential figure in cultural studies – Antoine Berman – and in particular to an important article by Berman entitled 'Translation and the trials of the foreign' in English (in Venuti 2000). Berman discusses linguistic variety and creativity and the way certain modes of translation tend to reduce

variation. He identifies twelve 'deforming tendencies' (p
marised in Munday (2001) as follows:

1. Rationalisation, involving a general tidying of syntac
   including punctuation and word order, as well as the nommansa—
   of verb processes.

2. Clarification, or opting for explicitation in an attempt to clarify what
   is deliberately left implicit in the original.

3. Expansion, a strategy which explains why TTs tend to be longer
   than STs, due to the use of such strategies as explicitation, over-
   translation and flattening.

4. Ennoblement, referring to the tendency on the part of certain
   translators to 'improve' on the original by rewriting it in a more
   'elegant' style.

5. Qualitative impoverishment, or the replacement of words and expressions with TT equivalents that lack the sonority and **iconicity** of
   the source.

6. Quantitative impoverishment, relating to the loss of lexical variation
   in translation.

7. The destruction of rhythms, with rhythm seen not as an exclusive
   property of poetry but as a quality that can pervade a text.

8. The destruction of underlying networks of signification, which
   invariably results from the translator's lack of awareness of the
   network of words that is formed throughout the text.

9. The destruction of linguistic patternings, an inevitable result of adopting a range of techniques, such as rationalisation, clarification and
   expansion which tend to make the TT linguistically more homogenous.

10. The destruction of vernacular networks or their exoticisation, a
    strategy which relates especially to local speech and language patterns
    that play an important role in establishing setting or portraying
    character in a novel, for example.

11. The destruction of expressions and idioms by replacing idioms or
    proverbs with fluent TL 'equivalents'.

12. The effacement of the superimposition of languages, or how transla-
    tions tend to erase traces of different forms of language that co-exist
    in the ST.

As Munday (2001) points out, Berman's work is important in linking
philosophical ideas to translation strategies and in raising issues relating
to the ethics of translation.

4.1.2 Translator invisibility research assessed

Research into translator **invisibility** and related issues has certainly been one of the more exciting developments in recent translation studies. It has reopened the debate on matters that have been sidelined for far too long, and has thus provided translators and teachers of translation with a rich store of insights. However, a number of problems remain. To begin, Fawcett (1995: 182) picks up the theme of translation and power and questions the wisdom of speaking of 'cultural imperialism', which tends to cloud the discussion of 'the role of the consumer in capitalism . . . (not a hapless pawn) and the complexities of individual firms working in a free market'. From a similar perspective, Pym (1996: 171) wonders whether we should be at all surprised that 'a culture as relatively major, prestigious and big as Anglo-Americandom tends towards fluency in translations' and concludes that, after all, 'there is nothing "radically English" about the phenomenon'.

At this point, it could legitimately be asked: has linguistics (much-maligned by commentators from a 'cultural studies' perspective) really failed to address ideological issues in translation? As Baker (1996) notes, the goal of **Critical Linguistics** and Critical Discourse Analysis, for example, has been simply to unmask ideological positions and attitudes in discourse. To achieve this, linguistic models and knowledge of social context are being systematically invoked, a development which can only support the point highlighted earlier that, as translation studies is a 'house of many rooms', so is linguistics.

4.2 Deconstruction: The plurality of meaning

Quote 4.2

Difference is never pure, no more so in translation, and for the notion of translation we would have to substitute a notion of transformation: a regulated transformation of one language by another, of one text by another. We will never have, and in fact have never had, to do with some 'transport' of pure signifieds from one language to another, or within one and the same language, that the signifying instrument would leave virgin and untouched.

Jacques Derrida (1981: 4)

4.2.1 Translation as transformation

It is often the case that what would be considered peripheral in a text is usually seized on by the deconstructionist in an attempt to bring out hidden meanings and concealed ideological values. Within this currently fashionable paradigm, and particularly in the area of literary translation, a new set of key concepts has emerged, describing translation by such epithets as 'transformation' and even 'transformance'. The notion is entertained that, in translation, it is the original text which is actually dependent upon the translation and not the other way round, since without translation the original would simply remain 'undiscovered'. Thus, the much sought-after text 'meaning' is probably not in the original and could well be found only in the translation. Furthermore, even after translations are produced, a particular rendering would only fix meaning in a particular way, which is valid until the next translation comes along and reshuffles the parameters (Gentzler, 1993: 144–5).

Concept 4.3   **The authority of the source**

In the tradition of language philosophers like Derrida, deconstructionists see the original not as a vehicle which carries the 'stimulus' in an unproblematic way, but as something which merely constitutes a 'response' from the translator. This reversal of roles has provided the theoretical arguments for undermining the notion of the 'author' and the 'authority' of the source.

Where does meaning come from, then, if it is not from the authority of the source? A Derridan answer would be that, in effect, meaning is constituted by the multiple forms and **intertextual** connections which the text must imply in order to say anything at all. The translator should therefore be in tune with those linkages that create meanings, not with meanings that are lifeless and fixed in some original. Whatever translators do, the deconstructionists warn, they must not stand outside the text doing their usual commentary, but must let that commentary come from within the evolving text.

4.2.2 Deconstruction and translation studies

In translation studies, American–Dutch translation theorist James Holmes was among the first to draw attention to the valuable contribution that the new approach of **deconstruction** had the potential to make to our understanding of translation. Holmes distinguishes between deconstruction and other interpretative approaches such as New Criticism and **hermeneutics**. While both the New Critic and the hermeneuticist clearly recognise all the paradoxes and contradictions interestingly inscribed in the text, these text analysts tend to postulate a notion of sublime unity as underlying the apparent chaos on the textual surface. Deconstructionists, on the other hand, make no such assumptions. Beneath the disunity of the surface, we are urged to look for the underlying contradictions and paradoxes and, more importantly, for 'the underlying motives, desires and frustrations which the author of the text has done his best to hide' (Holmes, 1985: 106).

In the context of literary translation, Holmes assesses the deconstructionist approach against the background of the tendency among translators to smooth away disturbances in the text they are translating. But it is these irregularities, the deconstructionist would argue, that make the text not only exciting but also meaningful. The problem for the translator is thus twofold. Translators must heed the motives which have given rise to these contradictions, and there will always be the translator's own motives to consider.

Situating the deconstructionist paradigm within a mode of anti-essentialist thought (i.e. truth is not eternal, but both variable and alterable), the Brazilian theorist Rosemary Arrojo (1998) identifies the central theme in the practice and theory of deconstruction as the constant questioning of the myth that meaning is intrinsically stable and fully present in texts, and that it is recoverable and can thus be 'transported' intact across linguistic and cultural boundaries. Arrojo asserts that the process of signification can be accounted for only in such tentative terms as meanings being reinterpretations of reinterpretations (Rorty, 1982: 92). This instability is transferable, not piecemeal or neatly, but in a holistic manner inevitably open to other co-influences. The process is interfered with by subjects performing the act of the transfer, and is contaminated by the diverse cultural, historical, ideological and political circumstances through which it must pass.

4.2.3   Deconstruction assessed

Pym (1995) assesses the deconstructionist argument and raises doubts as to the general pertinence to translation studies of the entire project. According to Pym, the debate should not be obscured by the tendency on the part of deconstructionists to equate 'equivalence' with the notion of the 'original' text. In other words, equivalence is not reducible to source text analysis, no matter how 'critical' this happens to be.

Another important issue addressed by Pym relates to the decon-structionist credo that source texts are semantically unstable points of departure. The notion of translation as the transfer of stable meanings tends to be constantly criticised, and terms such as 'transformation' are invariably suggested as an alternative to 'transfer'. But, as Pym (1995b) argues, the process of transfer is, after all, not a theorist's dream. It is an assumption which all readers of translations make. True, such assump-tions are social illusions, but these illusions are intrinsic to the use of translations as translations.

Pym stresses that the idea of transfer is not ubiquitous. Translators or translation critics probably do not even subscribe to the notion, yet they are aware of a powerful system of expectations at work among users for whom the existence of the original is beyond dispute. Thus, as long as there are different translators for whom source text meanings differ, plurality of meaning would be catered for most adequately.

4.3   Gendered translation: Production not reproduction

> **Quote 4.3**
>
> [Lucien] Francœur was the first and last male poet I translated. During the three years I spent on his poetry, I realized with much distress that my translating voice was being distorted into speaking in the masculine. Forced by the poems' stance, by language, by my profession, to play the role of male voyeur. As if the only speaking place available, and the only audience possible, were male-bodied. I became very depressed around meaning.
>
> Lotbinière-Harwood (1995: 64)

The context which has nurtured the approach that has come to be known as 'feminist translation' is one in which the Canadian scene in particular has seen a considerable volume of work by feminist writers who, in the majority of cases, have essentially sought to provide a critique of **patriarchal language**. Conventional vocabulary is etymo-logically dismantled and a new lexicon for the new experience of women developed. Language is fragmented at will and conventional **syntactic** and **semantic** structures are not simply disregarded, but rather examined more closely for concealed meanings. Put differently, language becomes a political weapon and conventional discourse targeted, since it is here that power is thought to reside.

4.3.1 The feminist paradigm: Tampering with usage

Within the feminist framework, translation is seen not as a neutral act of meaning transfer but, in the words of Barbara Johnson (1981, cited in Flotow, 1991: 81), as something much more 'strong' and 'forceful', a strategy that 'values experimentation, [and] tampers with usage'. This radical view of translation has prompted the need to restore an element of translator 'visibility' in the target text, a notion about which deconstructionists in general have never been in doubt. The translator's act of engaging with the text being translated is done deliberately and decisively, and it is now accepted that:

> No translation theorist or practitioner can but position him or herself –
> aesthetically, politically, ideologically . . . Indeed, it is this very positioning, be it overt or covert, conscious or unconscious, avowed, unavowed
> or disavowed, that enables us to go beyond dualist conceptions of translation in order to bring to the fore the ethical stance which translation both
> entails and implies.
>
> (Gillian Lane-Mercier, 1997: 63)

Feminist translation may thus be thought of as a practice in visibility, and the cardinal concepts are: production, subversion, manipulation, 'transformance'. It is an ethical code through which the translator learns to claim full responsibility for choices made – aesthetic, ideological or political. Traditional dichotomies, such as 'productive' vs 'reproductive' (referring respectively to 'original' and 'derivative' text production), are called into question, and the translator's 'authorial' role is widely promoted.

In this context, the role of the translator as an active text producer is asserted (Chamberlain, 1988) and the 'feminine' metaphors with which translation is described (e.g. translation is like a woman – beautiful, faithful, secondary) are questioned (Godard, 1990). This active form of **poetics** is also an active form of politics: the 'visible' feminist translator sees his or her work as an integral part of a commitment to a cause. The authorial role necessarily implicated in this configuration of roles runs counter, on the one hand, to the ideal of smooth, fluent readability in the target language and, on the other, to equivalence as a theoretical ideal (Homel and Simon, 1989: 50). The process is much less orderly than might be implied by any of these notions. It is one in which:

> The feminist translator, affirming her critical difference, her delight in interminable re-reading and re-writing, flaunts the signs of her manipulation of the text. Womanhandling the text in translation means replacing the modest, self-effacing translator. The translator becomes an active participant in the creation of meaning.
>
> (Godard, 1990: 91)

4.3.2   Feminist practices

In practice, feminist translation theory meant a rethinking of **gender** identity and a setting aside of 'natural', preconceived notions. The feminist translator would be working with whatever perceptions the source text might present, and translating is seen as an exercise in interrogating the complex ways in which gender becomes bound up with language and, consequently, with translation (Massadier-Kenny, 1997: 55). Feminist translators have openly discussed their role as interventionists in the texts they translate, openly admitting that they intervene when they see a need, for example,

- to mitigate offensive forms of machismostic or misogynistic discourse;
- to make explicit a subtle feminist rhetorical effect;
- to introduce an appropriate feminist angle on the source text.

This desire for what the feminist critic Barbara Godard approvingly refers to as 'shock effect' may be illustrated from the work of a prominent member of the group – feminist translator Susanne Jill Levine.

In her translation practice, Levine (1991) asserts that her intention is to subvert the text. Guillermo Cabrera Infante's *La Habana para un infante difunto* (a sexist novel bordering on pornography) provides Levine with an interesting forum from which to demonstrate her aggressive and creative approach to translation. According to Levine, Infante not only 'mocks' but 'manipulates' women and their words. The answer to this must be a *tradutore traditore*:

> Because of what is lost and can be gained in crossing the language barrier, because of the inevitable rereading that occurs in transposing a text from one text to another, a translation must subvert the original.
>
> (p. 92)

Levine (1991: 83) gives an interesting example of how she is able to question the male narrator's narcissistic posturing: his 'jaded' claim in the Spanish *no one man can rape a woman* (implying that women are willing rape victims) becomes *no wee man can rape a woman* (which focuses on the amusing alliterative aspects of the Spanish 'one' and 'wee').

To cite another case, it was in translating Nicole Brossard's play *La nef des sorciers* that feminist intervention achieved oft-cited notoriety. To take one particular line as an example, two versions might be envisaged – a conservative and a radical one. Operating within fairly traditional views of equivalence and fidelity, one might expect a **literal** rendering such as:

> *This evening I'm entering history without pulling up my skirt.*

Feminist translator Linda Gaboriau, however, chose to explicate the source text drastically:

> *This evening I'm entering history without opening my legs.* (Gaboriau, 1979: 35)

This liberty has raised a few eyebrows, but not from Godard who, as pointed out earlier, had praised such shock effects: commendable is 'the repossession of the word by women, and the meaning of the life of the body as experienced by women' (1984: 14).

In places, this unabashed embracing of manipulation takes the form of retaliation against traditional, **patriarchal** notions of translation: men do it, so why shouldn't we? Chamberlain looks at the politics of **gender** and the representation of translation in gendered terms. Turning to the politics of colonialism, she cites an English translation of Horace that was written in the sixteenth century. During that period, disregard for the original's language and culture was considered a public duty.

Quote 4.4

In his preface, the translator, Thomas Drant, has this to say:

> First I have now done as the people of God were commanded to do with their captive women that were handsome and beautiful: I have shaved off his hair and pared off his nails, that is I have wiped away all his vanity and superfluity of matter. . . . I have Englished things not according to the vein of Latin propriety, but of his own vulgar tongue. . . . I have pieced his reason, eked and mended his similitudes, mollified his hardness, prolonged his cortall kind of speeches, changed and much altered his words, but not his sentence, or at least (I dare say) not his purpose.

Lori Chamberlain, cited in Venuti (ed.) 1992

4.3.3   The feminist paradigm assessed

A striking example of the kind of concerted attacks on certain feminist translation practices might be drawn from Arrojo (1994) who took issue with what she variously labelled 'anxious', 'theoretically incoherent' and 'hypocritical' proposals. She criticised the feminist translators' tendency to intervene, sometimes wantonly, in the texts they are translating. The hypocrisy is seen most glaringly when it is these translators who usually claim some form of allegiance to a translation ethics whereby the author's meaning should be protected at all costs. This 'infamous double standard', Arrojo (p. 149) observes, is no different from the 'masculine' theoretical stance adopted by the traditional translation theorist.

Arrojo sees this 'ambivalent, rather opportunistic brand of "faithfulness"' (p. 152) to be closely linked with another form of double standard, this time relating to 'appropriation' which feminist translators have only too readily associated with colonialism and rape (see above quote). What is the difference between this usurpation and Levine's 'womanhandling' of Infante's text, which is an equally serious act of 'castration'? Is it not all a 'struggle for authority, a struggle for the right to possess and determine meaning?' (p. 154).

Flotow (1997: 7) replies to some of these criticisms by suggesting that, unlike what happens in patriarchal language and contrary to the impression given by Arrojo and others, the incidence of feminist interventions is in fact 'limited and highly focused'. Conceding that the political rhetoric of feminist practices does sometimes become overpowering, Flotow nevertheless asserts that the political investment and bias are done openly and are actually flaunted as 'the signature of a positionality' (p. 7).

Further reading

- On translator invisibility and general background to domesticating vs foreignising within the cultural model of translation, see Berman (1985/2000), Schleiermacher (1813/1992), Niranjana (1992), Gentzler (1993), Spivak (1993/2000), Pym (1996), Venuti (1998).

- On the theory and practice of the feminist translation trend, see Simon (1996), Kinloch (2007), Chamberlain (1988/2004), (1998/2001), Delisle (2002), Bauer (2003), Santaemilia (2005).

Chapter 5

From word to text and beyond

This chapter will . . .

- review James Holmes' seminal ideas on translation as product, process and functionality;
- describe work carried out within the 'continental' variety of 'cultural studies', and present the view of translation as a force which shapes culture and history and as an act of re-writing undertaken in the light of a dominant **ideology** and a dominant **poetics**.

Quote 5.1

Definitions of translation which postulate only correspondence in meaning as essential (semantic-correspondence definitions) are not valid definitions, since demonstrably not all texts generally accepted as translations conform to such a requirement. The same holds true for definitions postulating only correspondence in function (pragmatic-correspondence definitions), or for that matter correspondence in form (syntactic-correspondence definitions). Such definitions are in reality no more than codifications of time, place and/or text type-bound norms of an individual or a smaller or larger group, mistakenly elevated to the position of universal translation laws.

James Holmes (1978b: 101)

5.1   Translation as metatext

Until the mid-1970s, particularly in **domains** such as verse translation, the discussion of translation seems to have been focused on two extremes: 'equivalence' (in the sense of 'identity') and 'untranslatability'. With his theory of translation as metatext, James Holmes (e.g. 1969) steers a mid-course. It must be noted that, although the notion of 'metatext' is worked out with poetry and poetic translation in mind, the model proposed applies also to other forms of writing, other **genres** and other modes of translation.

Concept 5.1   **Translation as metatext**

Metatextual activity may be illustrated by *literature* – a form of writing which makes statements *about* reality. There is, however, another body of writing which communicates something *about* literature. This includes the various forms of explication (literary criticism, commentary, etc.), and literary translation falls under this *metaliterature* category.

Thus, the poem, which in a sense is a 'translation' of a given chunk of reality, is translated into another poem (a *metapoem*).

Of course, the poem is different from a commentary on the poem or a translation of it. Yet, the three forms are comparable in some meaningful ways. The relationship of the metapoem to the original poem is as that of the original poem to reality. It is in this way that the translator (the 'metapoet') may be seen as

- a critic, dealing with the **norms** and conventions embodied in the source;
- a poet, drawing on the norms and conventions of another literary system and attempting to reconcile the two sides – source and target.

According to Holmes, any act of translation attempts to overcome a number of hurdles. There will be linguistic interference relating to such features as source language **diction** and syntactic peculiarities. There will also be problems stemming from whether the languages involved are related or distant, and whether a language happens to be dominant or peripheral.

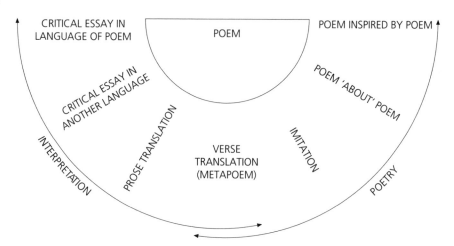

Figure 5.1   Spectrum of literary forms (Holmes, 1969: 24)

From the perspective of language dominance, little-known literatures tend to pose problems that are mostly related to the scant knowledge available regarding the background against which a text may be read and understood by the target reader. In these literatures, not only are the norms and models virtually non-existent or faintly present for the target reader, but they might also be inaccessible to the source reader. This is generally coupled with an inflexible set of attitudes on the part of target readers from certain cultural backgrounds: such readers would sometimes unreasonably expect to find the kind of experience which they have come to identify with poetry or certain genres.

The metatextual element identified above is not a static, catch-all concept, but one which covers a spectrum of activities. Holmes looks at the various phenomena involved in terms of a 'fan' of literary forms, as in Figure 5.1. From one edge of the fan to the other, we find:

- Form 1: the critical comment on the poem written in the language of the poem.
- Form 2: the critical essay, written in another language.
- Form 3: the prose translation of the poem.
- Form 4: the verse translation.
- Form 5: the imitation.
- Form 6: a translation drawing on the original in a partial way.
- Form 7: a translation vaguely inspired by the original.

In this spectrum of activities, the translator of poetry has a wide choice:

- Retain the form of the original.
- Focus on the **function** of the **form** within its poetic tradition.
- Opt for a **content**-based rendering.
- Settle on a deviant form.

In this respect, it is interesting to note (as Holmes does) that the various forms of interpretation mapped out in Figure 5.1 are not equally effective. That is, the overall effect which the translation achieves is closely bound up with the form the interpretation takes. By studying the various forms and correlating these with the kind of effect achieved, a great deal will be revealed not only about the nature of metapoetry but also, and perhaps more significantly, about the nature of the interpretive process in general (Holmes, 1969).

5.1.1 The nature of shifts

In this metaprocess, an important issue confronting both translator and analyst relates to the multi-layered nature of 'shifts' in going from source to target. There will be a shift simultaneously from one linguistic system to another, from one **socio-cultural** system to another, and from one literary or poetic system to another. Three contexts may thus be envisaged: the linguistic, the literary and the socio-cultural. The latter consists of those objects, symbols and abstract concepts that are bound to vary from one society or culture to another (Holmes, 1972/1994). Translation choices are made in all of these areas, not separately but cumulatively and in unison.

Concept 5.2   **Modernising vs historicising**

Particularly in literary translation, systemic incompatibilities are encountered and must somehow be reconciled on each of the three levels – the linguistic, literary and socio-cultural. A number of possibilities are open to the translator (Holmes, 1972a):

- To seek equivalence (seen in relative terms) and thus to create an air of contemporary relevance (*modernising* translation).
- To retain the specificities of the original, despite the apparent incompatibilities (*historicising* translation).

At this point, Holmes offers an important insight. Assuming that modernising older poetry would almost always be met with resistance, would this resistance to modernising be shown equally at the level of linguistic/literary form *and* at the socio-cultural level? In other words, transposing a poem of another day into a full-fledged modern meta-poem might, perhaps with good reason, be seen as gratuitous, but would the same be true if we were to leave the 'socio-cultural' alone and only modernise, say, the **genre** or, alternatively, tamper with the socio-cultural and leave the genre alone? This challenging research question is yet to be resolved. According to Holmes (1972b: 50), whichever permutation the translator deems appropriate, the end-result must satisfy two basic criteria:

• It must match the original to a degree sufficient for the label 'translation' to be applied (the matching criterion).
• It must be such that the end-product will be considered a poem (the poetic criterion).

5.1.2   The metatext model assessed

As pointed out earlier, the model proposed by Holmes is not restricted to poetic translation. Consider Holmes's idea of **micro-** and **macro-structure**, for example. At the level of the poem or the text, the translator will often find that the various parts form an integrated whole, and that dealing with a certain part in a particular way might make certain choices relating to other parts possible or impossible. This sensitivity to overall **text structure** is overriding; individual word choices and so on are so largely circumscribed by the macro-structure that they must be seen as secondary.

Thus, it is not 'textual' equivalence as narrowly defined by Catford, for example, that the translator seeks but what Holmes, Beaugrande and other text linguists would call a network of 'correspondences' or 'matchings', with varying **closeness of fit**. The translator searches for correspondences (**formal**, **semantic** and/or **functional**) and achieves these at various levels of text organisation. Of course any one of these kinds of equivalence could be a legitimate focus of attention, even a predominant one. In dealing with **actual** texts or parts of text, however, neither formal, nor semantic or even functional correspondence alone is sufficient in and by itself.

5.2   Translation: Shaping context and history

Quote 5.2

Linguists have moved from word to text as a unit, but not beyond. . . .
The overall position of the linguist in translation studies would be rather
analogous to that of an intrepid explorer who refuses to take any notice
of the trees in the new region he has discovered until he has made sure he
has painstakingly arrived at a description of all the plants that grow there.

Susan Bassnett and André Lefevere (1990b: 4)

Propelled by shared concerns regarding the role of translation in cultural innovation and social change, the 'cultural turn' is an all-pervasive phenomenon which has occurred gradually in many different parts of the world. To illustrate this universal appeal which the study of culture has had for the student of translation, it might be helpful to see the conceptual divide 'linguistic' vs 'cultural' through the eyes of a linguist-turned-culturalist: translation theorist Mary Snell-Hornby.

In her 'integrated approach', Snell-Hornby (1988) exhorts linguists to reconsider the 'scientism' of their statements about translation and to make the leap from the 'text' as the unit of translation to culture at large. The general trend in translation studies is clearly towards cultural rather than linguistic transfer. This entails that the process be viewed not as a transcoding of products but as a process of communication. The function of the target text must take precedence over a concern with the minutiae of the source text. From this perspective, the text would no longer be seen as an isolated instance of linguistic usage but as an act of genuine communication (taking in not only the textual-linguistic element, but also the entire cultural context). This last parameter, subsuming both text-world and language use, has come to be the hallmark of the integrated approach to translation as an 'interdiscipline'.

5.2.1   Reinstating culture

Translation as an interdiscipline is what, in their version of the 'cultural turn', Susan Bassnett and André Lefevere (1990b) meant by 'going beyond the text'. The integrated approach thus echoes viewpoints expressed all along by various European models of cultural studies. Promoted is an attitude which views translation studies specifically in terms of its potential to 'tackle the problem of **ideology**, change and power in literature and society and . . . assert the central function of translation as a shaping force' (1990b: 4). There is thus a common concern with the need to move away from a formalist position on translation and to turn instead to the larger issues of context and history.

A simple yet crucial assumption underlies this dynamically eclectic paradigm of cultural studies: like all activities to do with 're-writing', translation is never innocent. In theory, it is all too easy to see the process of translation in terms of a harmonious relationship between two different texts and contexts tied together by the bond of the emerging translation. In reality, the act of re-working a text is much more complex, and a number of issues, largely connected with aspects of the process of translation, have to be accounted for, including:

- the context in which the translation takes place;
- the history of the source and the future of the target;
- the place which the text had occupied in some literary system vs that which it will occupy once translated.

In order to account for this new translational reality, translation studies has had to adjust its focus radically. What came to be examined was no longer structural incompatibilities suspended in a contextual vacuum, but organic linguistic entities embedded within a network of cultural **signs**. While linguistics has a great deal to offer in this regard, the culturalists argue, the linguistic approach cannot be sufficient by itself, and the study of translation should therefore be channelled to move beyond it.

5.2.2   The anatomy of translation as a re-writing process

In the context of discussing the manipulation which all translations are said to undergo, André Lefevere's contribution to the debate is particularly noteworthy. As stressed above, Lefevere strongly argues for a view of translation as a form of 're-writing'. This refers to a range of processes which, in one way or another, 'interpret' (in the sense of 'impose a particular reading on', even 'manipulate') an original text. In Lefevere's view, translation studies as a discipline should thus concern itself with aspects of this manipulative behaviour as a way of accounting for the **socio-cultural**, ideological and literary constraints within which translation, and indeed all forms of writing or re-writing, operate.

Concept 5.3   **Image**

Central to the 'translation as re-writing' thesis is the notion of *image*, understood as the projection of any work or author into a given target culture in such a way that what is projected begins to exert more influence than that which the original has had in its own culture (Lefevere, 1992: 110). In fact, in one definition, translation as rewriting is taken to be 'anything that contributes to constructing the "image" of a writer and/or a work of literature' (Bassnett and Lefevere, 1990a: 10). This is inextricably linked to political culture (**ideology**) and literary power structures (**poetics**) operative in a given society.

Ideology and poetics, then, are two important constraints intrinsic to any act of manipulation. Within the framework of ideology, re-writing focuses on the original's **universe of discourse** or the 'objects, concepts, customs belonging to the world that was familiar to the writer of the original' (Lefevere, 1992: 41). Translation will be subject to the influence of a number of factors including (p. 87):

- the status of the original;
- the image that the target culture has of itself;
- the types of texts considered worthy;
- the levels of **diction** deemed acceptable;
- the intended audience;
- the cultural **scripts** with which the audience identifies or about which it is willing to learn;
- the translator's ideology in the sense of loyalty to particular modes of text reproduction: is meaning privileged over form, for example?

Ideology-related factors – such as the role of re-writing in dealing with the original's type of text, **diction** or cultural **scripts** – may also be seen in the light of the second constraint which Lefevere identifies in acts of manipulation: the dominant **poetics**. Within poetics proper, and striking at the heart of cultural conflicts, is the translator's attempt to ensure that a work acquires prestige through the use of a respected **genre**, a popular motif, a favoured set of literary devices or a set of symbols serving particular themes fashionable in a given culture (1992: 26).

Of course, all of this assumes that at some stage in the process of translation and publishing, the work has been 'admitted'. A work's symbolism, genre or character portrayal may militate against the status of such a work and deem it unworthy of translation in the first place. Aspects of a source text's poetics or ideology can and often do condemn works to oblivion or lead to their rejection.

In Lefevere's anatomy of manipulation, the two factors of poetics and ideology constitute a 'control factor' 'which sees to it that the [literary] system does not fall too far out of step with other systems society consists of' (1985: 226). Poetics actually belongs to the literary system and thus tries to control it from within. Ideology, on the other hand, lies outside the system but nevertheless sets the parameters which determine how the influence of poetics is to be channelled.

Ideology and poetics thus manifest themselves in the way texts are consciously or unconsciously brought into line with dominant world-views and/or dominant literary structures. Between them, political and literary pressures promote what literature (or the world, for that matter) should be like.

5.2.3   Appropriating the original: A case study

Manipulating **texture** (and consequently shifting **register** and overall pragmatic effects) is heavily implicated in the kind of discursive practices which drive ideologies. In a study of appropriation, Piotr Kuhiwczak (1990a) discusses a form of manipulation intended not so much to protect the reader from an indigenous ideology as to protect the reader from an alien poetics. The figure under scrutiny is the Czech writer, Milan Kundera.

Quote 5.3

In 1968 and 1969, *The Joke* was translated into all the Western languages. But what surprises! In France, the translator rewrote the novel by ornamenting my style. In England, the publisher cut out all the reflective passages, eliminated the musicological chapters, changed the order of the parts, recomposed the novel. Another country: I meet my translator, a man who knows not a word of Czech. 'Then how did you translate it?' 'With my heart.' And he pulls a photo of me from his wallet.

Milan Kundera (1988: 1)

Discussing Kundera's *The Joke*, Kuhiwczak (p. 124) points out that the English translation of the novel is inadequate and distorted,

An appropriation of the original, resulting from the translator's and publisher's untested assumptions about Eastern Europe, East European writing, and the ability of the Western reader to decode complex cultural messages.

Specifically, *The Joke*'s plot is not particularly complex; it reflects the writer's belief that novels should be about 'themes' served by narratives that are 'polyphonic, full of seemingly insignificant digressions and carefully crafted repetitions' (p. 125). These are textual manifestations which can be uncovered adequately only by a form of discourse analysis with a particularly rich cultural dimension.

The translator into English saw in this mosaic of features a bewildering array of 'irrelevancies' which had to be tidied for the prospective reader to make sense and discover a reasonably structured chronological order. For example, an important 'theme' – the folk music cultural element – is jettisoned, sweeping away with it the very thing which Kundera intended by this particularly long digression, 'to illustrate the fragility of culture' (p. 126).

5.2.4   The continental cultural model assessed

The cultural turn has alerted us to how standards of what constitutes 'good' or 'bad' translations tend to change rapidly, and how **norms** and conventions are constantly evolving. The mainstay of translator decisions and the proper domain of theorising the process cannot therefore be 'accuracy', based on purely linguistic criteria alone, but rather the variety of 'functions' which texts are intended to fulfil in real contexts. The range of constraints within which translation is undertaken would similarly have to be worked out in accordance with models developed within both literary studies and linguistics, seeking to account for such contextual factors as power relations and ideological manipulation.

Further reading

- On translation as 'metatext' and James Holmes' seminal ideas on the product, process and function of translation, see Holmes (1988).

- On the way linguistics-oriented approaches can give in to admit 'cultural' considerations, see Snell-Hornby (1988).

- On the continental brand of cultural studies, see Bassnett and Lefevere (1990 a and b, 1998).

Chapter 6

Literary and cultural constraints

This chapter will . . .

- discuss the implications which polysystem theory has had both for literary studies and for translation studies;
- look in more detail at the notion of translation 'norms' which underpins the predominantly target text orientation promoted by polysystemic descriptive work;
- introduce the 'functionalist' theory of *skopos* or translation purpose and highlight its concern with such issues as translation **commission** and the target text.

One important source of inspiration for research into the effect that institutions of prestige and power can have on the process of translation has been the work led by the Tel Aviv scholars Itimar Even-Zohar and Gideon Toury on literary **polysystems** and translation **norms**. In turn, the polysystem model owes a considerable debt to the vigorous intellectual activity which Eastern Europe saw in the 1960s and early 1970s. A valuable insight to emerge from this body of theorising relates to the losses and gains in translation. So-called 'shifts' in translation are not considered 'errors', as many a translation critic has called them. Shifts are seen as part of the process which is naturally embedded in two different **text-worlds**, intellectually, aesthetically and from the perspective of culture at large. As the Slovak translation theorist Anton Popovic (1970: 79) put it, shifts may simply be seen as 'all that appears as new with respect to the original, or fails to appear where it might have been expected'.

6.1   Polysystem theory and translation

Concept 6.1   **The polysystem**

Polysystem theory holds that literary systems (e.g. the **canon**, children's literature) tend to be in a state of flux, constantly changing status and fluctuating between a peripheral and a central position in their interaction with one another. The notion of the polysystem has emerged specifically to explain the way these systems function and evolve under a variety of societal constraints.

The interaction among literary systems is closely linked to the familiar tension which emanates from the way the various literary models (e.g. **genres** and traditions) interact with one another, all vying for recognition. There will always be a canonised form and a form which is less influential. Endorsed by an institutionalised aesthetic, the canonised form (e.g. the 'realistic novel' as a genre) will attempt to protect its prominence at whatever cost, while the non-canonised, usually innovative, form (e.g. 'popular fiction') tends to struggle for some form of prominence.

According to polysystem theory, it is necessary in dealing with the literature of any nation to account for the so-called 'low' forms as well as the 'high' forms. In addition to the widely recognised and respected models, non-canonic and seemingly peripheral forms must not be ignored. Genres such as children's literature, popular fiction and, perhaps more significantly, translated literature are no less worthy of attention than those systems which have traditionally occupied a central position.

Literary systems, then, invariably involve the struggle of a minor form to gain equality with the major form, and perhaps even hold sway. Obviously, translation is heavily implicated in all of this inter-systemic rivalry. Translated works usually occupy a peripheral position, but this is not necessarily always the case. Translations can at times assume a more influential role. Although often associated with the secondary function of merely propping up existing structures, genres, poetic traditions, etc., translated literature can be (and often is) capable of performing a primary function in the polysystem, bringing in new forms and innovative models.

According to Even-Zohar (1978a: 24), translation can achieve a primary position when, in a given society at a particular period of time, indigenous literature might be:

- too young or in the process of being established;
- peripheral or weak (or both) vis-à-vis world literature;
- going through a crisis.

The Israeli case is interesting in this regard. In the early stages of its development, modern Hebrew did not have an indigenous literature as such, and thus it virtually lacked a canon of literary forms. Given demographic and other political considerations, Hebrew was therefore heavily reliant on foreign language translations to fill serious gaps in literary thought and practice.

In such circumstances, which are all too common around the world, the new idiom of translated works tends to give rise to a variety of innovative forms of writing. Similarly, the repertoire of a burgeoning literature is never complete and translation serves as an important source of inspiration. There will also be factors such as generation gaps and changing **socio-cultural** mores which render certain forms obsolete and in need of rejuvenation, and translation fulfils this need.

The opposite of the conditions that make translation primary can also occur, relegating translation to secondary importance in the polysystem. In well-established, strong and dominant systems, translations might only be seen as peripheral, optional extras. This has serious implications for the theory and practice of translation. Polysystemists use the peripherality index to explore how and what kinds of texts are selected for translation by both the sending culture and the receiving culture. Research in this area has shown that texts are invariably chosen for translation if they are compatible with the canon (Even-Zohar, 1978b).

This dynamic search for homogeneity is evident in another aspect of the relationship between translation and the literary polysystem: the language of the translated work itself. The language of translation may be explored in terms of how responsive a translated text is to existing **norms** and models within the target system. In cases where translated literature is primary, what counts might not be the genius of the original work slavishly reproduced, but rather the 'version', the 'imitation' or even the 'adaptation' which assures an insecure receiving polysystem that it still has something to offer.

6.1.1   The development of norms

From the overall perspective of polysystem theory, and particularly in the work of Toury, translation shifts have come to be seen as indices pointing to the workings of norms and as attributable to a variety of influences, including translators' individual styles, translation policy, ideological considerations and political decisions.

Descriptive Translation Studies has emerged to deal with these issues and is totally at variance with the 'equivalence' proposals. In a similar way to what has happened under **deconstruction**, the equivalence argument is simply turned on its head. From the perspective of the descriptivists, the prime movers of the translation process are not source texts but socio-cultural norms and textual-literary conventions in the target language and culture, together with such factors as:

- the model within which the translator works;
- the presuppositions as to what counts as relevant;
- the decisions taken regarding the nature of the end-product.

Thus, literariness is never a concrete reality enshrined in the source text but a set of values that owes its existence to a wide range of factors. These factors are said to be facts of one system only – the target's. Toury insists that these 'translational facts' are linked only indirectly to the source text, and rarely to the source culture. This is how equivalence is effectively replaced by the notion of 'norms' (Hermans, 1985: 217).

Toury's crucial contribution to the debate regarding 'norms' may be set against the background of his own research experience. This began with an examination of a sizeable sample spanning a period of fifteen years of prose fiction translations into modern Hebrew from English, Russian, German, French and Yiddish. The aim of the investigation was to explore the kind of decisions considered to be instrumental in the making of a translation. This was one way of trying to unravel the polysystems at work in the receiving culture (Hebrew). The shifts between the source and target texts were an obvious starting point since it was here that the aesthetic underpinning translator decisions was thought to lie.

Concept 6.2   Norms

In dealing with the norm model as developed by Toury, it must first be recognised that, in the 1970s, concepts such as 'norms' were contentious issues in the study of translation. The literature on the subject of norms was extremely confused, and many contradictory normative models were in circulation.

Toury presented a straightforward tripartite model of normative translational behaviour: the category norm would be situated somewhere along the line between **'competence'** (rule-governed behaviour) and 'performance' (**actual** decision making, including lapses and idiosyncrasies) (1995: 54).

Toury then defined norms as strategic courses of action that were opted for with a noticeable frequency and chosen in preference to other available options within a given system of socio-cultural or **socio-textual practices** (1995: 54).

One of the more interesting findings of Toury's research emerged in the domain of 'shifts'. In the translations examined, very few straightforward linguistic changes were in evidence, and the minimal omissions or additions that were there tended in fact to be somehow irrelevant to the overall identity of the end product. More meaningful changes were observed in the area of style (e.g. **motivated** lexical choice, syntactic reformulation, etc.). For example, there was a tendency to upgrade language to avoid sounding common or vulgar: **register** was elevated and the general tenor of the text raised appreciably. Observation of this kind provided Toury with a rich hypothesis to work with and, in turn, lent further support for the existence and power of 'norms'.

The analysis of norms and of the way they are manifested in actual translations was an important source of insights for translation analysts and practitioners. The descriptivists hoped that a pattern would emerge to indicate how basic notions in the theory and practice of translation (e.g. equivalence) are dealt with in different traditions, by different societies or cultures and at different periods of time. In addition, they hoped that, through such empirical data, insight would be gained into whether true **universals** in translation practice existed. An investigation along these lines would shed light on the highly opaque relationship between major and minor forms and forces within given literary systems.

6.1.2   The ideology of what to translate

Operating within the general parameters of polysystem theory, Toury specifically deals with the factors at work in the selection of what is to be translated. Ideological reasons are found to motivate selection in most cases, with linguistic or even aesthetic criteria playing a minor role. For example, given the marginality and the crisis which Hebrew was going through generally, a tendency towards choosing social or socialist works was much in evidence in the first half of the twentieth century. Similarly, Jewish authors writing in the various European languages were selected first for translation, as were certain subjects and topics of national interest.

Literary and aesthetic criteria were not completely ignored but to be admitted, they had to be supplemented by other criteria. For example, literary reasons for the choice of certain works did feature fairly prominently but only in cases where compatible (i.e. comparable) indigenous literary models were not available. In fact, when this happened, translated works normally became a shaping force occupying the centre within the Hebrew polysystem. Other factors invoked in support of certain selections, and prompted by agendas other than the 'ideological', include the didactic appeal which the work might have and the adaptability of the work to jealously guarded norms in the target language.

6.1.3   Polysystem theory assessed

Within the polysystem paradigm, to talk of genuine linguistic or even functional equivalence seems irrelevant in most cases. What matters is the way texts come in, how they are translated and where in the target polysystem they are eventually found. Questions such as the **acceptability** of a translation as translation, and whether the translation is central or peripheral within the overall conceptual map, far outweigh considerations of correspondence and linguistic or aesthetic compatibility of source and target versions.

The value of examining a source text for evidence is certainly not ruled out, but the object of the analysis is to get to grips with the grounds on which operational decisions are taken, shifts effected and choices made. To the polysystemists, these are translational phenomena that legitimately belong to the target system and the receiving culture which operates it. The reason for the rather unenthusiastic attitude towards the source text and towards considerations of faithfulness, loyalty and so on, is not so much a lack of concern with the textual minutiae of the source text as it is a sociologically motivated plan to find out what actually happens when translations are made.

6.2   The Manipulationists

One group of scholars to take an active interest in the new development of polysystem theory and its implications for translation was what has come to be known as the Manipulation School. This unofficial designation refers to a trend associated with a particular approach to the study of translated literature and prominently represented on the continent by translation theorists such as Jose Lambert and Theo Hermans.

The assumption underlying the manipulationists' thesis owes a great deal to the notion of literature as a system (hierarchically structured elements). Within this configuration, translation holds a unique position in the system. In the competition which goes on between major and minor cultures, languages, or varieties and genres within the same language, it is assumed that power play is easier and more effective to act out in translation than in any other form of communication.

The manipulationists thus found an interesting niche in the unique position in which translation usually finds itself. From the perspective of the target literature, all translation involves some form of manipulation of the source text (Hermans, 1985: 11). This may be purposeful (the work of a translator prompted by a variety of motives) or it may be due to the various pressures exerted by different linguistic, literary and cultural codes impacting on one another.

An important factor motivating 'manipulation' research relates to the marginal role assigned to the study of translations, particularly in literary circles. There has always been a dominant poetics and a hierarchy of canonised texts in any national literature. This literary-critical fact has invariably meant that notions such as originality, creativity and aesthetic excellence are always valued above 'second-order' quality normally associated with such genres as children's literature, popular fiction and translation.

According to the manipulationists, the marginalisation of translators and translations is precipitated by factors such as the adherence to outmoded notions of equivalence and the insistence on the supremacy of the original. As a result, the manipulationists argue, myth is perpetuated regarding the original's outstanding qualities – an attitude which has in practice developed into an obsession with fault-finding in endless comparisons of source and target texts. Such attitudes are criticised as prescriptive, constantly directing the attention of the translator towards an almost sacrosanct source.

6.3   Translation purpose

> **Quote 6.2**
>
> An expert must be able to say – and this implies both knowledge and a duty to use it – what is what. . . . The translator is such an expert. It is thus up to him to decide, for instance, what role a source text plays in his translation **action**. The decisive factor here is the purpose, the *skopos*, of the communication in a given situation.
>
> Hans Vermeer (1989: 174)

6.3.1   *Skopos* theory

Functionalism is another influential trend in translation studies. The new focus on translation purpose emerged in Germany in the early 1980s and, under the general designation of ***skopos*** theory, came to be associated most notably with translation scholars Holz-Mänttäri, Hans Vermeer and Katharina Reiss.

Concept 6.3   *Skopos*

Skopos (Greek: 'purpose', 'goal') is an appropriate name for a theory which focuses on such aspects of the translation process as interactional dynamics and **pragmatic** purpose. The theory holds that the way the target text eventually shapes up is determined to a great extent by the function, or 'skopos', intended for it in the target context. Such a strategy can and often does run counter to orthodox equivalence-based procedures since in the light of *skopos* considerations, the end essentially justifies the means.

The *skopos* idea relies on key concepts in pragmatics, such as intention and **action**. Two basic assumptions are entertained as *skopos* conventions:

- *Skopos* Rule 1: Interaction is determined by its purpose.
- *Skopos* Rule 2: Purpose varies according to the text receiver.

Such a framework for translator decisions is governed by a number of factors, both textual and contextual. One such is **audience design**, which accounts for the way a target text is intended to be received. This largely determines which translation strategy is most appropriate. Different purposes may be served by different translation strategies, and translation proper, paraphrase (thin **glossing**) or re-editing (**thick glossing**), may respond to different communicative needs.

Is *skopos* theory source or target oriented? A great deal of confusion surrounds this area of research into *skopos*. Nord (1997: 29) suggests that a given *skopos* can be served equally adequately by a free or a faithful translation: 'what the [*skopos*] rule does not mean is that a good translation should *ipso facto* conform or adapt to target-culture behaviour or expectations'. Nevertheless, mainstream *skopos* theory insists that the target text must be produced with a given purpose in mind and that translations function well when shaped by a particular purpose:

> Translate/interpret/speak/write in a way that enables your text/translation to function in the situation in which it is used and with the people who want to use it and precisely in the way they want it to function.
>
> (Vermeer, 1989, cited in Nord, 1997: 29)

Three major kinds of purpose in translation are recognised within the *skopos* framework:

- the communicative purpose aimed at by the target text (e.g. to persuade, to inform);
- the strategic purpose aimed at in using a particular translation procedure (e.g. the option of a fluent, free rendering in a public relations exercise);
- the general purpose aimed at by the translator (i.e. whatever motivates that person).

Such purposes cannot all be equally important and must therefore be prioritised. According to *skopos* theory, the success or failure of a translation is ultimately decided by whether it can be interpreted successfully by the target recipient in a manner that is consistent with what is expected of it. Failing this, the translation would lead to what is referred to as 'protest'.

6.3.2   Success and protest

Skopos theory subscribes to a view of communication which posits 'feedback' (i.e. response by the text receiver) as an essential part of any form of interaction. The reaction to the message once it is delivered indicates the extent of its 'success'.

Concept 6.4   **Intention and function**

A message is deemed successful if, in the target situation, it elicits no 'protest' to indicate that the message is not received in the manner intended and/or expected. *Intention* is thus closely bound up with *function*, the latter being the use (or interpretation) assigned by the receiver to the incoming message in the light of his or her expectations, needs, prior **knowledge**, and so on.

(Nord, 1997)

As judged by the receiver, success is thus measured in terms of the coherence of content and intention (the latter encompassing 'use' or 'interpretation'). That is, a protest will ensue if coherence is impaired as a result of either the content of the message or the intention of the text producer/translator being below par for whatever reason.

6.3.3   Textual coherence

The concept of *coherence* is central to *skopos* theory. Two basic kinds of conceptual **connectivity** are distinguished:

- Intratextual coherence, relating to the integrity of the target text per se, with the 'coherence rule' stipulating that

    the message produced by the translator must be interpretable in a way that is coherent with the target recipient's situation.
    (Reiss and Vermeer, 1984: 113, cited in Shuttleworth and Cowie, 1997: 19)

    A target text which is inadequate because it is too literal, for example, will fail the intratextual coherence test and will elicit a 'protest'.

- Intertextual coherence (or fidelity), relating to the match which is presumed to obtain between the target text and the source text.

    Intertextual coherence is a direct consequence of the translator's ability to comprehend the source text and to engage with the *skopos* it is intended to have in the target language. A target text is judged to be intextually coherent to the extent that there is consistency between the **intentionality** of the source text producer, the way this is interpreted, and the way it is re-expressed in the target language. This is the 'fidelity' rule.

Within *skopos* theory, however, intertextual coherence is taken to be secondary to intratextual coherence. To a target-language reader who normally does not know the source text, what matters most is that the message received fulfils certain basic requirements. Central to *skopos* theory is the notion that such aspects of the source text as **text type**, **genre** or discourse style cannot automatically be considered a basis on which the fidelity rule operates. It is here that the notion of the source message, as containing within it no more than an 'offer of information', becomes relevant.

6.3.4   Information offer

The basic idea of the 'information offer' is underpinned by a number of assumptions:

- All texts exhibit plurality of meaning.
- Only some of a text's possible meanings are realised at any one time.
- The text is likely to generate meanings not physically present in it.

Within this view of communication, *skopos* theory holds that, on any given occasion of language use, no more than an 'information offer' is yielded by the text. In translation, a text has meaning only to a particular receiver since it is intended only for that receiver. Different receivers (or the same receiver at different times) find different meanings in the same linguistic material offered by the text. In short, a 'text' can be as many texts as there are receivers (Nord, 1992: 91).

In translation or original text production, it is of paramount importance to make the offer of information compatible with the presumed interests, expectations and knowledge of the addressees. *Skopos* theory holds that the translator is certainly not a mere conduit pouring meanings out of one vessel into another.

6.3.5   Holz-Mänttäri: Translational action

From a similar perspective to the *skopos* theories outlined above, translational action views translation as a purposeful, outcome-oriented human interactive activity, and focuses on the process of translation as a form of intercultural transfer:

> [It] is not about translating words, sentences or texts but is in every case about guiding the intended co-operation over cultural barriers enabling functionally oriented communication.
>
> (Holz-Mänttäri, 1984: 7–8; translated in Munday, 2001)

Involved in this actional process is a series of roles and players:

• The initiator: including those who need the translation.
• The commissioner: the issuer of the contract.
• The ST producer: the individual within the company who writes the ST, not necessarily always involved in the TT production.
• The TT producer: the translator.
• The TT user: the person who uses the TT; for example, as sales literature.
• The TT receiver: the final recipient of the TT; for example, the clients reading the translated sales literature (Holz-Mänttäri, 1984: 109–11).

In the 'translational text operations' (i.e. in the production of the TT), the ST is analysed solely for its 'construction and function profile'. Relevant features are described according to the age-old split of 'content' and 'form' (p. 126):

1. **Content**. Structured by what are called 'tectonics', content is divided into (a) factual information and (b) overall communicative strategy.
2. **Form**. Structured by '**texture**', form is divided into (a) terminology and (b) cohesive elements.

In this division, the needs of the receiver are the determining factors for the TT.

The value of Holz-Mänttäri's work thus lies in placing the process of translation within its **socio-cultural** context, including the interplay between the translator and the initiating institution. This has been well received in translation studies, earning generous praise from translation scholars such as Christine Schäffner who has this to say:

> Holz-Mänttäri's concept of translatorial action is considered relevant for all types of translation and the theory is held to provide guidelines for every decision to be taken by the translator.
>
> (Schäffner, 1999: 5)

6.3.6   Text typology and *skopos*

Who decides what the *skopos* of a particular translation will be? A straight answer to this question might be: the 'client' who initiates the process in cases where translation is done by assignment or **commission**. However, translation briefs are not always sufficiently detailed regarding what strategy to use, what type of translation would be most suitable, etc. To deal with such problems, *skopos* theory entertains the general assumption that, to accomplish a particular communicative goal, there will always be a 'normal' way of proceeding (sanctioned by the professional community, for example). This is also the case where no 'client' is particularly envisaged and no purpose specified.

Concept 6.5   **Reiss's text typology**

Reiss's text typology, originally intended as a set of guidelines for the practical translator, is envisaged within a theory of norms. Three basic types of text are proposed and are distinguished one from the other in terms of factors such as 'intention' or rhetorical purpose and 'function' or the use to which texts are put:

- *Informative* texts which convey information.
- *Expressive* texts which communicate thoughts in a creative way.
- *Operative* texts which persuade.

These contexts are said to have a direct consequence for the kind of semantic, syntactic and stylistic features used and for the way texts are structured, both in their original form and in the translation.

It is important to note that Reiss (1971) originally argued for a correlation between 'text type' and 'translation method' and that the predominant function of the text needs to be preserved in translation. To deal with informative texts, the translator needs to concentrate on establishing semantic equivalence and, perhaps only secondarily, deal with connotative meanings and aesthetic values. In the case of expressive texts, the translator should be mainly concerned with the need to preserve aesthetic effects alongside relevant aspects of the semantic content. Finally, operative texts require the translator to heed the extralinguistic effect which the text is intended to achieve, even if this has to be at the expense of both form and content.

Within her subsequent espousal of *skopos* theory, Reiss (in Reiss and Vermeer, 1984) departs from the above formulation slightly. It is now suggested that the correlation between text type and translation method is more likely to apply in cases of 'functional invariance' (e.g. in dealing with restricted registers such as weather forecasts). In such cases, there is nothing to justify a departure from the predominant function of the source text in the target language. Where this is not the case, functional change may be called for and source text function adjusted: the 'content' of 'informative' texts, the 'form' of 'expressive' texts, and the 'effect' of 'operative' texts are no longer sacrosanct and the translation *skopos* begins to play a crucial role in the way the material is translated. In fact, source-text function markers that are uncritically reproduced in the target text might signal an altogether different function.

6.3.7 Loyalty and *skopos*

Despite its avowedly target-language orientation, work within the *skopos* framework has shown that

- source text values may still be legitimately accorded a theoretical status;
- text types remain useful templates and continue to enjoy a special status in the work of the translator;
- equivalence (albeit of a highly flexible, functional kind) is not entirely moribund.

In practice, *skopos* functionality remains an overriding factor. The principle of loyalty is invoked not to persuade the translator to ignore cultural norms or the brief, but to place on him or her the moral obligation to explain any changes or to reveal any conflict of loyalties (in subtle 'textual' ways, or through negotiation with the communication partners, for example). Textually, the form which this explanation or negotiation might take, covers the entire spectrum of **'paratextual'** features, ranging from preface or footnotes to subtle hints in the text itself indicating what is happening. Loyalty thus commits the translator both to the source and to the target sides. But this should not be confused with 'fidelity' or 'faithfulness' (referring to the relationship between source text and target text). As Nord (1997: 125) puts it, 'loyalty is an **interpersonal** category referring to a social relationship between *people*'.

Concept 6.6   **Loyalty**

An interesting notion added to the vocabulary of *skopos* theory is *loyalty*. The term is introduced by Nord (1991b) to account for an attitude which translators are urged to nurture in their relationship with the source text's author and/or sender on the one hand, and the reader of the target text, on the other.

  The concept of loyalty is invoked in order to deal with *skopos* problems of the following type:

* A translation purpose as specified by the brief is at variance with the original author's intentions.

* The commissioning brief is incompatible with culturally sanctioned translation practices.

In such cases, it is incumbent upon the translator to inform the reader of certain decisions taken in carrying out the translation. This is a trust which the reader places in the translator, and which must be honoured; hence the moral nature of the principle of loyalty.

6.3.8   *Skopos* theory assessed

Despite the shift of focus in Reiss's model away from a rigid text-type orientation, towards a more functional approach to translation purpose, *skopos* theory has nevertheless been a timely reminder of how useful text-classifications are in sharpening the translator's awareness of discourse and other textual and extratextual factors. More specifically, text typologies continue to be seen as key variables in helping the translator to determine whether a given equivalence relation is or is not so important in a given context, with a particular translation *skopos* in mind. Indeed, as Nord (1997: 38) observes, even in the case of a much-needed functional change within a particular *skopos*, one would still be using 'function' and 'text type' as tools in assessing the various options.

  As we near the end of this tour through translation studies' 'house of many rooms', it is appropriate to claim that at no stage has equivalence been abandoned or text classification altogether jettisoned. In *skopos* theory, for example, these concepts are kept but are now related to 'adequacy', a term used in the non-technical sense of 'adequate to the job'. This has to do with the translation brief, and is seen as dynamic and **action**-based, a 'goal-directed selection of signs that are considered **appropriate** for the communicative purpose defined in the translation assignment' (Reiss, 1989: 163).

6.4   The circle closes: Linkages to other disciplines

In this book, the case that linguistics is capable of informing the study of translation is clearly stated. However, linguistics is not monolithic and a variety of models must be recognised as valid, each designed to achieve certain goals and not necessarily others. By the same token, translation studies has not remained a prisoner within one paradigm. As this survey has shown, different perspectives have systematically been adopted and different approaches invoked to shed new light on a constantly evolving intercultural and interlinguistic phenomenon.

One way of capturing this diversity is to see linguistics from the vantage point of how translation studies has opened up to a diverse range of influences. The following discussion will highlight those areas of interface between translation studies and a variety of adjacent disciplines both within and outside linguistics. Instead of focusing on what has been achieved, the emphasis will be on connections which can still be made. This entails that we follow to a natural conclusion the line already traced in portraying the way translation studies has evolved: from a narrower focus on languages in contact, to such broader issues as **gender** and **ideology**.

6.4.1   Contrastive analysis

Comparing or contrasting two or more languages at various levels of linguistic description has interacted with translation studies in two basic ways:

- It has provided explanations and solutions for problems encountered in translation practice (Nida, 1964).
- It has in turn received from translation a range of theoretical and practical insights, as well as **actual** data and specific information (James, 1980).

To play such an important role, contrastive analysis has had to broaden its scope, taking in pragmatics, text linguistics, discourse analysis, rhetoric. The translation data used has taken many forms: naturally occurring, fabricated or translated by the analyst. The level at which such data is elicited has also varied considerably, from word and lexico-grammatical features, to stretches of texts, entire interactions and communicative events.

6.4.2   Sociolinguistics

Sociolinguistics has contributed to the debate in translation studies from at least two perspectives:

1. The identification, description and explanation of how language relates to social situations and communicative events. This has to do with language in texts and, by extension, with features of the text with which translators constantly deal (e.g. regional dialect).

2. The analysis of:
   - how the translator as an individual sees his or her task in society (upholding **norms**, etc.);
   - the translator's response to the needs of a target audience operating in a different language and culture;
   - the implications of such attitudes in terms of translation strategy and the philosophy underpinning it.

Since such attitudes are by and large norm-driven, the kind of sociolinguistics involved here would not be one dealing solely with discrete and disparate elements found *in* texts. Rather, it is a sociolinguistics *of* texts relating to the entire concept of translation in all its complexity (Fawcett, 1997). This kind of sociolinguistics has subsumed work done on the language of translation, including:

- Modes such as fluent, dynamically equivalent translation when these emerge as norms.
- **Universals** of translation, evolving as norms in and of translations (Baker, 1995).

6.4.3   Psycholinguistics

The transfer of meaning involved in translation is certainly part of a mental process and thus relies in a major way on a complex form of information processing. Building on what happens in monolingual communication, psycholinguistic studies of translation proceed from an analysis of the constraints under which bilingual mediation works. Translation-specific components in the area of problem-recognition and problem-solving are added, and the process is seen in terms of analysis and synthesis (and revision if translation and not interpreting is being specifically studied). Drawing heavily on psycholinguistics, introspection (immediate retrospection and think-aloud) has recently emerged as an important area of research in translation process studies.

6.4.4   Corpus linguistics

Work on translation universals informed by the kind of sociolinguistics applied to the entire concept *of* translation (and not merely to what happens *in* translations) has recently emerged as an important research issue in corpus translation studies. This is partly modelled on corpus linguistics or the use of corpora in the scientific study of language in use. A number of concerns are shared by the two fields of inquiry, Corpus Linguistics and Corpus Translation Studies:

- Primacy is accorded to authentic instances of language use, and to a move away from introspection (Holmes, 1978b: 101).
- Texts are viewed not as idealised entities but rather as observable facts (Toury, 1980: 79).
- A concern with what corpora should consist of and with how to guard against such pitfalls as bias in the selection of materials.
- Recognition that computational and statistical tools are not sufficient by themselves, and that intuition and observation have a role to play.

In the specific area of design criteria for building corpora, certain developments in corpus linguistics have shaped thinking in corpus translation theory:

- In addition to random selection, which is still widely practised, a more active stance in dealing with the data is promoted. In both linguistics and translation, there has been a noticeable tendency to intervene purposefully in order to channel compilation of text samples in particular directions thought to be more suited to the specific concerns of the discipline.
- A more differentiated framework is employed to ensure that the material is 'representative', not only of such aspects as spoken or written language, but also of particular types of text or genre (Baker, 1993).

6.4.5   Text linguistics

The concept of a 'whole' language is now untenable, and such notions as register, text type, text function, **cohesion** and **coherence** have become common currency in debating translation issues. Together with insights from text linguistics, critical discourse analysis and genre theory, this new focus has sensitised translators to issues such as power, ideology and manipulation in translation.

6.4.6   Cultural studies and deconstruction

With the growing popularity of academic subjects such as cultural studies, the issue of ideology and the way it becomes bound up with translation strategy has come to the fore. The field of translation has benefited considerably from insights yielded by this kind of enquiry. Under what may be termed 'the ideology of translation', translation theorists have become interested in such aspects of the process as:

- the choice of works to be translated (what is valued and what is excluded);
- the power structure which controls the production and consumption of translations;
- who has access to translation and who is denied access;
- what is omitted, added or altered in seeking to control the message.

6.4.7   Gender studies

Gender studies and feminist scholarship have drawn attention to a considerable body of writing by women. As a result, women translators have begun to ponder what it means to be a woman translator in a male tradition. A number of factors long overlooked have suddenly emerged:

- the choice of texts to translate, a problematic issue particularly when the text to be translated is ideologically contentious;
- the languages involved, with issues such as the translation of **word play** acquiring a momentum of their own;
- textual practices across cultures.

Joining forces with post-colonial research and the study of popular culture, feminist translation studies has made a huge contribution to the study of the politics and ideology of translation.

6.4.8   Literature

Two phases in the relationship between literature and translation may be highlighted:

1. A traditional phase, in which literary translators have had to accept well-established hierarchies regarding what constitutes literature: poetry, prose, drama, high as opposed to low culture and so on. Modes of writing such as science fiction, children's literature and 'pulp' fiction would be excluded, with translation itself being treated with the low esteem accorded to derivative forms of text production.

2. A more recent phase, in which some of these ideas are challenged by new theories such as the polysystem model: any literature comprises not only the canonic, but also long denigrated forms such as soap operas.

Further reading

- On the evolution of cultural studies, and specifically on polysystems theory and its applications in translation studies, see Gentzler (1993), Hermans (1999).

- On such cultural studies developments as the Manipulation School, see Hermans (1985b).

- On functionalism and Skopos Theory, see the chapter by Hans Vermeer, and the chapter by Katherina Reiss in Chesterman (1989), Nord (1997), Holz-Mänttäri (1984).

Section

Research models

Chapter 7

Register-oriented research models

This chapter will . . .

- address the issue of 'translation strategy' as a research theme;
- describe how translation strategy has been dealt with by a range of research models informed by different paradigms and representing different translation trends.

Concept 7.1   **Translation strategy and context**

In the following discussion of research models, the issue of *translation strategy* is considered central to how translation research has evolved. As the discussion unfolds, the research scene will be shown to reflect a concern with:

- the notion of **'register'** and issues related to the 'use' and 'user' of language (although a target text orientation is not ruled out, this research focus is identified mainly within source text-oriented models of the translation process, represented by the left-hand side of the conceptual triangle in Concept Map III);
- **'intentionality'** and other aspects of pragmatics such as **'speech acts'**, **'implicatures'** and 'relevance' (shared by almost all translation models, this research focus is represented by the base line of the triangle);
- the broader notion of 'culture', with the focus shifting to the status of **'text'**, **'genre'** and **'discourse'** in the translation process (although a source text orientation is not ruled out, this research focus is identified mainly within target text-oriented models of the translation process, represented by the right-hand side of the triangle).

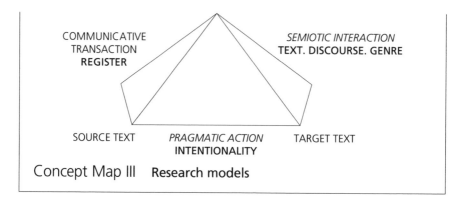

COMMUNICATIVE
TRANSACTION
REGISTER

SEMIOTIC INTERACTION
TEXT. DISCOURSE. GENRE

SOURCE TEXT   *PRAGMATIC ACTION*   TARGET TEXT
                   INTENTIONALITY

Concept Map III   Research models

As declared at the outset, the main aim of this book is to encourage translators and teachers of translation to reflect upon and, where necessary, to re-examine the practices in which they are engaged. The focus is thus on the kind of research which involves the practitioners themselves, and on the variety of approaches and techniques employed in such practice-driven inquiry. Of paramount importance in this mode of investigation (generally designated in the literature as **action research**) is the need to develop a 'research stance' which dispenses with unhelpful distinctions such as 'theory' as 'an exercise in reflection' versus 'practice' as 'what one normally does'.

7.1   The age of dichotomies

In discussing translation strategy, it is important to recognise that the distinction between 'literal' and 'free' translation has always been central in translation studies. It has informed a range of translation dichotomies, including Peter Newmark's 'semantic' vs 'communicative', one of the earliest treatments of strategy in the literature.

Concept 7.2   **Semantic vs communicative**

Semantic translation is a mode of text transfer which involves using 'the bare syntactic and semantic constraints of the TL to reproduce the precise contextual meaning of the author' (Newmark, 1981: 22).

Communicative translation is a mode of text transfer which seeks 'to produce the same effect on the TL readers as was produced by the original on the SL readers' (Newmark, 1981: 22).

Ever since it was introduced in the 1970s, the semantic vs commun- icative distinction has continued to exercise a considerable influence on the way translation strategy is viewed in writings on translation theory. At the heart of the debate is the extent to which the source text may or may not be altered in the process of translation. This is usually linked to whether the source text is aimed at the source culture receivers or designed for a wider audience.

To show how the notion of **'register'** has been pivotal to this think- ing, particularly in the early stages of current research into translation strategy, the following discussion focuses on a number of models which, while subscribing to different paradigms within translation studies, all revolve around factors such as the 'use' and 'user' of language and the role of the translator as both an analyst and a producer of texts. In addition to a shared interest in translation strategy, what these models have in common is thus a concern with the translator, the text and the audience, and with the kind of meanings generated in the process of this interaction (e.g. **interpersonal** and **ideational** functions or meanings).

7.2 *Skopos* and translation strategy

Building on the notion of 'loyalty' within the *skopos* model, Nord (1997) proposes a comprehensive functional framework for identifying and dealing with relevant features of the source text (see 6.3). Three aspects of the functionalist translation model are highlighted as particularly important to the practising translator (1997: 59):

1. The translation **brief**.
2. ST analysis.
3. A functional hierarchy of translation problems.

On the issue of the translation brief, Nord (1997: 59–62) notes that briefs are crucial in any ST–TT profile comparison which translators must conduct as part of the process of engaging in a translation. The translation **commission** should include some or all of the following information for both the ST and the TT:

- the intended text function(s);
- the co-communicants (sender and recipient);

- the time and place of text production and reception;
- the medium (speech or writing);
- the motive (why the ST was written and why it is being translated).

Once the ST–TT profiles have been compared, Nord (1997: 79–129) suggests, the ST can be analysed for:

- subject matter, content and specific terminology;
- background and presuppositions;
- microstructures, **macro-structure** and **cohesion**;
- dialect and register;
- sentence structure.

In the light of this information, translators should be able to prioritise what to keep or highlight in the TT, and what to gloss over or even jettison.

Such catalogues of features are always useful and cater well for the various dimensions of text in context. On the textual front, cohesion and **coherence** are taken care of. Contextually, register's use and user, as well as pragmatic **intentionality**, are adequately covered. Largely glossed over, however, is the cultural aspect of language as a social **semiotic**, or how a text or utterances within a text are processed (produced and received) as 'signs'. In dealing with this essentially cultural-semiotic dimension of context, the translator or translation analyst would be concerned not only with socio-cultural norms and conventions, but also with textual practices governed and regulated by higher-order norms and conventions. These practices would be ultimately responsible for textual effectiveness, efficiency and general sociolinguistic **appropriateness**. It is only within such a framework that a basis could be established for determining what features should be dealt with as a matter of translation priority, and how.

Such observations may not have escaped Nord's attention when, to account for what is here referred to as '**socio-textual** practices' at work in undertaking (or indeed analysing) a translation, she takes the next step in constructing a translation strategy model. This is to establish a **functional** hierarchy which basically relates to whether the intended function of the translation should be dealt with in a 'documentary' or an 'instrumental' manner.

Concept 7.3   **Documentary vs instrumental**

Documentary translation serves to document in the target language the communication which a source text contains (Nord, 1991a: 72). The source text is simply reproduced, with no special allowance made for the target context. To achieve this, various techniques may be used, including word-for-word, **literal** translation, and so-called exoticising translation. In this kind of translation, aspects of the source text such as wording, word order, cultural references and local colour, are bound to be the primary focus.

Instrumental translation is a freer method of translation which could be totally at variance with what the source text was intended to achieve in the source language. The target text might acquire a new communicative purpose, 'without the recipient being conscious of reading or hearing a text which, in a different form, was used in a different communicative **action**' (Nord, 1991a: 73).

In the instrumental mode, a translation can be made to act independently in a target culture by such translation procedures as:

- reproducing the ST function, although this may require some linguistic and cultural alterations (equifunctional translation);
- changing the function of the ST, as in translating adult literature for children (heterofunctional translation);
- seeking to recreate the aesthetic effect of the original, as in the translation of poetry (homologous translation).

Instrumental translation is a method fraught with difficulties: how far can one go on adapting, where does one stop, what differentiates a translation from re-writing or what Koller or Gutt would call 'non-translation'? These difficulties are compounded when distinctions such as documentary vs instrumental are seen in **binary** and not relative terms. Pym (1992b: 174) seems to pick up on such anomalies when he highlights a variety of restrictions involved in opting for one translation strategy and not another:

- Why do we translate in the first place, and which text should we translate when we decide to translate?
- How will a particular type of translation be recognised for what it is once it is made available to us?
- If it can be assumed that extratextual factors are involved, and that these are beyond the translator's control, whose control are they under?
- What role does the paratext (notes, interpolations, etc.) play in our choice of translation strategy?

7.3   Text reception and translation strategy

The binariness inherent in most translation strategy classifications (e.g. instrumental vs documentary) has been seen by a number of translation theorists as unhelpful. The choice of one translation strategy over another appears to be governed by a range of factors, both textual and extratextual, which have to be accounted for before any meaningful progress can be made regarding what 'translation' actually involves. For example, the receiver and the extent to which he or she becomes involved are important constraints, and a relevant question in this respect relates to the range of receiver types: What types of receiver do we theoretically envision when we write or translate, which do we assume, when, how? Is the choice of a given receptive mode determined only by the text, or only by the *skopos* of the translation, or are there other important factors to bear in mind? (cf. Pym, 1992b).

To illustrate the notion of receiver status, Pym cites the example of an English-language advertisement placed by the State of Kuwait in *Le Monde*, inviting international contractors to participate in a tender. Somewhere below the English text, three lines appeared in small print describing in French what the advert is about (*La publicité ci-dessus est relative à . . .* – 'The above advertisement concerns . . .').

Pym focuses on the appended French text and assesses it in relation to the main English announcement. He notes that, even though the French text enables its readers linguistically to understand what the English advert is about, it remains a mere **gloss** which, in and by itself, does not pragmatically function as an 'invitation to take part in a tender'. What kind of text is the French gloss, then? Is it a translation? Could it become translational? These and similar issues have a great deal to do with the type of receiver envisaged in writing or translating.

Concept 7.4   **Receiver status**

In a context such as that of the *Le Monde* English advert and the appended French gloss, Pym identifies three receptive positions:

- An *excluded* receiver (e.g. a reader for whom the French text was obviously necessary).
- A *participative* receiver (e.g. a reader who can genuinely respond to the English text, with or without the French text).
- An *observational* receiver (e.g. a reader not genuinely able to respond to the invitation in the English text).

Given this configuration of receiver positions, Pym suggests that the French text could be considered translational in that, like all translations, it uses **code switching** to overcome the excluded receiver status. On the other hand, it cannot strictly speaking be translational since a **deictic** element such as *the above advertisement concerns* . . . rules out participation and confers only an observational status on the receiver.

Note that this observational status cannot be changed into full participation merely by removing the problematic deictic. As Pym (1992b) points out, the English **performative** in the larger advertisement would still be overriding and no tenders would be accepted from companies not wishing to do business in English (pp. 176–7).

Several assumptions about translation emerge at this point:

- Texts are translated in order to overcome the exclusion of an implied receiver.
- A translation can convert an excluded receiver into an observational receiver.
- A translation can convert an excluded receiver into a participative receiver, 'although there might be doubts about the commercial **acceptability** of the result' (Pym, 1992b: 178).

It is pertinent to point out at this juncture that the issue of receiver status raised by Pym above could, perhaps more productively, be explored from a text type perspective. The participative status accorded to those for whom the French gloss was unnecessary is safeguarded by the 'instructional', 'operative', type of text. The French gloss, on the other hand, is a token of a different text type: 'expository', 'informative'. This 'monitoring' type of text is pragmatically intended for 'spectators' and is thus optimally suited for the observational status accorded to someone for whom the French gloss was necessary. This text type focus is important since to confuse receiver status in such a context can have daunting implications for the work of the translator: turning the instructional thrust into one serving an informative function or the other way round is behind a great deal of diplomatic litigation regarding what a treaty, for example, said or did not say. Text type restrictions are picked up again and discussed in greater detail in 9.1.4 and in Part III of this book under research applications.

7.4   Quality assessment and translation strategy

The model of translation quality assessment proposed by Juliane House represents a well-established approach to translation strategy seen specifically from the vantage point of linguistics and equivalence. The model is primarily concerned with contextual meaning in translation: it is grounded in **register** theory and is informed by a theory of pragmatic function. From this perspective, details relating to conveying information, ideas or experience (i.e. **ideational** meanings) and using language to establish particular relationships (i.e. **interpersonal** meanings) form an important part of source and target 'textual profile'. Translation quality assessment examines equivalence in terms of:

- the linguistic and situational particularities of source and target texts;
- a comparison of the two texts;
- an assessment of the relative match.

Concept 7.5   **Function**

Within the scheme proposed by House, an important distinction is made between *language function* and *text function*. Language function captures how language is used to convey information, express feelings, persuade, etc. This may be illustrated by Bühler's well-known categories 'representational', '**expressive**' and '**persuasive**' functions. Halliday's 'ideational', 'interpersonal' and 'textual' components also represent language functions. Text function, on the other hand, attends to the rhetorical purpose of entire texts (e.g. counter-argumentative texts). While a particular language function (say, the representational) may well predominate in a particular text, other language functions cannot be completely excluded, and the two senses of 'function' must therefore be kept distinct.

Classifications of 'language' function, such as those given in Concept 7.5, have nevertheless provided the basis for a number of 'text' classifications. For a text typology to be adequate, however, 'language' function should not be equated with 'text' function. In other words, the assumption must be resisted that the text is a longer sentence, and that what applies to sentences individually should apply to entire texts. As we have pointed out above, and as House demonstrates, such an equation is flawed since we rarely encounter texts that use one language function to the exclusion of others (that is, purely 'ideational' or purely 'interpersonal', for example) or are exclusively of one or the other type (e.g. strictly 'representational' from beginning to end). The way texts function may thus be more helpfully seen along a cline between two extremes – **referential** and non-referential. This is bound to have important implications for translation strategy.

7.4.1   Covert translation

Concept 7.6   **The covert strategy**

Covert translation is a mode of text transfer in which the translator seeks to produce a target text that is as immediately relevant for the target reader as the source text is for the source language addressee. Although functional equivalence is the objective, anything which betrays the origin of the translated text is carefully concealed. This strategy is said to work well with source texts which do not rely for their relevance on aspects of the source language and culture, such as traditions, societal mores or institutional structures.

In a covert translation, it is thus possible to reproduce the function or the overall purpose of the source text. This may be achieved through what House calls a 'cultural filter', a form of translator mediation which seeks to recreate a cultural model equivalent to that of the source text. However, if such an intervention turns out to be unjustified (e.g. a misreading of the original's intention or a miscalculation of likely target reader reactions), then the translation is no longer 'covert', but will have moved along the continuum towards 'free translation'. This extreme includes what House calls a 'covert version', a translation said to be inadequate almost by definition.

Examples of texts which lend themselves to a covert translation strategy include advertising, journalistic writing and technical material. A great deal of Bible translation also falls within this category, and the cultural substance of the biblical text is often relativised to make the biblical message more accessible.

7.4.2   Overt translation

Concept 7.7   **The overt strategy**

Overt translations cater for situations in which the source text is specifically directed at source culture addressees and can thus be dealt with only within the socio-cultural setting of the original. In handling this kind of text, the translation would aim for a narrowly defined form of equivalence, with the target addressee being quite 'overtly' sidelined (House, 1986: 188). The translation would be a 'translation' and not a 'second original'.

Source text function cannot be preserved intact in **overt translation**. A text so firmly anchored in its own socio-cultural environment cannot be replaced with an alternative model which always works well in all respects for a different audience in a different context. In dealing with texts that are bound to a specific historical occasion, for example, the translator must try to match what House calls a 'second level function'. This recognises that the two texts are removed from one another in time and place ('displaced **situationality**').

Second level function involves an **audience design** based on what would be acceptable both to the contemporary speakers of the target language and to contemporary language users in the source culture (who also happen to be text receivers not originally addressed by the text). That is, the target text could well include certain 'alienating' features, and the onus is on the text receiver to filter away those aspects of text meaning which are perceived not to be relevant. Quite a portion of the cultural content would be left for the target reader to sort out. Historic sermons, great political speeches and a substantive body of good litera-ture provide us with examples of this kind of overt translation strategy at work.

7.4.3   Cross-cultural pragmatics: A case study

The way different languages and cultures perceive reality has been approached from a number of perspectives. House (1977, 1997) deals with the issue from the standpoint of **cross-cultural pragmatics** and subscribes to the notion that 'overt' and 'covert' translation strategies cannot be seen as separate from the context of culture. These transla-tion procedures are closely tied to cultural and linguistic norms, and an intercultural perspective is therefore necessary.

To demonstrate the value of cultural input, House analyses a letter in English addressed to the shareholders of an investment company, requesting them to adopt certain organisational changes which, if truth were told, would not be to their advantage. The use of language is subtly manipulated to relay careful evasiveness and polite distance (e.g. *Your assistance is required; It is anticipated that . . .*).

In the original study which House published in 1977, the translation of the letter was found wanting. The German rendering projected an image of the writer that was much more forceful, active and direct than indicated by the source text, where the action requested had been cast in highly abstract and indirect terms (e.g. *bitten wir Sie, Sie müssen die Bank bitten*).

At the time, the assumptions entertained by the translator concerning the German readers' different expectations were judged by House to be unwarranted. The translator's perceptions were found to be based on stereotypes not substantiated by facts. More recently, however, ethnographic evidence corroborating the translator's intuition has come to light. As House points out in her latest 1997 'model re-visited', several cross-cultural studies have since been carried out, suggesting that communicative preferences actually exist across cultures. In the English–German context, for example, variation may be detected along five basic dimensions: directness, self-reference, focus on content, explicitness and reliance on communicative routines.

7.5   Translation strategy dichotomies assessed

Insightful as it certainly is, House's model of translation quality assessment, informed by the overt–covert distinction, has come under some concerted criticism over the years. Nord (1991a), for example, suggests that the strategy of her own 'instrumental' translation and that of House's 'covert' translation are not in fact the same 'in that [instrumental translation] only requires the [target text] function to be compatible rather than identical with or equivalent to that of the [source text]' (p. 72). Furthermore, the commitment of a target text to a documentary or an instrumental translation strategy is not simply dictated by the text type to which the source text belongs.

To date, the debate on these and related issues is far from conclusive. This underlines the need for what Holmes called 'research into research' to evaluate the various models constructed. For example, research is still scarce into such issues as how effective a particular dichotomy is in shedding light on:

- the nature of the relationship between source and target texts;
- the way texts relate to the human user (author, reader/translator and target reader);
- the essential difference between what is and what is not 'translation'.

The position held by translation theorists such as House (covert vs overt translation), Nord (regarding instrumental vs documentary translation) or Venuti (with respect to **domesticating** vs **foreignising** translation) can now be usefully reassessed in terms of whether it represents any real advance on what is already in place with distinctions such as communicative vs semantic translation proposed by Newmark decades ago. From the perspective adopted in this book, the parallels between the various schemes appear to be particularly striking, and any difference found must therefore be seen merely as a matter of focus.

Further reading

- On such translation dichotomies as 'instrumental' vs 'documental', see Nord (1991a).

- On the assessment and critique of the various forms of translation strategy and text receiver status, see Pym (1992c), Fawcett (1995).

- On Translation Quality Assessment and the overt-covert distinction, see in particular Chapters 4, 5 and 6 of House (1997), House (2007), House (2009).

Chapter 8

The pragmatics turn in research

This chapter will . . .

- describe research into 'translation strategy' informed specifically by pragmatics and the theory of relevance;
- look in some detail at '**communicative clues**' and how the analysis of such features has been central in translation practices which seek to account not only for what is said but also for how something is said.

Concept 8.1 **Pragmatics and relevance**

Discussion of translation strategy from the perspective of such aspects of translation as purpose, the receiver, text type, **register** membership, has necessarily highlighted the *pragmatic* dimension of context (**intentionality** and language use as **action**). Pragmatics is concerned with how the transmission of meaning depends not only on linguistic knowledge (e.g. grammar, lexicon), but also on the context of the utterance, including most significantly the inferred intent of the text producer. This focus will now become clearer as we move next to research into *relevance* and translation (Gutt, 1991).

Research issues relating to pragmatics occupy the base line of the triangle in Concept Map IV. This reflects how, in accounting for the pragmatic dimension, the analysis of such contextual factors as intentionality has always served a bridging function and is subscribed to by almost all models of translation: it has enriched models of register analysis and has at the same time been foundational in the analysis of discursive practices.

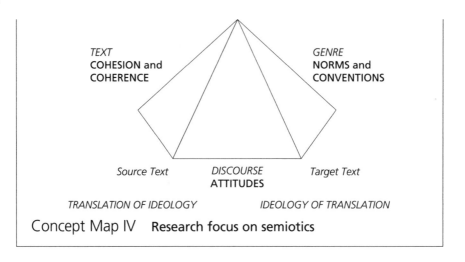

TEXT
COHESION and
COHERENCE

GENRE
NORMS and
CONVENTIONS

Source Text   *DISCOURSE*   *Target Text*
ATTITUDES

TRANSLATION OF IDEOLOGY   *IDEOLOGY OF TRANSLATION*

Concept Map IV   **Research focus on semiotics**

8.1   Translation strategy and relevance theory

In section 3.3, **relevance** in translation was considered in terms of two different methods:

- Descriptive translation: a translation intended to survive on its own without the receiver ever being aware that there was an original.
- Interpretive translation: a translation intended to relate in some, often conspicuous, way to an original.

In the model of translation informed by relevance theory, translations which involve descriptive use are considered 'not really translations' (Gutt, 1991: 65). This leaves us with interpretive use as the legitimate mode of translation proper. To limit the scope of interpretive use, two kinds of translation are distinguished:

- Indirect translation, where the translator is free to elaborate or summarise.
- Direct translation, where the translator has to stick to the explicit content of the original.

On the basis of the general view of translation and relevance outlined above, Gutt (1991) discusses the issue of **covert translation** and focuses on an English translation of a German tourist booklet, originally analysed by House (1977). The brochure is appropriately translated in a covert way since it is a kind of text that, in translation, ought to be maximally relevant to its target readers. The information contained in the source text is presented in as clear and accessible a manner as possible, allowing the target reader to see the translator's own effort at interpretation in a number of places throughout the target rendering. For example, in a reference to the age of the mastersingers, the source text speaks about '*die Zeit des Meistergesanges, die Zeit des Schuhmachers und Meistersingers Hans Sachs*' ('the time of mastersinging, the time of the shoemaker and mastersinger Hans Sachs' (Gutt, p. 45)). The translation, on the other hand, opts for: 'the age of the mastersingers and their best known representative, the shoe-maker Hans Sachs'.

In her assessment, House concludes that this particular translation leaves implicit certain elements of cultural information and that, as a result, it has failed to reproduce, for example,

- the effect of flattering the reader's cultural **knowledge**;
- the pseudo-poetic exaggeration typical of travel advertising.

House notes the discrepancy and considers the rendering a case of tampering with the **interpersonal function** of the source. Gutt finds such conclusions unconvincing. The interpersonal dimension (with fuzzy categories such as 'flattery' or 'exaggeration') and how this finds expression in **actual** texts are not clear-cut issues, particularly when the different cultures involved conduct interpersonal relationships differently. This prompts Gutt to pose the question: How can the translator be so sure that the implicitness in the German text actually flatters the average German reader and that this effect is part of the overall strategy?

One could of course argue that such effects can never be quantified, yet people have always managed to perceive and react to them. However, Gutt's main point is that, whether in translating or assessing translations, a reading of the source text is not sufficient by itself, since meaning is not a static entity that can be recovered mechanistically. Furthermore, **compensation** is not entirely unproblematic as long as the main aim remains to be one of seeking to establish **functional equivalence** and using this as a basis for translator decisions:

> [functional equivalence] leaves unanswered a rather basic problem – and that is, that the preservation of a function may not, in fact, make the translation functionally equivalent: for example, maintaining the function of flattery can make the translation non-equivalent with regard to other functions.

> (Gutt, 1991: 50–1)

Such discrepancies are at the heart of intercultural miscommunication. The 'relevance' account may shed light on some of the complex issues surrounding this area of translation.

8.2 Translating the direct way

What **direct translation** is intended to achieve may be seen against the backdrop of a perennial question in the study of translation: Can assumptions intended specifically for a particular audience ever be optimally communicated to a different audience and if so, how? In mainstream translation studies, this is often dismissed as a non-issue on the grounds that, at least in principle, any message or interpretation can be communicated to any audience.

Relevance theory finds such 'pseudo-universalistic' claims problematical (for a fuller discussion of the conceptual background to the relevance model, see 3.3). To be communicated successfully, the set of assumptions conveyed by the target text must yield adequate contextual effects (i.e. benefits). This must ultimately depend on the context in which the message is processed, and unbridgeable gaps are bound to emerge. As Gutt (1991: 97) puts it:

> We cannot communicate the same thoughts to just anybody, regardless of background **knowledge**. When addressing different audiences, we tend to change *what* we want to convey, not only *how* we say it. (Italics added)

Assuming for the sake of the argument that this contextual problem can somehow be circumvented (there is always the **indirect translation** option), the question which is still unanswered by relevance theoreticians and others is: What if the translator is particularly concerned with the *style* as well as the *content* of the message to be translated (that is, what if a translation situation involves the translator in dealing not only with *what* is said but also with *how* it is said). It is this area of language use that has often led translators, particularly of sacred and sensitive texts, to opt for a **literal** approach almost by default, and often with what consequences! (For a more detailed discussion of this set of issues regarding translating what is said and how, see Chapter 15 in this volume on the translation of style.)

8.3   Communicative clues

> **Quote 8.1**
>
> A contextualization cue has been defined as 'any feature of linguistic form that contributes to the signalling of contextual presuppositions' (Gumperz, 1982: 131). For instance, it might be a rising intonation signalling a need for encouragement (Gumperz, 1982: 147) or the switching between T-type and V-type pronouns to signal how one wishes to be seen on the dichotomy between power and intimacy (Ostermann, 2003). . . . In any case, the contextualization cue serves to activate and retrieve the necessary background **knowledge** base so that a contextually appropriate process of **inference** can take place.
>
> Andrew Wilson (2004: 1)

To deal with such translation anomalies as those raised above in Gutt's discussion of **covert translation**s, and to salvage the direct–indirect distinction in the 'relevance account, Gutt further refines the notion of direct translation by introducing the concept of the **communicative clue** which, as Quote 8.1 makes abundantly clear, may be traced back to Gumpertz's work on 'contextualization cues'. In the 'relevance' model of translation, it is suggested that it is not only the intrinsic value of a given stylistic property that matters but the communicative clues which such a property yields (Gutt, 1991: 127). These clues, which can arise from either form or content, are aimed at guiding the audience to the correct interpretation of the utterance. Consider, for example, the issue of **focus**. This might be relayed in English by employing **stress**:

THE DEALER stole the money
The dealer STOLE the money
The dealer stole THE MONEY

[Upper case indicates 'stress']

In certain languages, these effects cannot be achieved by 'stress', but by syntactic means such as 'clefting':

It is the dealer who stole the money
It is stealing the money which the dealer did
It is the money which the dealer stole

Clefting (like stress) would be a crucial communicative clue which must be heeded, not necessarily by translating **cleft sentence** for cleft sentence, but by preserving the pragmatic 'effect' which clefting is intended to convey. This can be achieved by the use of a comparable communicative clue intended to spark off a comparable effect. In the direct mode of translation, unless there is a good reason to do otherwise, the 'function' is kept constant and preserved intact through the use of a similar or a different clue, but a clue of some kind must always be in evidence nonetheless (cf. Nida and Taber, 1969, and the discussion of 'dynamic equivalence' in 2.2).

To see these factors at work, the following is a typology of communicative clues identified by Gutt in terms of the linguistic level at which they may be manifested. To present these different style markers in some order, it might be helpful to start with lower-order linguistic expression located at the level of sounds, and move up the scale to the higher level of the word, to syntax and eventually to wider aspects of style such as connotation and emotive meaning.

Concept 8.2   **Communicative clues**

In the same way as it relates to Gumpertz's 'contextual cues' as indicated in Quote 8.1, the notion of 'communicative clues' might usefully be related to Goffman's 'footing' (1981). Footing, which is important in orchestrating social interaction (both in fictional and in non-fictional texts) is represented by various cues in the surface text. For example, authorial shifts in the fictional text may be signalled by shifts in voice or **focus**.

Communicative clues are thus not just any properties of the text, but features built into the text for the purpose of guiding the audience to the intended interpretation. They are textual features which vary in degree of subtlety and which are perceived to be particularly significant for the intended meaning. A number of factors are involved in determining the non-incidental nature of source text communicative clues, and whether or not they should appear in the translated text as communicative clues (Gutt, 2000). These factors include:

- the intentions of the original communicator;
- the translator's notion of his or her task – how well the translator's strategy matches the expectations of the audience.

8.3.1   Phonology and style

Phonetic properties are cued by their **graphological** counterparts in written texts. They serve to indicate how a word is pronounced or spelled, and are thus useful in dealing with such features of the text as proper names. Transcription of such elements has been a standard procedure in translation (Levy, 1969). Whether this is acceptable as fulfilling the conditions of what translation proper is continues to be controversial. Newmark (1988: 70), for example, holds the view that:

> In theory, names of single persons or objects are 'outside' languages, belong, if at all, to the encyclopedia not the dictionary, have . . . no meaning or connotations, [and] are therefore, both untranslatable and not to be translated.

However, what if semantic meaning is felt to be particularly relevant and translation is therefore necessary? In the German translation of Sheridan's *The School for Scandal*, for example, *Careless* becomes *Ohnsorg*. The German name is intended to convey something about the person's character.

Within relevance theory, whether to opt for translation or transliteration is a matter to be settled in the light of processing factors such as 'cost and benefit' or 'effort and reward' associated with the principle of 'relevance': Is it rewarding for the reader to learn that a particular name carries given connotations?

8.3.2   Poetics and style

Sound-based **poetics** (rhyme, rhythm, etc.) involves expressing in language that which does not have semantic properties. As with all such forms of expression, communicative clues must always be 'negotiated' by the translator. How explicit such translator mediation is can only be determined by invoking contextual criteria such as 'relevance': should a description of the utterance (i.e. a **gloss** of what is involved) be supplied, or is the utterance alone capable of conveying its own 'significance'? For example, no translator has ever been able to bring the hearer closer to the 'thudding of hooves of a galloping horse' than that conveyed by the well-known line from Virgil 'with galloping sound the hoof strikes the crumbling ground'. Such glosses influence, indeed become part of, the overall interpretation.

Relevance theory looks at these poetic effects in terms of a cumulative effect, which the audience is usually invited to experience. This freedom to interpret a text is vital in poetic communication. Syntax would be left inert because, if allowed to impose its precision, it could inhibit poetic effect, reducing rather than extending interpretive potential. Sound patterns such as rhyme and rhythm neutralise syntax and the relations they suggest are always unspecified and liberating. Once again, however, the question is: Should these added cadences be explicated in translation or should they be simply approximated? The relevance model is clear on this: different procedures will have implications for overall meaning which becomes part of the contextual information the translator should not tamper with.

8.3.3 Onomatopoeia

Two kinds of onomatopoeia are distinguished by Levy (1969: 91): ad hoc and functional. Functional onomatopoeia carries conceptual values and word-like characteristics (e.g. the 'language' of pets, the most common sounds of nature). In translation, this form of conceptual onomatopoeia may be illustrated by the following example. In *The Waste Land*, Pierre Legris replaces the onomatopoeic allusion to a nightingale, 'jug, jug, jug, jug, jug, jug', by the French equivalent 'Toi, Toi, Toi, Toi, Toi, Toi' (Levy, p. 90). Neither the English form nor its French counterpart is, strictly speaking, 'conceptual', yet they have something of a 'conceptual value' about them: they enjoy the status of a **sign** as things which mean something to someone in some respect or capacity (Grice 1975).

In terms of relevance theory, this is bound to be part of the 'relevant' encyclopaedic entry and, as such, to yield appropriate significant communicative clues. The expressions are therefore translatable if the other language has an expression associated with this information and not necessarily with the form the utterance takes.

8.3.4 Style and semantic representation

Semantic representations (e.g. whether a word is abstract, too abstract, concrete, or even what a word evokes) serve as a rich source of **inferential** hypotheses (i.e. it makes the hearer wonder why like this, why here). The question now is: How can the translator work directly with mere mental blueprints (which is what 'semantic representations' effectively are, at least initially), and with communicative clues, of which one may not be physically aware?

Relevance theory suggests that the translator has to be careful, particularly in dealing with cases where there is a so-called 'lack of fit' (non-correspondence) between what is inferred to be the interpretation (we know what is being implied, what the **implicatures** are) and the communicative clues adequately provided or not, as the case may be. That is, meaning may not be always derivable from the stimulus alone but from the interaction of this stimulus with the **cognitive** environment. (For the way these terms are used within relevance theory, see 3.3.)

To illustrate the role of contextual assumptions in this area, Gutt (1991) provides the example of translating a poem from the Japanese **genre** *haiku* into English. The problem word is *furuike*, a compound noun consisting of 'old' and 'pond'. The translator felt that the English equivalent was far too abstract and general to capture an important semantic element relating to the 'landscape' evoked by the original word.

The solution opted for was therefore 'to say more than "an old pond" to give a little more sense of the presence of the poet by the pond' (Yuasa, 1987: 233; cited in Gutt, 1991: 132). The translator added the word 'silent' which, to him, was one way of suggesting 'by implication the presence of a listening ear' (Yuasa, p. 234; cited in Gutt, p. 133).

In 'relevance' terms, the meaning communicated by the above text is not attributable to *furuike* = 'old pond' (i.e. the stimulus alone) but to the interaction between this and the original scenery which may not be part of the target reader's cognitive environment. Such relationships are important to preserve, but this cannot be achieved simply by making everything explicit, as communicative approaches to translation are prone to doing (Gutt, p. 133). In fact, the translator of the above example is taken to task for the liberty he took, spelling it all out, as it were. In any case, the 'explicitation' strategy is certain to misfire if implemented as a way of bridging the gap between original and receptor receivers regarding 'background knowledge'. If an element of information is part of what in relevance theory is considered the 'encyclopaedic knowledge', then this information will belong to the context 'and so . . . would fall outside the scope of a translation concerned with the preservation of communicative clues' (Gutt, p. 136).

Thus, the interaction between original utterance and original context should not be pre-orchestrated for the target reader. It should be given free rein as one way of facilitating inferencing. Only in this way will direct translation legitimately become part of interpretive use, but at a price that may even render the principle of 'minimum processing' redundant. The choice between direct and indirect translation remains an option linked to what the translator sees as relevant to the audience. Once chosen, however, direct translation absolves the translator of the responsibility to compensate for contextual mismatches and puts this responsibility squarely on the audience who have to familiarise themselves with the context assumed in the original communication (Gutt, p. 166).

In a nutshell, the relevance argument regarding these issues would seem to run as follows: If a text or part of a text is felt to be suitable for direct translation (e.g. historically important texts like the war speeches of Winston Churchill), but the translator nevertheless feels that it is his or her responsibility to help the reader along, say, with certain cultural references, where should this help stop? That is, where do we draw the line between direct and indirect translation? Chapter 15 on the translation of style suggests answers to some of these questions, but further research into relevance and translation is certainly needed to unravel the constraints governing the process of translation in this area.

8.3.5   Formulaic expressions and style

Set forms such as formulaic expressions and standard openings and closings of communicative routines convey meaning by activating the hearer's knowledge about language and culture (e.g. what we know about the word *hello* in English). **Communicative clues** indicating such meanings are part of encyclopedic knowledge which becomes the basis of handling such expressions in direct translation. We look for expressions that have similar information in the other language and act accordingly.

Memory plays a part in dealing with this aspect of language use. The more often an expression is used, the more it is likely to be remembered. When used subsequently, however, these expressions tend to yield fewer contextual effects. The fewer the contextual effects, the less relevant the utterance, hence the clichéd nature of formulaic expressions.

8.3.6   Syntax and style

Syntax can generate its own communicative clues. Such methods as inter-linear translation have stood the translator in good stead when dealing with syntactic properties (e.g. word order), but syntactic structures include much more than surface manifestations.

For example, in the discussion of the translation of a passage from Dickens's *Tale of Two Cities*, Gutt (citing Chukovskii, 1984) sees syntactic structures as vehicles for the expression of pragmatic meanings such as irony. When the Russian translation of *The Tale of Two Cities* opened with *It was the best and worst of times . . .* for Dickens's *It was the best of times. It was the worst of times . . .*, the ironic quality of the original was severely undermined. Source text ironic effect is largely attributable to sentence structure and specifically to how Dickens uses a string of sentences in juxtaposition. Preserving the relevant syntactic properties can be one way of responding to syntactic **communicative clues**. However, the solution to the problem of conveying intended meaning in translation is much more complex than mere **iconicity**. Languages differ not only in the patterns of structure employed, but also in the values assigned to those patterns. That is, the way texts are structured can in and by itself produce cumulative effects which carry meaning and thus may vary across languages and cultures. From the perspective of relevance theory, the effect of repetition, for example, is seen in terms of 'the cost–benefit correlation between the effort needed to process a stimulus and the contextual effects to be expected as a reward' (Gutt, 1991: 140). According to Sperber and Wilson (1986: 220):

> The task of the hearer faced with these utterances is to reconcile the fact that a certain expression has been repeated with the assumption that optimal relevance has been aimed at. Clearly, the extra linguistic processing effort incurred by the repetition must be outweighed by some increase in contextual effects triggered by the repetition itself.

The balance between processing cost and benefit is influenced by a number of factors, including the structural complexity of the stimulus. The relevance principle may now be reformulated as follows: If a communicator uses a stimulus that manifestly requires more processing effort than some other stimulus equally available, the hearer can expect the benefits of this stimulus to outweigh the increase in the processing cost – otherwise the communicator has failed to achieve optimal relevance (Gutt, 1991: 32).

This complexity principle goes hand in hand with, and may even be overridden by, the all-important factor of frequency. Regardless of complexity, the deployment of a more commonly used type of structure is bound to demand less processing effort than a less commonly used structure. If **focalisation** in English, for example, has '**stress**' as a common mode of realisation (thus requiring minimal processing effort), then the alternative of using a 'cleft' in a given target language would be adequate *only* if clefting also happens to be as commonly used in that target language.

8.3.7   Connotation and style

The notion of encyclopedic information and its availability to the language user has important implications for the way stylistic or **connotative** meaning is handled in direct translation. This kind of meaning relates to register, dialect, accent, etc. For example, in Shakespeare's *Julius Caesar*, Brutus's wife reproaches her husband, thus:

> You've urgently, Brutus, Stole from my bed:
> And yesternight, at supper
> You suddenly rose, and walk'd about. (II.i)

In his Russian translation of the tragedy, A.A. Fet used the word *nevezhlivo*, 'impolitely', for 'urgently', the colloquial word *vechor* instead of *vecher* for 'yesternight', and the ultra-formal word *trapeza* for 'supper'. Critics at the time noted the stylistic disparity. The problem, however, is not semantic, but rather contextual, and the associations specified in the source are thus part of the encyclopaedic entries of these words.

8.4   The pragmatic view of translation strategy assessed

In any examination of the translation process, the particular cognitive environment of the receptor is always a crucial part of the equation. The first issue to take up in this regard relates to what Gutt calls a 'primary communication situation' which justifies a direct translation. This is where, for proper **inferences** to be made, utterances would have to combine with the original context. Two consequences flow from this:

- the need on the part of the target audience to familiarise themselves with the context assumed by the original communicator;
- absolving the translator of the responsibility to compensate for contextual mismatches, etc.

Such requirements, however, raise an important question which Gutt seems to sidestep: What has become of the principle of minimum processing effort? This is not to speak of the difficulties already there with regard to the choice between direct and indirect translation which remains unclear and is still left for the translator to make (Fawcett, 1997: 139).

The notion of audience features prominently as an important constraint on what is or is not 'adequately relevant', what is or is not 'necessary effort', etc. But what if the audience constitutes 'the great unknown masses', as Newmark (1993: 106) suggests, or what if authors write for themselves rather than for their readers, as Benjamin observes (Fawcett, 1997: 137)?

A positive development in the way the 'relevance' model of translation has evolved is Gutt's rehabilitation of text typologies broadly defined (e.g. novels, eulogies, summaries, commentaries). Gutt (1998) sees these **macro** units of interaction as templates which help in coordinating the intentions of communicators and the expectations of the audience. Gutt further suggests that, used appropriately, such **genre** labels can guide the audience in their search for optimal relevance. For example, when given something like a novel to read, one would not look for the relevance of the text in the historical accuracy of what is said, but in the values and attitudes of what is portrayed. That is, certain kinds of texts and utterances yield what Gutt refers to as 'relevance-enhancing' communicative clues.

These are some of the questions which future research needs to address (see Part III of this volume). Worth noting is how relevance theory has re-opened the debate on an important issue in the theory and practice of translation:

Should the outward form of a given source text feature be preserved in translation and, if this is not always possible, what are the constraints?

Further reading

- On 'relevance' in translation, the role of 'inference', and the phenomenon of 'communicative clues', see Gutt (1998).

Chapter 9

Focus on the text

This chapter will . . .

- describe discourse-oriented research into translation strategy;
- focus on models designed specifically to analyse **ideology** in translation.

Concept 9.1 Semiotics in translation research

With models of **text, discourse** and **genre** occupying centre stage in recent translation studies, research into **register** and pragmatics has extended outwards, taking in aspects of language as a social **semiotic** such as 'signs' and '**intertextuality**'. Research models in this area of translation studies (Concept Map V) are located on the right-hand side of the conceptual triangle, under 'the *semiotics* of culture'. It is important to recognise that, while a source text orientation is not ruled out, problems encountered in the area of discourse and genre have been addressed within predominantly target-oriented approaches to the translation process.

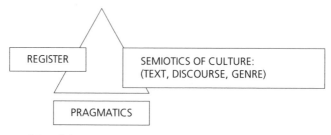

Concept Map V   **Semiotics research models**

9.1   Text processing and the process of translation

> **Quote 9.1**
>
> [Meaning is] the kingpin of translation studies. Without understanding what the text to be translated means . . . the translator would be hopelessly lost. This is why the translation scholar has to be a semanticist over and above everything else. By semanticist we mean a semanticist of the text, not just of words, structures and sentences. The key concept for the **semantics** of translation is *textual meaning.*
>
> Albrecht Neubert (1984: 57)

The relationship between translation and linguistics has never been easy. As the survey of translation studies in Part I has shown, there have always been competing pressures coming, on the one hand, from translation practitioners whose training has not included extensive exposure to a theoretical study of language and, on the other, from professional linguists of a **structuralist** or **transformational-generative** persuasion who saw translation as an irksome distraction (Bell, 1991).

The 1970s to early 1980s, however, was a time which saw translation studies thoroughly re-examining established orthodoxies in such areas as equivalence and translatability. The possibility of translation began to be discussed more openly, and support grew for the contribution which more enlightened brands of linguistics might make to the analysis of the process. Contemporaneously with this shift in thinking which made possible a wider perspective on notions such as equivalence, **text linguistics** gradually emerged, ushering in new ways of looking at language, texts and the process of translation.

9.1.1   Translation: product vs process

Support for an interactive view of texts preceded the development of full-fledged text-linguistic models of the translation process. As far back as the late 1960s, James Holmes questioned the usefulness of distinguishing between translation as a *product* and translation as a *process*, and argued that dealing with texts as products must ultimately depend on an understanding of the process of textual communication.

Concept 9.2 Planes of processing

Looking at a variety of models of translation, Holmes reached the important conclusion that a text is a string of units, essentially serial in nature, but one which operates on two planes with which translators work (1978a: 82–3):

- A serial plane, in which the text is transformed sentence by sentence.
- A structural plane, in which the translator abstracts a 'mental conception' of the original text.

On the structural plane, abstracting an overall mental conception is a process which the translator shares with every reader and in which the source text features prominently. Holmes calls this mental conception Map One.

Another kind of map, an evolving map of the prospective target text, is used as part of the compositional strategy which the translator shares with every writer. Holmes calls this Map Two, and invokes the 'correspondence' criterion which determines the way the target-text map is developed from the source-text map.

According to Holmes, the concept of 'map' (in the singular) can be misleading. In reality, what we have is a 'conglomerate of highly disparate bits of information: a map of a linguistic artifact . . . , a map of a literary artifact . . . , a map of a socio-cultural artifact' (1978a: 83). Each map yields its own norms, which are best seen in relative terms, since compliance with or violation of norms is always relative. For example, there are always form-function choices to make at each level. In linguistic, literary or socio-cultural terms, translation may involve:

- a feature corresponding in form but not in function leads to a homologous translation;
- a feature corresponding in function but not in form leads to a monologous translation.

It is interesting to note that Holmes's 'homologues' tend to be more common when dealing with **socio-cultural** features (i.e. **cultural objects**), whereas 'analogues' predominate in dealing with many linguistic, **socio-textual** features (e.g. **genre** characteristics).

In this maze of textual activities, it is important to work out **a hierarchy of correspondences**, where particular relationships can be seen as more salient than others. Modelling the translation product/process in this way applies to both literary and non-literary texts. For example, **informative** (referential) texts tend to accord priority to semantic correspondence, heeding other kinds of correspondence as long as they do not interfere with overall text function (cf. Reiss, 1971). In the case of what Holmes calls a '**vocative**' (appellative or operative) text (e.g. a TV commercial, a sermon), the translator will accord priority to correspondence of appeal even if this means completely ignoring semantic integrity.

Holmes recognises that this text-type orientation is an idealisation and that skewing of function is often the rule rather than the exception. Particularly in the translation of literary texts, the various restrictions identified above can be, and often are, overridden. At various points in its development or simultaneously, a literary text can be **informative**, **vocative** or **expressive**. Defining and assigning priorities thus become much less clear-cut, hence the flexibility which characterises solutions proposed for the problem of literary meaning (1978a: 86).

9.1.2   The contribution of text linguistics

Text linguistics has already been introduced in this book as an important trend in translation studies, and the main features of the approach to translation are outlined and illustrated in Part I (see 3.2). In translation research, the new focus on text in context has necessitated that attention shift away from 'incidental incompatibilities among languages', towards 'the systematic communicative factors shared by languages' (Beaugrande, 1978: 12). This cross-linguistic common ground may be illustrated by:

- how contextual factors such as **intentionality** and **intertextuality** operate universally across languages and cultures;
- how these factors systematically inform expression in **actual** texts and serve as templates within which inter- and intra-linguistic and cultural specificities may be examined.

From this perspective, the minimal unit of communication or translation is seen to be the *text*. In his approach to poetic translation, Beaugrande (1978: 7) demonstrates the value of such an orientation to any analysis of communicative behavior in general and **textual competence** in particular. The inquiry sets out with the specific aim of describing the process of translation 'explicitly enough to indicate what factors human competence should contain and whether these factors can provide a basis for translation strategies'.

Reading is seen as a privileged skill in the practice of translating. In fact, what takes place in reading has always held a special fascination for translation theorists concerned with text in context. Reading provides an ideal testing ground for how texts are structured and meaning constructed, not only by text producers but also by text receivers. The text receiver brings to the act of reading his or her own knowledge, belief and value systems, etc. – an activity which, if properly appreciated, is likely to shed useful light on such issues as equivalence and translatability.

The view from text linguistics on reading suggests that, although a text appears as a linear sequence of elements, the various components are not dealt with as autonomous units of information in the sequence in which they occur. Furthermore, comprehension involves much more than understanding what the words which make up the text point to in the external world. There are, for example, inner feelings and thoughts to consider.

Perhaps more significantly, there are the so-called redundant elements in the text. The term **redundancy** is borrowed from information theory, where it refers to the amount of information communicated over and above the required minimum. Language tends to use redundancy as a way of controlling the flow of information when this becomes unmanageable or when channels of interaction are blocked for whatever reason (cf. Nida, 1964). The necessary 'noise' generated by the redundant elements thus goes beyond what is necessary or unnecessary simply as a means of transmitting information or guaranteeing comprehension. Redundant words are primarily intended to provide the reader with sufficient background to make the integration of new information possible. If reading is to be **efficient**, the text linguist argues, it must be undertaken in line with how factors such as redundancy work in texts.

Readers, then, do not move from one element to the next in an orderly, predictable fashion. They tend to move forwards and backwards in the text, and to group and regroup the various components into a variety of information clusters. Some information will be perceived as more prominent, other information less prominent. As Beaugrande (1978: 32) explains, 'it would be more accurate to assume that the mind retains not a *level sequence* but a *topography*, with some information stored higher' than other information in the text (italics added).

The topography of reading (Figure 9.1) rests on the notion of semantic and syntactic **salience** or the degree of relative importance accorded to the various elements of the text. As reading gets under way, such prominence assignment is undertaken in the light of specific communicative

$$T = c_1 \quad c_2 \quad c_3 \quad c_4 \quad c_5 \quad c_6 \quad [\ldots]$$

Text as a linear sequence

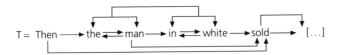

$T =$ Then ⟶ the ⇄ man ⟶ in ⇄ white ⟶ sold ⟶ [...]

Information is redistributed

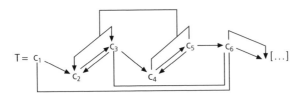

A topography with some information becoming perceptually more prominent

Figure 9.1   **The process of reading**

requirements. This implies that what the text physically contains and what the mind **registers** are not necessarily, if ever, identical. Efficient reading must capture these fluctuations, and readers must constantly be on the alert, rearranging bits of information and redistributing attention accordingly.

The assumption that the information one needs is all contained in the text must therefore be resisted. Readers themselves supply information, drawing upon experience and knowledge of the world. Similarly, texts exhibit varying degrees of 'dynamism' which can defy readers' expectations and thwart predictability (see 3.2.2).

Different reading strategies are employed, depending on the kind of text one is dealing with. In general, there seems to be:

> A gradation moving from a reading which is based predominantly on reader-supplied information toward a reading based predominantly on text-supplied information.
>
> (Beaugrande, 1978: 87)

Schmidt (1975b) describes this interaction between text and reader in terms of a distinction between what happens during the initial stages of beginning to 'comprehend' a text, and the subsequent stages of assign-ing 'interpretation' to a text. The achievement of this ultimate goal tends to be informed by an increasing input of 'text-based' information. As the reader gets further along in the text, 'reader-supplied' informa-tion tends to diminish, allowing text-based material to predominate (cited in Beaugrande, 1978: 87).

The performance of different readers and their varying degrees of efficiency may be accounted for in terms of the kind of reading they do on a given occasion (e.g. how much of the information gathered is 'reader-supplied' and how much is 'text-supplied'?). The important point here is that the interaction between the reader and the text never ceases: 'The reader is likely to discover not one definite meaning for the text, but rather an increasing range of possible meanings' (Beaugrande, 1978: 87).

A corollary to this observation, which is crucial for the work of the translator (see deconstruction, 4.2), is that:

> Only if the reading process is consistently pursued to the point where the interpretation is maximally dominated by text-supplied information can a truly objective translation be produced.
>
> (Beaugrande, 1978: 88)

It is precisely in these terms that Beaugrande defines the notion of 'equivalence'. An 'equivalent' translation is 'a translation which validly represents the perceptual potential of the original' (1978: 88). But, can reading ever be consistently pursued to such a degree? To answer this question, we need to assess what precisely is meant by 'text-based information'. This issue was dealt with by relevance theory from the vantage point of effort, reward and **communicative clues**. In a similar vein, Beaugrande (1978: 95) had already suggested that text-based information cannot be equated with purely formal features and must rather be seen as the result of evaluating the communicative relevance of formal features. Translation is an activity in which 'meaning' must take precedence over 'form' in specifiable contexts.

9.1.3   The notion of text in translation

Work on the status of 'text' in the process of translation has been fairly eclectic, drawing on a variety of different approaches to text in context. Beaugrande and Dressler's (1981) model of the textual 'standards' which all well-formed texts must meet has been particularly influential in this regard.

Concept 9.3   **Standards of textuality**

The effectiveness of textual communication is related to the extent to which a text upholds some if not all of the following standards of textuality:

- **Cohesion**: the diverse relations which hold among the words, phrases and sentences of a text.
- **Coherence**: the range of conceptual relations underlying surface continuity.
- **Situationality**: the way utterances relate to situations.
- **Intertextuality**: the way utterances relate to other utterances and ultimately to other texts performing relevant functions.
- **Intentionality**: the purposes for which utterances are used.
- **Acceptability**: text receivers' response.
- **Informativity**: the extent to which texts or parts of texts may be expected or unexpected, known or unknown, etc.

Reiss's text-type model (1971) and House's model of translation quality assessment (1997) have demonstrated that pragmatic notions such as 'communicative purpose' (a sender-oriented concept) and 'text function' (a receiver-oriented concept) are crucial for research into the nature of text in the translation process. In more recent approaches, the two perspectives have merged in the idea of **rhetorical purpose** (e.g. narration, argumentation), a notion seen as pivotal both in the processing of texts and in the process of translation (Hatim and Mason, 1990, 1997).

The model of translation developed by Hatim and Mason subscribes to the view of textuality outlined above and endorses the notion that, although texts are essentially **hybrid**, one particular function tends to predominate in any given occasion of communicative use. Texts tend to exhibit what Werlich (1976: 19) calls a 'dominant contextual focus':

> Texts . . . conventionally focus the addressee's attention only on specific factors and circumstances. . . . Accordingly, texts can be grouped together . . . on the basis of their dominant contextual focus.

Concept 9.4   Monitoring and managing

For texts to function efficiently, effectively and appropriately, only one *predominant* rhetorical purpose is usually served on any one occasion of use. Other purposes may well be present, but they are bound to be subsidiary to the overall function of the text (Hatim and Mason, 1990: 146). The distinction between *monitoring* and *managing* is a useful framework within which the issue of text **'hybridisation'** may be understood (Beaugrande and Dressler, 1981):

- If the dominant function of the text is to steer the situation in a manner favourable to the text producer's goals (as in various forms of argumentation), 'managing' would be performed.

- If the focus is on providing a reasonably detached account (as in various forms of exposition, such as the typical summary or review), 'monitoring' would be performed.

Monitoring and managing form the basis of the text typology with which Hatim and Mason work. In this model, texts are situated on a cline of varying degrees of **evaluativeness** (i.e. involvement) on the part of text users. If communication is stable (i.e. expectation fulfilling), texts can readily be slotted at either end of the cline (i.e. they would be predominantly 'evaluative' or 'non-evaluative'). However, it is often the case that the text receiver is subtly moved away from one pole towards the other, with expectations being constantly defied in subtle and intricate ways. Faced with such **hybrid** forms, translators need to determine when a shift away from a particular function and towards another is significant.

To illustrate **monitoring** and **managing**, consider the following excerpts from two different kinds of text, one argumentative, the other expository:

The University of . . . and The University of . . . have a proven track record which this collaborative venture can only enhance. (From a Dean's address at a reception on the occasion of inaugurating a new joint centre.)

The University of . . . and The University of . . . have a proven track record which this collaborative venture is intended to enhance. (From a press release announcing the inauguration event.)

In his address, the Dean, through the use of an emphatic assertion, tries to 'manage' an audience (an audience that is possibly 'sceptical', 'eager', 'bored'). The reporter in the press release, on the other hand, cannot afford to be as indulgent, and he or she thus merely 'monitors' the situation.

This is all undertaken within norms sanctioned by the community of text users. Encroachments or excesses are immediately spotted and shunned as 'over the top' (a label which our reporter would have earned had he opted for the emphatic 'this venture *can only* enhance') or as 'coy' (with which the Dean would have been described had he opted for the passive 'this venture *is intended* to enhance').

9.1.4   Text-type criteria: A case study

The pragmatics of notions such as receiver status dealt with by Pym (see 7.3) has been investigated from a variety of other perspectives. Hatim (1988), for example, adopts a text-type approach to the problem and focuses on discourse errors made by advanced English/Arabic translator trainees. To extrapolate from the findings of this study, it appears that distinctions such as 'excluded', 'observational' and 'participative' status, or even receivers of **covert** or **overt** translations (see 7.3 and 7.4), can all be equally and most adequately accounted for within current text typologies.

In Hatim (1988), two different kinds of text were analysed:

[1] Jean-Jacques Rousseau was one of the greatest thinkers of the 18th century whose writings inspired the leaders of the French Revolution and influenced what became known as the Romantic generation. As a philosopher, he tried . . . In politics, he . . .

(Encyclopaedia Britannica, 1974)

This encyclopaedia entry is seen as an example of monitoring (detached exposition) and may thus be usefully compared with a sample taken from an 'evaluative' biography of Rousseau:

[2] Jean-Jacques Rousseau was the revolutionary, the impertinent, who, for the first time, directly and effectively, challenged the accepted rationalist view held by the enlightened century in which he lived. He made a real breach in that long tradition of reasonableness which . . . Partly under Rousseau's pounding, the formal structure of . . .

(Bronowski and Mazlish, 1974)

In Sample [2], the essential properties of 'exposition' are clearly in evidence. However, monitoring is shifted subtly to serve a **managing** function (e.g. to argue a point through, to promote certain beliefs).

In this study, the value for the translator of contextualising texts and specifying text-type focus in this way is shown to be extremely valuable. Functional shifts in the source text are slightly problematical and difficult to identify with any precision. Shifts will also be difficult to 'negotiate' in the target text. However, it is suggested that this inevitable **hybridisation** lends credence to, and does not detract from, the value of using 'pure' types as conceptual pegs on which to hang the myriad cases of text 'impurity'.

The kind of texts described in terms of 'monitoring' within detached exposition, or 'managing' within argumentation, enjoy a reasonable measure of psychological reality. To relate the discussion to the point at issue here, the text classification proposed is not at variance with such classifications as Pym's 'observational' vs 'participative' receiver status (see 7.3). In fact, the parallels between Pym's classification and text typologies such as that proposed in Hatim and Mason (1990) are striking. To put this in simple experiential terms, we can use language either as 'participants' or as 'spectators' (Pym's 'participative' and 'observational', respectively). When the goal is to get the text receiver to do something, or even to change his or her opinion about an issue or set of issues (Text [2] above or Pym's 'invitation to tender'), then we become participants, and invite others to become participants, in the affair in question. If, on the other hand, we merely want to 'inform' the text receiver (Text [1] above or Pym's appended note in French), then not only do we invite the text receiver to become a spectator, but we also become spectators of the experience in question (cf. Britton, 1963: 73).

9.2   The genre–text–discourse triad

Hatim and Mason subscribe to a source text orientation made compatible with a communicative approach to the process of translation. The approach is informed by a broader **semiotic** perspective on translation, and is thus concerned with the wider issue of cultures in contact. Alongside its commitment to a text-type slant, the scheme is designed to cater for a range of **socio-textual practices** dealt with under the triad of **macro**-signs: **text–genre–discourse**.

9.2.1   Socio-textual practices vs socio-cultural features

Socio-textual modes of language use are distinguished from the no-less-important but generally 'static' socio-cultural features. A number of translation theorists have employed the latter in an attempt to account for cultural non-equivalence. Newmark (1988), for example, adapts Nida's classification of the various aspects of culture and presents his own scheme along the following lines:

1. *Ecology*: animals, plants, local winds, mountains, etc.
2. *Material culture*: food, clothes, housing, transport and communications.
3. *Social culture*: work and leisure.
4. *Organisations, customs, ideas*: political, social, legal, religious, artistic.
5. *Gestures and habits*: how to signal 'yes' or 'no' in certain languages and cultures.

Within the translation model proposed by Hatim and Mason, such lists are considered important and useful, yet incomplete and certainly insufficient as a way of defining culture or accounting for the process of intercultural communication. The alternative model advocated supplements this catalogue of **cultural objects** (artifacts) with a socio-textual dimension (**sociofacts** and **mentifacts**), which subsumes the form and function of such **macro**-signs as **discourse** and **genre**.

9.2.2   Textual practices: A case study

In putting forward a model of 'socio-textual practices', Hatim and Mason (1997) build on the critical-linguistic assumption that, to communicate effectively, language users rely on their ability to deal with:

- rhetorical purposes through **texts** (e.g. counter-argumentation);
- attitudes through **discourse** (e.g. racism);
- rules of **appropriateness** in conventionalised communicative events or **genres** (e.g. a letter to the editor).

A speech by Ayatollah Khomeini of Iran (along with its published translation) is analysed to illustrate the various aspects of socio-textual practice (the text–genre–discourse triad). Essentially, the analysis is intended to highlight the cultural specificity of what we do with 'texts' in the process of translation. The study examines the striking mix of genres and the shifts in discourse which Khomeini's speech clearly exhibits, and shows how this **hybridisation** has proved to be particularly problematic in the translation of the speech into English.

The study starts with the socio-cultural domain and examines features such as the sustained use of the 'blood' metaphor (a religious theme). This is seen in terms of the cohesive chain created throughout the text by a series of doublets ('*crimson and blood-stained commitment*', '*crimson of martyrdom and the ink of blood').* The incessant recurrence of an image is a device which could be crucial to the construction of a **text-world** specific to a given text. However, unless **motivated** and seen to be substantially contributing to a discourse theme, socio-cultural references tend to be rather static, culture-specific, difficult and often unimportant to convey in translation (see 3.2.2). As the analysis shows, it is hard to see how the image of blood in this context can be transferred intact (as the English published translation has attempted to do) without giving rise to numerous unintended effects.

In socio-textual terms, rhetorical conventions are considered overriding, and the use of certain lexical and grammatical devices within texts as important indicators of the workings of textual norms. For example, the lexical token 'of course' is conventionally associated with text-initial concession in English, but its token-for-token equivalent in other languages (e.g. Arabic, Farsi) often introduces not a concession to be countered, but a case to be argued through. Consider the first in a sequence of sentences taken from the translation of Khomeini's speech:

> *Of course this does not mean that we should defend all clergymen.* Dependent, pseudo and ossified clergy have not been, and are not, few in number. There are even persons in the seminaries who are active against the revolution and against pure Mohammedan Islam. There are some people nowadays who, under the guise of piety, strike such heavy blows at the roots of religion, revolution and the system, that you would think they have no other duty than this.

For the English-language reader, the sentence (in italics) sets up an expectation that a counter-argument will follow, something along the lines of 'However, the majority of these men are good, God-fearing people'. As can be seen from the sequence cited above, however, no such pattern is in evidence, and what is involved is simply a point consistently argued through. That is, a 'through-argument' and not a 'counter-argument' is how the argumentation is intended in Farsi. In this study, it is suggested that the translator of this text could not have been responding consciously to socio-textual norms, but was rather reacting mechanistically to surface format (see the discussion of 'descriptive' vs 'interpretive' use in 3.3.3).

Seen from the vantage-point of discourse, the various features and devices which facilitate the expression of 'attitudes' (i.e. perspectives) seem to be fully accounted for by the translator of the Khomeini speech. To illustrate the form mediation takes in handling discursive features, Hatim and Mason look more closely at 'recurrence' as an aspect of cohesion. The function of such a device (which has not been thoroughly researched to date) can be to reinforce a point of view and display commitment or attitude. For example, the element *It was through the war that* . . . is repeated no fewer than six times in a short stretch of utterances. Faced with this unconventional degree of recurrence, many translators tend to erroneously opt for variation, relexicalising certain elements and conflating others.

The study concludes that the translator of this text has probably felt that only full recurrence could provide the target-text reader with access to ST discourse, hence the rendering of the whole sequence intact in English. But might this not simply be a **literal** strategy which the translator, working for the BBC Monitoring Service, felt he had to adopt? Evidence produced by the analysis reported in this study suggests that, given the many anomalies with which the translation is riddled, the strategy adopted by the translator is probably straightforward literalism and not something that is critically and consciously undertaken or contextually motivated.

Similarly, mediation in terms of **genre** appears to be minimal in the published translation. This is significant because, although the translator has limited scope to modify genres in translation, possibilities nevertheless exist at the level of genre-upholding lexical selection (collocations, imagery, etc.). Hatim and Mason suggest that this lends further support to the conclusion that the translators of the speech have opted for a fairly **literal** hit-or-miss approach.

Concept 9.5   **Interdiscursivity**

Discourse is the linguistic, socio-textual expression of 'perspective' on or 'attitude' towards socio-cultural areas of language in social life. Feminism, sexism, racism are all discoursal **mentifacts** – 'statements' articulating a 'stance' on the various issues involved. But discourses are not self-contained, hermetically sealed units of linguistic expression. Rather, discourses interact in subtle and intricate ways, not only with other discourses but also with other units of linguistic interaction (from word to text). With varying degrees of implicitness, discourses are interrelated, hence the term 'interdiscourse'. In complex ways, religious fundamentalism and political neo-conservatism, for example, interlock and mesh together (i.e. is the interdiscourse) in the thinking and language use of many well-known political or religious leaders (e.g. George W. Bush, Bin Laden).

Those aspects of a discourse that explicitly or implicitly exhibit virtual or actual points of resemblance or difference between one discourse and another serve as **communicative clues** to relations subsumed by what has come to be known as 'interdiscursivity'. This may take the form of what Fairclough (1989, 1992) calls 'horizontal **intertextuality**' (e.g. a government Minister of the Environment referring 'chapter and verse' to other specific speeches on a specific issue). But interdiscursivity could also be much more subtle, complex and dynamic. Fairclough calls this 'vertical' intertextuality', with the reference being not so much to other concrete instances of discourse as to entire 'types of discourse'. Here, the Minister of the Environment's use of language could (invariably implicitly) conjure up impressions or images of the 'style' conventionally recognised as characteristic of the 'analytic exposition' of multinational companies, as opposed to the 'hortatory' argumentation of Greenpeace, for example) (Martin, 1991).

For the sake of clarity, it might be helpful to reserve the term inter-textuality for the former, 'horizontal' kind of specific allusions, while adopt the term 'interdiscursivity' for the 'vertical' type of intertextual relationships (Fairclough, 1989).

9.2.3   Pitfalls in researching ideology

Within the parameters set for the discourse model of translation illustrated above, Hatim and Mason see the notion of **ideology** as one of the more salient manifestations of discursive practices. From the perspective of text linguistics, a basic assumption has been that ideology shapes discourse and is in turn shaped by it (Fowler, 1996), with a variety of discursive practices helping to maintain, reinforce or challenge prevalent ideologies. The assumption is also entertained that these ideological-discursive formations play an important role in the decision-making process undertaken by translators and in the choices made when dealing with **text-worlds** in transition.

Discourse analysis in this area of ideological meaning is fraught with difficulties (see works cited under Candlin and Crichton), and researchers must guard against a number of pitfalls in the study of ideology in translation. Some of these pitfalls, discussed in detail by Hatim and Mason (1997), are listed in outline form below.

Distortions: Are they conscious or accidental?

There is first of all the question of whether the writer's manipulation of discourse or the translator's intervention to foreground or sideline certain features is consciously undertaken or whether discourse uncon- sciously filters through. In the scheme proposed, this should not be seen as an insurmountable hurdle. It is safe to assume that the individual (text producer or translator) is envisaged as operating within discursive practices which have been somehow internalised by individuals and which in the process have become established among diverse social groups and institutions. As Gee (1990: 174) sees it, a two-way process is involved in which the user is 'at one and the same time an active (agent) in the discourse and passively subjected to its authority'.

Of course, this does not imply that language use is wholly predeter- mined and that users are always at the mercy of ideological forces, having no control whatsoever over their own discourse. By and large, however, manipulations or interventions can plausibly be seen as emanat- ing from an individual who has absorbed the mores of society regarding these discursive practices and has in turn contributed to them.

Determinism

In analysing discursive effects, researchers would also have to be wary of positing any form of determinism between the **ideology** or world- view of a text producer and the **actual** linguistic structures of the resulting text. Nevertheless, it is legitimate to see a particular linguistic feature (e.g. passives with **agent deletion**) in terms of how it system- atically serves a particular function in a given context. That is, it is appropriate to scrutinise the way a given feature is used and to see this function served by different text producers in different contexts but for similar purposes and similar effects. Patterns and trends can emerge, and it is desirable to relate assumptions made by text users to contextual factors at work, as evidenced by discourse **texture**.

Generalisations that are too powerful

Caution must also be exercised to prevent claims from becoming too powerful. There is always the user, the discourse, the ideology and society to consider.

- The use of certain devices such as 'passive **agent deletion**' might be unmotivated and incidental, and the cause could simply be such external factors as linguistic 'incompetence'.
- Devices such as agent deletion might easily be a 'convenience' of the writing process (you have just used a particular feature too many times and you feel like some variation is needed).

- The issue might be related to idiosyncrasy and idiolect (some speakers are given to verbosity).
- Fashions of speaking tend to be culturally induced and therefore **motivated** only by the sociolinguistic conditions which have engendered them. For example, residual orality in certain cultures encourages its own modes of speaking or writing, and language use has to be assessed within these parameters and not in the light of such criteria as universal logic.

Further reading

- On text-related insights into the translation process prior to the emergence of text-linguistics, see Holmes (1994).
- On text-linguistic developments, see Nord (1997) (with a brief introduction to Reiss's text typology (see Chapter 3).
- On text theory, see Beaugrande (1995) (Chapter 5 on 'interlinguistic discourse' has an important section on 'translation').
- On the cross-cultural angle, see Hatim (1997a).
- On reading, see Grabe and Stoller (2nd edition, 2011).
- On discourse theory and practice, see Moore et al. (2001).
- On discourse and the translator, see Mason (1994), Hatim and Mason (1990).

Chapter 10

Translation and ideology

This chapter will . . .

- describe research into **ideology**, not only *in* translation, from the perspective of Critical Discourse Analysis, but also *of* translation, from the perspective of Cultural Studies;
- highlight the common interest in discourse equally shared by text-linguistic models of translation and models subscribing to the cultural paradigm on both sides of the Atlantic.

> **Quote 10.1**
>
> Translation requires the recognition of discourse typologies in order to ascertain the fundamental characteristics of particular texts to be translated. That is to say, the conscious theorization of the problematic embodied in a particular source text is a useful and, I would argue, necessary step in achieving a 'satisfactory' translation.
>
> Donald Bruce (1994: 47)

10.1   The ideology *of* vs *in* translation

In researching translation and **ideology**, two different perspectives may be identified:

1. The *translation of **ideology***, with the focus on how 'ideology' *in* the text to be translated is dealt with, and how best to convey this *in* translation. From this perspective, the various discursive formations at work *in the text* are focused on. The constraints tend to be related to the use of language in social life, including value and belief systems shared collectively by given social groups (e.g. racism, feminism).

2. The *ideology of translation*, with 'ideology' becoming a cover term for what is essentially not *in* the text or *in* the translation, but *of* the text and *of* translation. The constraints in this domain tend to be *translational* (i.e. those which a translation, like all translations, function under). For example, 'target text fluency' as a translation aim is closely bound up with an ideology subscribed to by certain translation traditions.

Within this distinction, the question of the extent to which translators can or should mediate in the process of translating becomes important. Mediation is a facet of the translator's work which straddles the two perspectives outlined above. Translator mediation can be ideological in itself:

- In the discursive, 'language in social life' sense defined under (1) above (e.g. the translator mediates to express her own feminism or racism).

- In the translational sense defined under (2) above (e.g. the translator mediates to uphold the mores of the translation tradition or the prevailing ethos).

This two-way representation (the translation of **ideology**, the ideology of translation) and the extent of translator mediation are apparent in any appraisal of translation practice. For example, feminist translators (4.3.1) would subscribe to an ideology that determines not only value and belief systems (e.g. feminist ideals), nor only translation methods (translation as text production or re-writing), but also the degree of latitude enjoyed by the translator (feminist translation practice being highly interventionist). In fact, whichever analytic perspective on ideology is adopted, what is involved will inevitably relate to how a given **text-world** is preserved or altered for the benefit of a text receiver operating in a different cultural and linguistic environment.

Chapter 9 dealt with the 'translation of **ideology**' and presented this from the perspective of text linguistics. This chapter shifts the focus slightly and turns to the 'ideology of translation' as seen from the perspective of cultural studies. To show how, like linguistics and translation studies itself, the 'cultural' model is 'a house of many rooms', this chapter sets the scene with an example of the kind of work on **ideology** and translation conducted within what we have in this book generally referred to as the 'continental variety' of cultural studies (see 5.2).

This is followed in the second and third part of the chapter by work coming out of North America within such frameworks as cultural politics in translation (10.2) and feminist translation (10.4). The various approaches presented here have one thing in common: they all subscribe to the notion that translation method is itself ideological. That is, in addition to the racism or the feminism of the source text, there is something about how translations are made, or how they sound, which shows allegiance to a particular translation method or tradition.

10.2 The ideology of translation: A cultural studies perspective

Within the framework of both continental and North American cultural studies, important research questions addressed include:

- How do cultural context and linguistic expression become intertwined?
- In what ways do translations become impoverished if the texts to be translated are stripped of intellectual or emotional overtones?

10.2.1 Expropriation

Vladimir Maccura (1990a) looks at the Czech scene and challenges the myth that the function of translation is merely the transfer of information (i.e. the exchange of **signifieds**). In the context of nineteenth-century Czech culture, for example, readers did not really need translation from most adjacent European tongues, but strongly felt that to translate is to prove one's national identity (expropriation), and that a language is capable of rendering the treasures which other more prestigious languages (in this case German) possess.

It is suggested that cases such as this cannot be argued simply on the basis of current notions of 'translation function' as dictated by the precepts of translation theory. According to Maccura, the transfer of information is not the sole purpose of translation, and to subscribe to

such 'utilitarian' views would be failing to notice, for example, that the
aim behind translating *Paradise Lost* into Czech was because it

> represents an amalgam of different cultures. In his epic Milton shows
> pagan, Christian and Jewish traditions side by side, reconciling medieval
> romances with biblical history and heathen myths with theological con-
> cepts of his time.
>
> (p. 69)

10.2.2   Mimicking target discourse

The subject of language and identity also occupies Mahasweta Singupta
(1990a) in her study of the Bengali poet Tagore's autotranslation. The
study outlines the pitfalls of a translation in which faithfulness is exclusively shown towards the target language and culture. To mimic the
dominant discourse of English, Tagore (winner of the Nobel Prize for
literature in 1933) would translate his own work, changing not only
the style of the original but also the imagery and tone of the lyric. An
entirely different **register** emerges, matching as closely as possible the
target language **poetics** of Edwardian times.

It was Tagore's emulation of Western values which earned him approval
in the West. He was accepted, first, as a mystic or religious prophet
and, second, on the grounds that he translated his works 'in a manner
that suited the psyche of the colonizer' (p. 61). This was not to survive
the onslaught of time, however. In the words of Singupta (p. 62), 'he
was forgotten as fast as he was made famous': when he began to lecture
against nationalism, thus challenging an important Orientalist super-
structure, the master–servant relationship with which he had imbued
his poems was no longer in fashion.

10.3   The North American scene

10.3.1   Ideology and the choice of what to translate

A number of factors surround the act of translation and influence the
conditions under which translations are made:

- The role of the critical establishment, both in the choice of what to
  translate and how to translate.
- The kind of interventions which translators make.

- The economics of the exercise.
- The influences which translations exert on or receive from the dominant **poetics** or **ideology**.

The cultural theorist and translation scholar Donald Bruce (1994: 7) sets his research within such parameters, and specifically seeks

> to enquire into a familiar question of cultural politics which returns repeatedly to haunt translators and cultural historians: what factors determine whether a text will be translated or not?

The texts which Bruce discusses are major literary works belonging to the Paris Commune of 1871. These are Jules Valles's *L'Enfant*, *Le Bachelier* and *L'Insurge*. The first was translated with an introduction by Douglas Parmée only fairly recently in 2005 (*The Child*, NYRB Classics). To date, however, no complete English translation of the other two major texts exists.

Bruce traces the reasons for this absence back to the circumstances surrounding the publication of the trilogy and the kind of reception it had in France. This was one of 'ideological marginalization and delegitimisation of these novels within the French educational apparatus itself' (p. 48).

Valles's exclusion from the canon may explain why a taste for his writing had not in fact been generally cultivated. This certainly served as another possible reason for the marginalisation of his writings. Bruce (p. 56) lists and illustrates some of the textual manifestations perceived as problematical in the French writer's work:

- The heavy use made of journalistic devices was seen by Valles's critics as 'inferior' and not 'belletristic'.
- The texts are strongly 'referential' (inaccessible when portraying the social upheaval in the Commune, for example).
- The texts are politically morbid, problematising social conflict instead of providing an escape from it.

10.3.2   Discourse in translation: A model for analysis

Bruce (1994) develops a working model for the analysis of the discourse of the Commune in particular. The basic discursive categories proposed are said to be 'central to the discourse of the Commune where they are formally and functionally instantiated' (p. 64), It is, however, also suggested that the discursive features which emerge from such an analysis are areas which the translator must account for in practising discourse analysis more generally. The model sketched below is applicable to contexts beyond that within which it was originally envisaged, and the features illustrated are in fact typical of many texts.

In this study, Bruce discusses the role in translation of a heightened awareness of how text and context constantly interact with each other in the production of meaning. In the specific case of anarchist discourse in nineteenth-century France, the cross-fertilisation in evidence between text and context constitutes the linguistic dimension of the Commune culture, which is crucial to an appreciation of the cultural politics that was instrumental in marginalising Valles and his work.

Bruce believes that contextual awareness of this kind is highly relevant to the work of the translator, and suggests that 'conscious theorization of the problematic embodied in a particular source-text is a useful and . . . necessary step in achieving a "satisfactory" translation' (p. 47). To translate the culture of the Commune, translators must first thoroughly acquaint themselves with the cultural politics surrounding an issue. Literary and cultural theory are particularly beneficial in laying the foundations for conceptually more valid translation methodologies, a trend which, according to Bruce (p. 47), can be enhanced by enlisting discourse analysis.

Bruce poses a number of research questions:

- How can discourse analysis help the translator to cope with the range of complex issues encountered in the kind of situation exemplified by Valles's Commune writing?
- Does the analysis of Commune discourse shed light on the reasons why (with the exception of a fairly recent translation of *L'Enfant*) there has not been an English translation of Valles's work to date?

These are important questions that need to be answered by future research with reference to numerous writers marginalised for one reason or another in various parts of the world and within a variety of cultural milieux.

An important set of factors at work in reading and translating writers such as Valles has to do with what, in the case of the Commune, Bruce describes as the formal and functional specificity of the discourse of the Commune – that is, the qualities which render them 'subversive' (p. 57). This 'historical specificity' resides not only within the cultural politics enveloping the text but also in the **actual** minutiae of language **texture**. Contextual matters such as class struggle or competing world-views find immediate expression in discourse. Bruce illustrates this from the work of Valles and identifies the following sets of discourse manifestations:

1. 'Radical decentralisation' of the discourse. This is brought about by writing in a certain **defamiliarising** way (e.g. by breaking up the narrative flow and generally fragmenting the discourse of the novel).

Bruce emphasises that 'it is absolutely essential that the translator maintain this deceptively simple but fundamental discursive feature' (p. 64). Cited here is the case of the German translation of one of Valles's works in which 'the translators have not rigorously adhered to this principle of narrative fragmentation which corresponds clearly to such "anarchistic" notions as decentralization, autonomous experience, spontaneity' (p. 64).

2. Tense shifts in Valles's work also become powerful ideological clues to 'different **narrative voices** [which] take charge of the **narrative** (Jacques as child, as young man, as insurgent, as retrospective exile, as "omniscient" third person narrator)' (p. 66).

Bruce suggests that the translator must decide whether to follow English tense uniformity closely or to preserve the temporal discordance of the French. Anomalies should not be 'smoothed out', and tenses should be left alone unless logical comprehensibility is totally impeded.

3. Semantic **fields**. These are key semantic domains which 'must be maintained if the lexical integrity of the discourse is to be protected' (p. 66). Included here are the various juxtapository and oppositional relationships and their distribution.

For example, in Valles's *L'Enfant*, antinomy is established through the use of such juxtapositions as *blouse/redingote, province/ville, boulevard/rue, mouvement/stabilité.*

4. **Word play**. The semantic ambiguity inherent in the use of this rhetorical device, which in the kinds of texts we are considering is bound to be ideologically **motivated**, must somehow be preserved (through functional equivalents if necessary):

> What is essential here is the translator's recognition of the functional role of lexical ambiguity in the trilogy: both form and function are re-semanticised in terms of counter-discourse. They are subversive and that subversion must be maintained by the translator. (Bruce, pp. 67–8)

An example of the semantic ambiguity inherent in ideological word play is *carrière* > *quarry*. Also, *la lutte* [*pour la vie*] versus *la lutte* [*des classes*], which mix and oppose two discourses: the socio-Darwinism of the state ideological apparatus and the Marxism which defines class struggle.

5. Interdiscursive mixing. This is an ideological weapon which draws heavily on the way signs 'signify'. Subsumed under this category are most of the features discussed so far: the ambiguity of competing discourses in the ideologisms, discursive juxtaposition and conflict, the hijacking of other discourses and the inherently subversive thrust of the currently unfolding discourse.

As Bruce acknowledges, the repertoire of discursive features discussed here is far from comprehensive and should be extended to account for numerous other characteristics present in ideologically **motivated** statements. It would be useful to include:

- figurative expression (especially metonymy);
- the use of spatial metaphors to represent the text in a non-hierarchical fashion (horizontal rather than vertical);
- cultural references specific to counter-culture (and consequently typical of counter-discourse);
- shifts in perspective and positionality.

10.3.3   Striking parallels

The way Valles has been rejected is not unique, and striking parallels exist around the world. In modern Arabic literature, for example, we have the case of the Arab novelist Abdul Rahman Munif, whose name was floated as possibly a more meritorious candidate for the Nobel Prize in literature than the Egyptian novelist Naguib Mahfouz who was awarded the prize in 1988. So what is it that prevented Munif from being even considered by the Nobel Prize committee (or any international prize-awarding body for that matter)?

This is still a matter of conjecture, and further research is needed into this and related issues, but one thing is certain: Munif was for a long time not a favourite of Western publishers. By the mid-1980s, he had had only one or two of his novels translated into the major European languages, a picture that has not appreciably changed to this day. Furthermore, it has to be noted that the bulk of the few translations made so far are decidedly 'fluent' and thus largely unresponsive to source text intended and highly creative complexity (see, for example, *al-nihayat*, translated into English as *Endings* by Roger Allen). Further research is needed to shed light on the kind of translation shifts affected in such translations.

But, the deeper, underlying reason for the neglect which Munif suffered at the hands of a translation publishing industry and consequently prize-awarding bodies must ultimately be found in the kind of texts Munif wrote. Munif's work is strongly **referential** (i.e. generally inaccessible and not easy to appreciate by the outsider) and politically morbid (i.e. problematising and not sufficiently escapist). This is confirmed by textual evidence which even a cursory discourse analysis of Munif's work yields, and which, to extrapolate for the purposes of the present discussion, seems to lend credence to Bruce's theory regarding the reasons why and how Valles was marginalised.

The parallels with Valles's situation stop here. In the case of Munif, the Arab critical establishment has systematically praised the quality of his work. Characteristics such as political morbidity have become part and parcel of a kind of fictional writing held in high esteem: the so-called 'catastrophe fiction' (*adab al-nakba*, in the wake of the Arab defeat in the Six-Day War with Israel). But, as Venuti and Bruce have strongly argued, it is such qualities that always seemed sufficient to render a writer's work uninviting, if not totally alien, to the publishing and translation establishment in the West.

10.4   The ideology of translation: A feminist perspective

> **Quote 10.2**
>
> [O]ne of the challenges for the feminist translators is to move beyond questions of the sex of the author and translator. Working within the conventional hierarchies . . . the female translator of a female author's text and the male translator of a male author's text will be bound by the same power relations: what must be subverted is the process by which translation complies with gender constructs.
>
> Lori Chamberlain (1992: 72)

10.4.1   Feminist translation strategies: first attempts

In keeping with the way feminist thinking itself has evolved over the last two or three decades, feminist translators have begun to address a variety of issues never properly aired before. For instance, an important question to come to the fore is whether all women share similar concerns regarding such social ills as oppression, or whether the scene is more differentiated? In an article in *The Translator*, feminist translation theorist Françoise Massadier-Kenny (1997: 55) argues for the need to recognise difference (ethnic or otherwise) and challenges the basis of traditional distinctions within feminist thinking on translation:

> The use of 'feminist' or 'woman' provides an unstable point of departure for translation practice. Active translation does not depart from predetermined **gender** definitions but must lead to an interrogation of such gender definitions and roles.

As discussed in 4.3, the history of feminist translation has been a struggle for visibility, 'to make the feminine – i.e. women – visible' (Lotbinière-Harwood, 1991: 101). To pursue this goal, feminist translators discussed the creative aspects of their work and underlined how the writers they translate are colluded with or challenged.

Concept 10.1   **An early model of feminist translation**

A number of interventionist strategies are used by the feminist translator (Flotow, 1991):

- *Supplementing* the source text, a strategy to which politically conscious feminist translators would resort in dealing with areas such as **word play** (Le Vine, 1991).

- *Prefacing* and *footnoting* as important instruments of active engagement with the source and participation in the creation of meaning (Godard, 1988: 50).

- *Appropriation*, or what has sometimes been disapprovingly called 'hijacking' someone else's text (Homel and Simon, 1989).

The question now is whether there is anything specifically feminist about the strategies mentioned in Concept 10.1, except the use to which they are put. As Massadier-Kenny (1995: 57) observes, 'supplementing . . . looks very like the old strategy . . . "compensation"', and it appears that, to make the feminine visible, the translator turns to adapting existing translation strategies rather than inventing new ones. Massadier-Kenny presents a comprehensive scheme setting out major strategies which have been or can be adapted to advance a feminist agenda. Such a framework is useful not only for researching feminist translation issues, but also for describing the process of translating ideology in general.

10.4.2   Author-centred strategies

Author-centred strategies serve the original author's intended purpose and seek to make the reader appreciate the source text for what it is. Such methods are important in the work of the feminist translator since, among other things, they reinstate women as legitimate producers of texts. The idea of 'production' is central to feminist thinking on translation; it merges the notions of 'author' and 'translator' into the all-encompassing category of 'active co-producer of texts'.

Recovery

This relates to the way women's experience has been excluded from the canon. In the context of feminist translation, to 'recover' is to widen and thus reshape the canon (Massadier-Kenny, 1995: 57), with women's experience providing the pivotal point (Lotbinière-Harwood, 1991).

Commentary

Involved here is 'the metadiscourse accompanying the translation to make explicit the importance of the feminine (. . .) in the text translated' (Massadier-Kenny, 1995: 59). 'Prefaces' and 'afterwords' are part of the metadiscourse which have consistently been shown to enhance translator visibility. Massadier-Kenny (p. 59) mentions two important functions which are served by 'commentary' through the metadiscourse. In the 'preface', the reader is reminded of the authority or the image of the writer and of how this projection has become possible only through the mediation of a translator who is a critic in her own right. Furthermore, such metadiscourse makes it possible to counteract the immediacy of the translated text and the feeling of familiarity which a translation necessarily induces to some degree. This immediacy and familiarity often lead us to forget about the difference that the source text presented.

Resistancy

Resistancy involves 'making the labour of translation visible through linguistic means that have a **defamiliarising** effect and that work against fluency' (Massadier-Kenny, p. 59). This is not restricted to the translation of works that are post-modernist and innovative, but can be adapted to cater for the 'feminist' in those texts which do not use stylistic innovations as part of the usual repertoire (e.g. most pre-contemporary texts).

Framing

This refers to the material which individualises the translation, thereby enabling it to become part of text meaning, contributing to its very resistancy, 'pushing against its automatic insertion in the target culture' (Massadier-Kenny, p. 61).

Annotation

As part of 'framing', annotation also serves the feminist project. Relevant in this respect is Appiah's (1993) notion of **thick glossing**: a translation 'that seeks with its annotations and its accompanying glosses to locate the text in a rich cultural and linguistic context'. This has a pedagogic value since a thick translation invites the reader to interact meaningfully with source cultures.

10.4.3   Translator-centred strategies

Dealing with feminist translation strategies in terms of author-centredness has highlighted the notion of the translator as an active co-producer of texts. This awareness has facilitated the recognition by feminist translation theorists of *translator*-centred strategies and not merely of *reader*-centred strategies. Massadier-Kenny lists some of these specifically 'translator-centred' strategies:

Commentary

Seen from the perspective of the translator, commentary allows feminist translators to describe their motives and show how these have influenced the way they translate. This strategy comes under what has been called the 'standpoint theory' whereby the translator acknowledges her 'positionality . . . , identity politics and the awareness of the necessary losses that such politics inevitably entails' (Bauder and McKinstry, 1991: 4).

Parallel texts

These include:

- source texts and their translations;
- original texts belonging to the same **genre** in the source language;
- texts of the same genre in the target language (p. 64).

The use of parallels enhances the metadiscourse of **thick** commentary and thus enables the translator to define her priorities, desires and the need to document her own choices.

Collaboration

Collaboration could involve working with other translators or with the author.

10.4.4   The feminist translation framework assessed

The notion of 'feminist translation strategies' (Flotow, 1991) has pushed to centre stage values pertaining to women which, if present in the source text, must somehow be carried over. But if such values are not explicitly there, are we entitled to 'hijack' the target text, and 'feminise' texts deliberately, often wantonly, sometimes even violently? These have been fairly controversial issues in writings on the subject and recent debate suggests that such strategies obfuscate rather than illuminate the process. The 'use' factor (Massadier-Kenny, 1995) is thus obviously crucial in the strategic design of the feminist translation.

Issues of identity and positionality have recently come to the fore in sexual politics. In declaring her hand, however, the feminist translator runs the risk of usurping textual power, an activity in which her male colleague has arguably been engaged for a long time. This strategy has been criticised as counter-productive. Adopting a more responsible stance, the critics argue, does not imply that the feminist translator has succumbed or acquiesced to authorial power structures. On the contrary, the translator would still be openly taking full responsibility for her own ideological/psychological position and for the text she happens to be translating (Massadier-Kenny, p. 63).

Such a prudently active stance should answer those who have charged feminist translators with hypocrisy (cf. Arrojo, 1994, 1995): while through such procedures as **thick translation** the feminists would certainly move into a new experience, they would not be colonising the new territory as their male counterparts are said to have done. Still, some feminist translators may see this as an attempt to relativise their newfound positionality and regained status. However,

> it can also be considered as a way of elevating the translator: super-reader/ author . . . [a function which] includes feminist questioning of universal categories in the translation project.
>
> (Diaz-Diocaretz, 1985)

The 'collaboration' strategy identified above is relevant to the issue of the legitimacy of the entire feminist translation project. This answers the critics who take feminist translators to task on the issue of control of meaning, a trap similar to that into which **patriarchal** translation theory has allegedly fallen. According to Massadier-Kenny (p. 65):

> Collaboration in the context of feminist translation means that, while the translator claims her agency in the metadiscourse surrounding the translation and the awareness of creating a tradition, she can also avoid the traditional dichotomy between two subjectivities (author/translator) which seek control of meaning.

Constant negotiation thus ensures that the stance adopted by the feminist translator flaunts its presence without being too obtrusive, and interrogates without being too oppressive.

Further reading

- On continental Cultural Studies and the study of ideology in translation, see the body of work best represented by Bassnett and Lefevere (1990a, b).

- The North American scene on discourse, ideology and translation is best portrayed by Bruce and Butler (1993).

- Work on feminist analysis of translation is best represented by such volumes as Simon (1996).

Chapter 11

Translation of genre vs translation as genre

This chapter will . . .

- describe research models which have addressed the theme 'genre in translation' vs 'genre of translation' (along similar lines to the distinction 'ideology in translation' vs 'ideology of translation') from the perspective of both applied linguistics and cultural studies;

- look more closely at research into the issue of translation 'norms' which has underpinned approaches to translation as a genre in its own right.

Quote 11.1

Translation is what goes on in the space between reading the SL text and writing the TL text, and that therefore it is on this interface that we ought to be concentrating, and not on reading and writing as assumed preconditions for translation skill.

Carl James (1989: 39–40)

An important insight to emerge from the discussion of 'the translation of ideology' vs 'the ideology of translation' relates, on the one hand, to the translation of the various textual **genres** encountered (e.g. cooking recipes, Mills & Boon fiction) and, on the other hand, to how translation itself as an act might be seen as a genre in its own right. That is, two distinct levels of abstraction might be distinguished in dealing with the notion of genre in translation:

- A translation might be seen in terms of the minutiae of source or target genres and the translation shifts affected. Thus, genre as a macro-sign provides translators with a framework within which **appropriateness** is judged and the various syntactic, semantic, pragmatic and **semiotic** structures handled.

- A translation might be seen in terms of how closely it represents all that is 'translational' (that is, what all translated material tends to look or sound like, as opposed to what happens in monolingual communication, for example).

Of course, the second sense of 'genre' may be derived from the first and vice versa, but the focus of the investigation would be different in each case. In the first sense, the *translation of genre* would be involved; in the second sense, *translation as genre* is the issue. We will deal with these two aspects in turn.

11.1   The translation of genre

From the perspective of genre theory, Carl James (1989) convincingly argues for the distinction between the two levels of abstraction outlined above. On the one hand, there is the more detailed sense of **genre** as a purposeful activity revolving around conventionalised social occasions or communicative events (i.e. a *textual-linguistic* issue, as in what typifies a 'cooking recipe', a 'letter to the editor', and so on) (see Hall and Kies, forthcoming). On the other hand, translation may be seen in the abstract as a function of the total effect of choices made and felt to be intrinsic to any act of transfer (i.e. a *translational* issue, as when we talk of something which looks or sounds like a translation, sounds foreign, reads fluently).

Dealing with the linguistic sense of the term, James subscribes to a notion of genre which covers a spectrum of textual-linguistic manifestations such as the conventional 'formats' of writing (e.g. a *haiku*, a sonnet) and the 'texture' involved (e.g. discourse markers). Genre may also refer to 'types' of writing (e.g. the lab report, the academic abstract), fairly general 'organisational' activities within these modes of writing (e.g. the 'preparation' part or the 'analysis' part in articles describing scientific experiments), or more specific 'moves' (e.g. summarising previous research). But whichever linguistic sense of genre is adopted, one thing is clear: genres carry traces of their identity and, through a variety of linguistic features (lexical and syntactic), tend to signal and insist on their textual presence. In academic writing, for example, there will be conventional markers of what 'abstracts' (as opposed to a straightforward 'summary' or an 'overview') would look like. And, of course, there will be differences between abstracts in academic English and those abstract formats recognised as appropriate in Arabic, for example.

Concept 11.1   **What is a genre?**

In genre analysis, the emphasis is 'on the conventional, formulaic, routine, labour-saving aspect of language use' (James, 1989: 32; Bhatia, 2004). This makes *genre* distinct from:

- **cognitive**-linguistic structures such as **schemas**, **frames**, **scripts**;
- rhetorical–textual modes such as description, narration, argumentation;
- the range of **registers** and their **ideational**, **interpersonal** and **textual** profiles.

These structures and templates tend to have a broader scope, and are rather more open-ended, than what we strictly recognise as 'genre'. For one thing, they involve more than just the language used (e.g. 'entering the place', 'eating', 'paying the bill', as some of the non-verbal aspects usually involved in the 'restaurant' script).

11.1.1   The translation of genre: A training perspective

Focusing on non-literary issues and the translation of so-called 'pragmatic' texts, James (1989) looks at the translation of genre in relation to reading and writing as skills that are central in working with non-proficient translators, particularly in the early stages of training. The option that the trainees may do their own translation in **fields** such as science and technology is underlined and closer links between learning the conventions and coping with them in translation are highlighted.

Approaching the matter from the vantage-point of teaching English for Special Purposes, James (1989: 40) suggests that activities such as reading and writing in such fields as science and technology, on the one hand, and technical translation, on the other, should be better streamlined. It might not be the most efficient use of resources to present the non-native student of science and technology with the stark choice of either to learn the rhetorical conventions in English or (if cheaper or quicker) to read ready-made translations.

Within the area of genre in translator training, James suggests that shifts and changes haphazardly introduced in the translation can irreparably dislocate the text from its intended genre and thus distort the rhetorical structure of the original. One way of dealing with this kind of 'genre violation' (p. 31) is to provide the translator with genre-based experience. The role of contextual specifications is often neglected in the training of translators, and the focus has invariably been on the 'words on the page', and not on the need to instil an awareness of larger discourse structures and genre specificities.

11.1.2   The translation of genre: A cultural perspective

The linguistic approach to issues of genre in translation has had echoes further afield in disciplines such as linguistic stylistics and cultural studies. Within the wider framework of cultural studies, genre theory has been exploited in rewriting and manipulation, and in the analysis of these phenomena. The examples which Maria Tymoczko (1990a) cites in her study of '*Hamlet* in West Africa' deal with the theme of resistance to faithful translation and bring up the issue of 'orality'. What has proved difficult for the oral tradition to cope with in the case of *Hamlet* was the transfer of certain concepts (e.g. *ghost*), values (*chastity of Ophelia*), customs (the Western concept of *mourning*), motivations (Hamlet's *madness*) and material culture (*swords* vs *machetes*).

In addition to socio-cultural artifacts of this kind, however, particular textual practices also resisted transfer (e.g. plot sequences, rhetorical and linguistic structures) (p. 49). It is shown that conceptual structures such as the 'plot' and the 'rhetorical sequence' tend to reflect cultural values in some meaningful ways, and that, in focusing almost exclusively on socio-cultural manifestations, research has at best been one-sided.

Tymoczko deals with such **genre** elements and the difficulties involved in their rendering within the framework of oral translation traditions. The translation of Welsh **narratives** into a Latin genre (the 'historical chronicle') provides an interesting example. The translation was undertaken by Geoffrey of Monmouth, who let his Latin historiography shape the way time, space and causality are handled. Alongside the choice of genre and rhetorical conventions, source text 'fatalism' and the theme of the 'messenger' gave way to the motif of *fortuna* and plotting.

This is important since it shows that certain socio-cultural features (e.g. 'fatalism' in this context) do acquire a dynamism of their own and can consequently enhance the effectiveness of structures such as genre. As Tymoczko (1990a: 51–2) puts it,

Geoffrey manipulates the heroic values of his source materials. . . .
Moderation, compassion and mercy are more in evidence . . . ; honour
gives way to the notion that 'there is nothing better or more enjoyable
than life itself'. . . . Themes that are characteristic of the French epic are
introduced.

The complexity which seems to be inherent in the process of cultures coming into contact through translation puts a different slant on
'faithfulness'. It is no longer possible to account for the notion in terms
of mere equivalence of words or even texts. Rather, faithfulness may now
be seen as an attempt to make target texts function in particular ways:
translators can be said to be faithful when, for example, they deliver
what those who commission the translation want. The receiving culture
is one such important client which can take over and assign different
functions to the translation of different texts.

Palma Zlateva (1990a: 30) picks up this point and cites the example
of *Peter Pan* in Bulgaria: this is said to have

> failed to attract the interest and win the admiration of its Bulgarian
> readers. Its heroes did not become part of their **universe of discourse** in
> the way Winnie the Pooh did.

This has little to do with translation quality. Zlateva's concept of the
pre-text is relevant here, subsuming the cultural assumptions which act
as indicators of the way the work is likely to fare in the target culture
(p. 29). The notion of the pre-text is a research issue which can usefully
be pursued along similar lines to Bruce's 'conscious theorization of the
cultural politics' enveloping the source text (see 10.3.1, 10.3.2).

11.2   Translation as genre

Can a translation be regarded as a genre in the same sense as a cooking
recipe or a letter to the editor would be? James suggests that 'there is
a genre "translation", but that it has a special status' (p. 35). Toury's
(1982) notion of 'ideological translation' is invoked in support of this
point: For ideological reasons, Russian and German Jews preferred to
read Hebrew translations of German and Russian texts rather than the
originals which they were perfectly capable of reading. Although such
evidence might shed more light on nationalistic fervour and less on the
appeal of translation as a genre, there is the helpful suggestion that
there must be something about translation itself which does something
to readers, something in the language that translators typically use,

something to do with a kind of textural 'feel' to translations, the intrinsically 'once removed' impressions created and which all translations seem to possess and exhibit.

In his argument for the possibility of a translation genre, James highlights characteristics typically associated with translation and cites Toury, this time on the issue of '**pseudotranslations**'. These are defined as 'target-language texts which are presented as translations although no corresponding source texts in another language, hence no factual relationships, exist' (1982: 67). The point adduced from this phenomenon is that pseudotranslations would not have been possible had it not been for the fact that 'it is only when humans recognise the existence of an entity and become aware of its characteristics that they can begin to imitate it' (p. 35).

The discussion of parody as a particularly interesting kind of **imitation** provides a further illustration of this 'genre within genre' manifestation. It is suggested that parody may be seen to have a dual significance: 'parody not only exists as a genre *per se* but its very existence depends on the assumed existence and the real knowledge of other genres which get parodied' (James, 1989: 35). When what is being parodied is a sermon, a political speech or a particular mannerism, **intertextuality** is fully tapped in order to account for, on the one hand, the 'outer' genre (the art of parody) and, on the other, the 'inner' genres (whatever happens to be parodied).

This duality becomes even more complex in the translation process. As James (1989: 36) points out, translators should be aware of what parody does, and what is being parodied (e.g. a sermon). Translators must additionally be conscious of the fact that it is not the production of 'an' original (let alone 'the' original) that should concern them but rather an act of doing something which must ultimately depend on the existence of something else.

11.2.1 Translation norms

> ### Quote 11.2
>
> The translation process is seen to be an example of discursive production determined by the full range of texts and translations which already exist in any given culture, and the cultural adaptation they entail.
>
> Lance Hewson and Jacky Martin (1995: 32)

Concept 11.2 **The norm model**

In Descriptive Translation Studies, norms have come to be seen as 'internalized behavioural constraints which embody the values shared by a community and govern those decisions in the translation process which are not dictated by the two language systems involved' (Hermans, 1995: 216). As such, norms are recognised as the mechanisms which inform a variety of decisions, including judgements relating to the ideology of translation:

- whether the translation is intended to follow source rather than target textual and literary norms (what Toury calls the *initial norm*);
- the use of an existing translation into another language as a likely source, and whether this is acceptable in a given culture (what Toury calls *preliminary norms*).

It has to be noted that, despite the label and the assumption that it is perhaps logically prior, the 'initial norm' does not have to precede other norms. Nevertheless, this type of norm tends to provide the backdrop against which the act of transfer is strategically played out. According to Leuven-Zwart (1989: 154), the initial norm subsumes

> the translator's (conscious or unconscious) choice as to the main objective of his translation, the objective which governs all decisions made during the translation process.

For Toury, this is intimately related to whether the translator can afford to remain 'faithful' to the source text or has to adjust his or her strategy in the direction of the target language and culture.

As part of gauging the reactions of the target culture to the **acceptability** of certain translation procedures, preliminary norms are invoked, governing such matters as whether or not a coherent translation policy is in place within a given culture or language at a particular time. Such a policy does not always have to be formalised and may merely derive from preferences regarding individual authors, genres or schools in given languages and not in others, or among certain cultures and at a particular period of history.

Concept 11.3   **Acceptability and adequacy**

The idea of norms is conceptually set against the background of two basic ways of judging a translation, proposed by Toury (1980): **acceptability** and adequacy. These may be explained in the light of a fundamental principle underpinning the polysystems theory: specifically in literary translation, the notion that there is one 'proper' way to translate is to be utterly rejected. What should be addressed instead is whether and to what extent the translation is 'acceptable'. Acceptability is distinguished from adequacy:

- *Acceptability* is a function of the adherence to those norms and conventions (both linguistic–textual and literary–aesthetic) which operate in the target system.

- *Adequacy* applies if, for whatever reason, source rather than target norms are followed throughout.

But translations can never be purely 'acceptable' or purely 'adequate', and are more likely to occupy a place somewhere between the two poles. The question of which orientation predominates and informs the decision-making process is one which is settled by invoking the initial norm (see Concept 11.2). As Toury (1980) succinctly puts it, translations which tend towards the 'acceptability' pole may be thought of as fulfilling the dream of 'reading as *an* original', while those which tend towards 'adequacy' meet the condition 'reading as *the* original' (p. 75) (italics added).

11.2.2   Alternative views on norms

Quote 11.3

Translation is increasingly seen as a process, a form of human behaviour. A theory, therefore, should seek to establish the laws of this behaviour.

Andrew Chesterman (1993: 2)

Toury's notion of norms has been an important source of inspiration in translation research, and in the last three decades or so has informed a number of proposals which explore some of the more interesting theoretical ramifications.

Concept 11.4   **Conventions**

Nord (1991b) sees *rules, norms* and *conventions* hierarchically in this order, with the lower parameter (e.g. conventions) being less binding than the one above it (norms). Conventions may thus be seen as 'specific realizations of norms . . . not explicitly formulated, nor are they binding' (p. 96).

In the model proposed by Nord, translation is said to be an act of carefully juggling three distinct sets of 'conventions':

- those related to the source-culture;
- those of the target-culture;
- those which govern the translation process as a whole.

Translational conventions may be 'constitutive' – that is, having to do with 'what a particular culture community accepts as a translation (as opposed to an "adaptation" or "version" or other forms of inter-cultural transfer)' (p. 100). Conventions can also be 'regulative', related to 'generally accepted forms of handling certain translation problems below the text rank' (p. 100) (e.g. proper names, culture-bound concepts, quotations).

In a study in *Target*, Andrew Chesterman (1993) approaches the issue of norms from a slightly different angle to that adopted by Toury or Nord. He postulates what he calls 'laws' defined as observable regularities seen in purely descriptive terms: laws 'would take the general form: under conditions ABC, translators (tend to) do (or refrain from doing) X' (p. 2). Such 'general descriptive laws' are bound to be probabilistic, catering for behavioural regularities identified in any type of translator (regardless of degree of competence) and for any kind of translation (as long as it is a 'translation' and not an adaptation or some other form of 'reworking' a text). What is needed, then, 'not instead of, but in addition to these general descriptive laws, is what makes a good translation' (p. 4).

How do we go about developing the kind of translation norms which would fulfil the primary condition for the existence of norms in general – namely, the problem-solving function? As with all matters of language use, this must involve developing ways of enhancing the possibilities of communicative success. To apply this to translation, Chesterman (p. 7) suggests that we need to:

- identify a group of individuals who translate and whose translations can be taken to represent optimal performance; this may be represented by a notional category appropriately labelled 'competent professional translators';

- identify a collection of translated texts which can similarly be taken as an accepted 'model', presumably of the kind which our competent group of translators normally produce.

The group of competent professional translators (defined behaviourally) and the output of model translated texts (defined text-linguistically) both become important sources of translational norms, yielding (according to Chesterman, 1993: 8):

- *professional norms*, involving criteria worked out on the basis of the behavioural aspect;
- *expectancy norms*, involving criteria developed on the basis of the text linguistics relevant to the collection of translations.

Concept 11.5 **Professional and expectancy norms**

Professional norms cater for the optimal conditions within which good practice is said to be grounded, that is, 'the accepted methods and strategies of the translation process' (p. 8). The process involves a series of tasks, ranging from source text analysis to needs analysis, and even to the evaluation of reference materials in use.

Professional norms ultimately serve three higher-order sets of criteria:

- accountability (an ethical norm subsuming loyalty to original writer, commission, etc.);
- communication (a social norm requiring the translator to optimise communication);

- relation (establishing and maintaining an appropriate level of equivalence).

This diverse range of textual and extratextual activities is distinguished from what is involved in 'expectancy norms'. These have more to do with the nature of the 'product' than with 'production' per se. Once again, higher-order criteria govern this kind of norm: What is expected of a translation or of a given type of translation? What do translations (as opposed to original writing, for example) look like?

Chesterman concludes that 'translation studies should be normative, norm-describing and indeed norm-refining' (p. 13). The question now is: How do conventional frameworks such as 'professional norms' actually come about in the first place? When regularities are detected in translator activity, these must be seen as akin to

> a normative law (with a prescriptive force), a norm-directed strategy which is observed to be used (with a given, high, probability) by (a given, large, proportion of) competent professional translators.

Being thus empirically oriented, normative theory of translation behaviour and the normative translation laws which emanate from it have both a predictive and an explanatory power (p. 15). The predictive aspect lies in the fact that the theory is probabilistic and that translation law is 'thus strictly speaking a hypothesis that has not yet been disconfirmed' (p. 15). As for explanation, the theory must be capable of demonstrating not only 'what' but also 'why'.

Further reading

- On the general climate of thinking surrounding such issues as norms vs laws, see Andrew Chesterman (1997) (Chapter 7 is devoted to 'translation ethics', with the discussion of norms featuring prominently).
- On genre theory and the practice informed by the various models of genre description, see Bhatia (2004), Devitt (2004), Frow (2006), Swales (2004).
- On the translation of genre, see Hatim and Mason (1990, 1997), Hatim (1997).
- On translation as a genre, see Toury (1995), Hermans (1991).

Chapter 12

Empirical research in translation studies

This chapter will . . .

- describe models of empirical research into such issues as 'translation universals' undertaken within corpus translation studies;

- report on research into the translation process which has focused on the process of what goes on in the translator's mind.

12.1   Corpus research into translation universals

The investigation of norms, and the empirical data yielded, have cast new light on the existence of 'translation universals': whether, regardless of the language pairs involved, translations function in specific ways which distinguish them from ordinary language material composed independently of source text constraints. Research into this aspect of translation has been driven by a number of working hypotheses which corpus translation studies is addressing at present.

12.1.1   Types of corpora

In translation studies, corpora generally refer to 'collections of texts held in machine-readable form and capable of being analysed automatically or semi-automatically in a variety of ways' (Baker 1995: 225). This material tends to be lumped together under the rather unhelpful heading of 'parallel texts'. A closer look at textual data reveals that other forms of corpora are also widely in use.

Concept 12.1   **Types of corpora**

Parallel bilingual corpora, consisting of original texts and their translated versions, have traditionally been the most popular data for research in translation studies. They can tell us a great deal about those patterns of language use specific to certain target texts, and should thus be very informative regarding particular translation practices and procedures used by the translator.

Multilingual corpora are sets of two or more monolingual corpora in different languages and, as such, can be exploited in finding out more about the typical means employed by two or more languages to express similar meanings. In a sense this limits the theoretical value of multi-lingual corpora when what is being investigated is the phenomenon of translation itself.

Comparable corpora can help to overcome the difficulty involved in researching the nature of translation. This kind of corpora refers to two separate collections of texts in the same language, one consisting of original texts, the other of translations in that language. Comparable corpora are useful research tools in investigating the kind of linguistic features which are typical of translated texts. This is central to research into translation universals.

12.1.2   Translation universals

Research using translation corpora is informed by the basic assumption that translating is not simply language use in the ordinary sense, and that the language of translated texts therefore reflects more than knowledge of, and competence in, the languages concerned. That is, 'approximating to the patterns of the target language, or any language for that matter . . . is not the only factor at play in shaping translational behaviour' (Baker, 1993: 242). As discussed in 6.1, this position has been vigorously argued by scholars working within the descriptivist paradigm. Even-Zohar (1978a: 77), for example, notes that, in translation 'we can observe patterns which are inexplicable in terms of any of the repertoires involved', that is, those of the source and target languages.

Can this form of translational behaviour point to the existence of 'universal' features of translation? Corpus translation studies assumes that this is conceivable. It is also suggested that the identification of such features is likely to be useful for the explication of the translation process and of notions such as translation competence. This kind of enquiry has thus set itself the specific goal of identifying those features which typically occur in translations rather than in original text production and which are not explainable in terms of factors such as interference from specific linguistic **systems**.

On the basis of evidence obtained thus far, Baker (1993: 243–4) has compiled a list of hypotheses which corpus-based work might further investigate:

- Translated texts tend to exhibit particular patterns of **texture** (e.g. source text repetitions tend to be omitted or reworded) (Shlesinger, 1991; Toury, 1991).

- Translated texts tend to be more explicit than the specific texts from which they are derived or texts originally produced in the languages concerned (Blum-Kulka, 1986: 21).

- Translated texts tend towards a higher degree of disambiguation and simplification. Potentially ambiguous pronouns, for example, are replaced by more precisely identifiable forms and complex syntax is made easier (Vanderauwera, 1985: 97–8).

- Translated texts tend to be more standardised: an element of conventionality in the use of language is generally observed (Vanderauwera, 1985: 93). In oral translation, for example, unfinished sentences get invariably rounded off, ungrammatical utterances 'grammaticised' and interactive features such as false starts and self-correction ironed out (Shlesinger, 1991: 150).

- Translated texts tend to 'level out' by gravitating towards the centre in situations characterised by such modes as orality (Shlesinger, 1989).

- Translated texts tend to flaunt certain conventions and overuse certain features known to be stylistically favoured in the target language. Toury, for example, notes the overuse in texts translated into Hebrew of binomials composed of synonyms or near-synonyms, which is a common feature of Hebrew writing (1980: 130).

These hypotheses are likely to lead to some interesting conclusions as to what we do when we translate and the kind of constraints that operate in translation, as opposed to freer and less controlled monolingual language production. For example, if a corpus of translated texts were to display a high **type-token ratio** (i.e. low lexical density, or low sentence length) compared with that found in other texts in the same language, then this would support the 'simplification hypothesis' (Laviosa-Braithwaite, 1997). By the same token, an increase in text length and a noticeably more substantial amount of glossing, use of explicit conjunctions, etc., would support the 'explicitation hypothesis' (Baker, 1997: 180–1). The 'standardisation hypothesis' will find support in the attested frequency of certain vocabulary items not noted in original text production (Gellerstam, 1986). Similarly, the 'conventionality thesis' will be upheld if what is found is a consistent effort at maintaining use of certain collocational patterns in translation.

12.1.3   Corpus research assessed

There is a substantial area of shared interests between corpus linguistics and corpus translation studies. However, to be relevant to translation research, criteria developed by linguists on the basis of general mono-lingual corpora would have to be heavily refined and adapted (Baker, 1995: 230). For example, criteria such as 'typicality' and the text producer/translator factor would have to be supplemented by an awareness of such variables as:

- the range of translators represented in a corpus;
- the level of expertise;
- **directionality** (whether the translator is working into or out of the mother tongue);
- the spectrum of **macro**-textual structures represented (**genre**, **text type**, **discourse**).

It is in this diversity of contexts and textual practices that the greatest challenge to the use of corpora in translation studies lies. Such a broad perspective is not yet fully catered for in corpus linguistics, which has invariably been data-driven, proceeding from the bottom up, and using concrete facts to make generalisations about particular languages. Much current translation scholarship, on the other hand, has found it more revealing to proceed top down: theorists are interested in finding evidence to support abstract hypotheses (Baker, 1997: 185).

In using corpora as research tools for investigating the nature of translation, a number of translation scholars have urged caution. Specifically regarding parallel corpora, Malmkjaer (1993) alerts us to the danger of letting one's selection acquire a momentum of its own, beginning to affect what the observer notices. We are also warned against relying too readily on statistical evidence and, in the process, ignoring problematic cases which might well be 'one offs'.

Within 'comparable corpora', difficulties have also been noted regarding such factors as working with lesser-used languages where the spectrum of text variety is limited and where no adequate supply of texts exists with which to compare translations. Politics, economics and the whole issue of 'cultural imperialism' also feature here; for example, 'a wider variety of texts have been translated into Norwegian, but fewer the other way round' (Malmkjaer, 1993).

12.2 Process research

> **Quote 12.1**
>
> The distinction [between the product and the process] cannot give the scholar leave to ignore the self-evident fact that the one is the result of the other, and that the nature of the product cannot be understood without a comprehension of the nature of the process.
>
> James Holmes (1978a: 81)

Process research has provided translation studies with another forum for addressing the issue of what goes on in the translator's mind. Techniques from **cognitive** science and information processing are being increasingly used in probing the mental activities involved in translating. Various forms of introspection are employed to get translators to verbalise as many of their thoughts as possible, either while doing the translation (Think Aloud) or more or less immediately afterwards (Immediate Introspection). The verbal protocols thus produced are recorded or videoed and analysed for the insights which they might yield into what goes on inside the black box of the translator's mind.

In terms of what process research is intended to achieve, two basic directions may be identified:

1. A psycholinguistic orientation, where the object is to conceptualise performance and thereby explicitly describe language processing rather than actual translating (e.g. Lörscher, 1991b).

2. A pedagogical orientation, where the research aim would be to concentrate on the practical aspects of training translators and thus on working with trainers or trainees as subjects of experimentation (Fraser, 1993, 1994).

The general assumption underlying the theory of recall in verbal reporting is that information needed, activated and actually used in the performance of a task is usually held in **short-term memory** and thus remains accessible to the subject (Ericsson and Simon, 1980, 1984, 1987).

Concept 12.2   **Types of recall**

Recalling information can take many forms. Subjects may engage in:

- 'self-reporting' by giving a generalised account of how they went about, not the specific task allocated, but a task-type;
- 'self-observation', retrospectively going through the steps applied in the execution of a particular strategy;
- 'self-revelation', an unedited verbalisation of whatever comes into one's mind.

Insights gained from such research might relate to:

- how subjects conceptualise translational problems;
- how dictionaries and reference works are used;
- the kind of semantic analysis which subjects perform on source text items;
- the way various target language equivalents are assessed and selections made;
- the kind of assumptions translators make with regard to editing source- and target-language texts to cater for specific translation purposes.

12.2.1   Think Aloud and Immediate Retrospection

An important methodological issue facing process research relates to the mode of verbalisation. Fraser (1996) focuses on the distinction between Think Aloud Protocols (TAP, or verbalising at the same time), and Immediate Retrospection (IR, or verbalising some time later). IRs are thought to be superior in many respects: the accounts tend to be more structured, inferential and thus much more revealing than the instantaneous TAPs. The accounts yielded by TAPs are not generalisable even when the difficulties are placed within a broader context (e.g. within a particular translation strategy).

In the context of community translation, for example, TAPs are likely to yield information about the difficulties of translating particular cultural terms. Through IRs, on the other hand, subjects might be able to deal with broader issues which relate to the cultural aspects of the text as a whole.

Nevertheless, concurrent TAPs have their uses too. They seem more appropriate for the identification of the principles that an individual translator systematically adopts in dealing with recurrent difficulties. For example, how elements of an individual translator's professional practice are revealed by the kind of decisions made in response to a working **brief** is an area which TAPs can handle adequately (Fraser, 1994).

The preference for Immediate Retrospection (IR, or verbalising thoughts more or less immediately after doing the translation) is argued by Fraser (1993) on the basis of a study which adopts the technique in looking at cross-cultural aspects of the translation process. Twelve community translators were asked to translate a public information leaflet written in English into seven of the minority languages spoken in the UK. Target receivers of such documents normally vary in terms of their level of competence in English and assimilation into British culture. The range of issues addressed in eliciting the protocols for this study include whether and how to translate the titles of the various social security benefits and how to deal with references to members of religious communities for Sikh speakers of Punjabi.

In this specific professional setting, an IR approach is found to be most revealing. In fact, in the particular study reported, only one TAP (verbalising while doing the translation) is obtained and it is here that the translator commented almost exclusively on the adequacy or inadequacy of particular cultural terms. Given the context of community translation in which the study is conducted, this aspect of cultural meaning is relatively minor. The issues addressed are broader and relate in the first place to 'the cultural aspects of the text and the difficulty in rendering [cultural terms] meaningfully in the community language' (Fraser, 1996: 68). IR is thus ideally suited to investigating how translations of a particular kind are tackled (e.g. in dealing with literary or emotive texts). That is, IR is superior where strategic decisions are important.

The issue of introspection methodology as a whole remains only partially understood. Very little research has tried to compare Think Aloud data with Retrospective data, for example. A future line of enquiry could be to ask TAP subjects also to engage in IR in order to determine whether and how the IR protocols produced then differed from their TAP accounts (Fraser, 1996: 75).

12.2.2   Informant constituency

Another methodological issue, and one commonly proving to be problematical, relates to the composition of informant groups. This is also related to the choice of verbalisation mode and thus to research aims. For example, students or language learners are consistently reported as ideal subjects for the kind of introspective data which focus not on broader strategies but on the specifics of translation such as lexical choice, grammatical restructuring, or the use of idiomatic expressions (Fraser, 1996: 71). Mixed samples of intermediate-level translation students and bilinguals have also been used with such purposes in mind (Gerloff, 1988).

A more widely studied category has been translation students vs professionals. Within a strategy-based problem-solving framework, Lörscher (1993) reports predictable yet interesting differences in the kind of strategies adopted by members of these two groups. For example, while professional translators mainly check target versions for stylistic and text-type adequacy, learners tend to focus on lexical and syntactic well formedness, almost to the total exclusion of text-level criteria (p. 210).

Jääskeläinen (1993) extends student vs professional samples to include 'educated laymen' (that is, people with a high level of aptitude in the source foreign language but with no translation experience). In this context, a new set of strategies emerges, which have more to do with goal-orientedness than simply problem-solving, that is, with the best way of achieving a given interactive goal in the process of translation. In this respect, professionals and educated laymen are found to be more concerned with global strategies (e.g. **brief**-driven priorities) than with such lower-level vagaries of the language code as lexical choice. This finding receives ample support from Fraser (1993, 1994): professional translator subjects emphasise:

> Cross-linguistic contextual issues such as readership, stylistic conventions, and textual norms. Recognition of such factors facilitates the attainment of professional standards and provides the translator with a framework within which individual difficulties may be solved.

12.2.3   Researcher intervention

Two extreme cases of researcher intervention may be cited to show the kind of variation in approach likely to be encountered in process research. Konigs (1987) represents an almost totally non-interventionist approach. Except where some culture-specific terminology detrimental to the completion of the exercise is encountered, students' verbalisations are allowed to run unimpeded. Fraser's (1994) study, on the other hand, has the researcher prompting the subjects if they fall silent for more than a few seconds. According to Fraser, subjects' reactions to such prompting vary: some find it helpful, others feel it to be too intrusive.

12.2.4   The status of rationalisation

Particularly in TAP research, and to guard against subjectivity, it has been customary to instruct subjects to refrain from 'rationalising' what they are thinking. However, TAP research on natural discourse involving two professional translators points us in a slightly different direction. Séguinot (1989a) notes that in such situations (with the two subjects being responsible for the act) the translation is usually negotiated, with overt reasoning being sometimes the dominant mode. To include rationalisations as part of TAP, or any other form of retrospection, does not therefore invalidate the approach, but can in fact enhance it: rationalisations 'flow naturally from a situation in which participants have a need to maintain an ongoing relationship' (p. 76).

12.2.5   The translation brief

A more striking feature of the comparison between professionals and students of translation relates to the status of the 'brief' in the process of translation. Briefs vary, with some experiments simply instructing students to translate and produce an 'acceptable' version in the target language (Konigs, 1987). In contrast, the brief in Fraser's study (1994) was sufficiently explicit, reflecting awareness of the need to define the nature of the readership in professional translation.

   The nature of the assignment plays an important role in modulating style and pitching register at the right level, particularly in dealing with non-formulaic and non-technical texts. For example, in dealing with social security documents in a context such as community translation, translators would automatically work to a 'universal' brief, assuming the kind of readership normally addressed by the texts translated.

12.2.6   The use of dictionaries

In settings where professional concerns such as deadline pressure and **brief** feature prominently, the use of dictionaries and other reference works is a matter which merits attention (see Hartmann, 2001). This is particularly the case when 'novice' and 'professional' samples are compared. The use made of such materials, and whether access to them is allowed at all, can be valuable indicators of subtle qualitative aspects of translator performance. The approach to reference materials used by Fraser's (1994) commercial translators is worth noting: dictionaries are used not so much to establish meanings but as a catalyst in the complex process of refining meaning and checking for **appropriateness**. This is in stark contrast with the use that student subjects have been reported to make of reference materials: almost exclusively to establish meaning.

12.2.7   Process research assessed

One basic weakness in process research is that subjects' verbalisations can be, and often are, incomplete, most probably due to the fact that invariably they are attempts to produce commentaries on processes which are to a large extent unconscious (Krings, 1987: 163). TAP in particular involves a certain element of risk – namely, that 'strategies which had become completely automatic through lengthy and repeated use would not be available for verbalization and hence investigation' (Fraser, 1994: 132).

A way around this problem is suggested by Fraser (1994): texts chosen for translation must as far as possible contain a number of challenges that do not encourage default reaction. For example, the text chosen in Fraser (1994) is a non-technical, non-formulaic text, containing a number of socio-cultural references to France. The **field** (higher education) is lively and controversial and not the staple diet of freelance translators. The journalistic style used is also particularly distinctive and does not follow the predictably clichéd mode normally associated with such writing. These factors have all been framed within a **brief** that is also challenging: 'translate for the foreign news section of *Times Higher Education Supplement*'.

Researcher intervention remains a controversial issue and further research into 'research strategies' is needed. Gerloff (1988) proposes that future studies find out more about the possible differences in the process data elicited under various conditions, including researcher presence. A list of such varying conditions would also include type of introspection methodology (TAP vs Immediate Retrospection) and assignment or non-assignment of a brief.

A most fruitful line of enquiry awaiting further research is the inclusion of text-type criteria among translator decision-making strategies:

experiments may be conducted to ascertain the status of **text type**, **genre** or **discourse** in the translation process.

Further reading

- On research into translation universals, for an overview, see Baker (1993); for a research methodology, Toury (1991); for a description of a specific area of practice, Vanderauwera (1985).
- On process research and such methodologies as TAP, see Tirkkonen-Condit and Laffling (1993), Lörscher (1991).

Chapter 13

Theory and practice in translation teaching

This chapter will . . .

- set translation didactics against the background of recent developments in learning theories such as Problem-Based Leaning;

- describe models of research into translation didactics;

- assess research evidence relating to such pedagogical issues as the feasibility of translation into the foreign language, the nature of translation errors and the status of text type in translation teaching;

- look in some detail at curriculum design in translator training, and examine a number of syllabuses.

Quote 13.1

Translators can be trained. It is pure speculation to say that a good translator is born and that a good translation cannot be accomplished under pressure. In this age of discipline, translations are performed under time and quality controls. Translators can no longer indulge in reverie and infinite finishing touches.

F.K. Pan (1977: 40)

It is important now to look more closely at translation didactics and view this in the light of how research in translation studies has evolved. Translation teaching is a varied activity that subsumes the training of translators and interpreters, not only within institutionalised settings (e.g. universities) but also outside (e.g. self-learning). The contexts in which these activities commonly take place also vary, ranging from degree courses to in-service training for national and international organisations. Translation may also be used as a mode of achieving other goals (e.g. mastery of the foreign language in language teaching). In all of this, a number of tasks are usually performed: curriculum design, materials writing, course delivery and implementation (selection of candidates, teaching, testing, etc.).

These issues, which have been debated fairly intensely in the field of translation pedagogy, culminate in the question of how new research and developments in translation studies could be integrated to become part of (a) individual practices and (b) the general requirements of educational training. That is, how can meaningful interaction be fostered between the two domains of 'action' and 'reflection'? A host of questions are usually raised in this respect:

- Are translators or interpreters born or made?
- Is a theoretical input desirable?
- When is training most optimal (e.g. undergraduate or postgraduate), and in which department (linguistics, literature, other)?
- What do we ultimately want to achieve (academic, vocational or professional competence)?
- Should training be specialised or generalist?
- What criteria to use in the selection, grading and presentation of materials?
- How much language teaching or interpreting should there be on a translator training course?
- How much language teaching or translating should there be on an interpreter training course?
- What requirements do we make of candidates (aptitude, previous experience)?
- What qualifications should we require of teachers of translation?
- What should be tested and how should it be tested?

An important assumption currently entertained in applied translation studies is that, in the training of translators, it is critical to include some theoretical input. The nature of such an input varies from country to country and even from institution to institution. However, it is true to say that theoretical models informed by factors such as text in context (e.g. the register membership of texts, discourse texture) are becoming increasingly popular in the training of translators worldwide.

Three main themes may be singled out as being particularly important in applied translation research today:

1. Translation into the foreign language: Is it feasible?
2. Language teaching vs translation teaching: Are there qualitative differences in assessing performance in these two different pedagogic settings?
3. Text type models in the training of translators: In what way are they superior to other teaching methodologies?

13.1   Translation into the foreign language

Concept 13.1   **Directionality**

The issue of *directionality* relates to whether translators work from their mother tongue into the foreign language or the other way. It is generally assumed that working into one's mother tongue (the 'A' language) is the 'natural' order. Such assumptions build on an important theoretical claim in bilingual education – namely, that bilingual linguistic competence is rarely symmetrical (i.e. that functioning in one's native language is bound to be superior to performing in a second language). To be realistic and to respond to job market demands, however, teachers and employers alike seem to look the other way: to all intents and purposes, a translator should have no difficulty translating fairly competently in both directions, that is, into and out of the foreign language.

The debate concerning whether translators should only work into language A thus continues, with serious implications for the pedagogy of translation. Ladmiral (1979: 46), for example, does not set much store by the efficacy of working into the foreign language, except as a pedagogical exercise to test performance in that language. Similarly, Newmark (1988: 3), while acknowledging the existence and value of what he calls 'service translation', believes that 'translating into the language of habitual use is the only way you can translate naturally and accurately and with maximum effectiveness'.

13.1.1 Practical considerations

In most European translator-training institutions, the general perception is that translation into the mother tongue is the 'normal' direction – a stance promoted by international translation associations and enshrined in UNESCO's recommendations. There are dissenting voices, and some compelling arguments have been put forward for the need to recognise the intrinsic value of translating out of one's native language (*inversa translation*).

According to McAlister (1992), for reasons to do with national pride or sheer economic survival, there is a pressing demand for translating from a minor language (e.g. Finnish) into a major one (e.g. English). The demand usually exceeds the number of those who are native speakers of English and who also have Finnish as a second language. A survey conducted in Finland has revealed that between 69.7% and 91.7% of the 18 text types included in the questionnaires sent out to translation agencies were translated into, or directly composed in, the foreign language. Also noted in the survey is the fact that only 6% of the members of the Finnish Translators and Interpreters Association did not have Finnish or Swedish as their mother tongue (McAlister, 1992).

A further argument for the need to develop translation into the foreign language relates to the kind of receiver usually envisaged for the bulk of translated texts within the context of the so-called 'service translation' sector. As McAlister (pp. 292–3) points out, quite a number of translations (tourist brochures, trade magazines, etc.) are not undertaken with a specific target language or culture in mind, but for a worldwide audience. This renders the insistence on native competence in the major languages (e.g. English or French) unnecessary and perhaps even undesirable. Interestingly, McAlister notes, the kind of translation produced by non-native speakers of the target language is likely to be more accessible in terms of both language and cultural content.

In an earlier study, Ahlsvad (1978) reaches similar conclusions. Focusing on the situation of translating Finnish forestry texts into English, he mentions a number of points which suggest that it is both unreasonable and undesirable to insist that the work be done by native speakers of the target language (also English in this case). Apart from the issue of the availability of such translators, the matter of passive command of a minor language is relevant: this is seldom good or reliable.

On the question of producing translations that are accessible, Ahlsvad makes the interesting point that, particularly in technical fields, translation done into the second language (say, from Finnish into English) may even be preferable since non-native readers find non-native writing in the target language easier and more comprehensible. There is also the matter of technical expertise which is bound to be easier to secure from locally recruited translators who are native speakers of the source language. Related to 'technicality', Ahlsvad highlights the quality of 'accuracy', which is considered to be more important than stylistic 'felicity'.

13.1.2 The cultural dimension

Beeby (1996) approaches the issue of directionality from the standpoint of culture. She proposes discourse analysis as the framework within which the selection, grading and presentation of texts in a course designed to meet the objectives of translating into the foreign language (inversa) are carried out. According to Beeby (1996: 121), native translators working into the major languages enjoy the distinct advantage of intimately knowing the indigenous (source) culture:

> Those who stress the importance of native speaker competence in the culture and language of the target text often do not attach enough importance to understanding the culture and language of the source text, particularly when discourse patterns differ greatly from one culture to another.

A kind of **contrastive textology** is proposed as a basis for training in this domain. Beeby (1996) describes the inversa translation course content of the Barcelona UAB School of Translation as comprising a variety of subject fields and discourse types for which there is market demand. Parallel texts are used to develop skills in discourse processing and documentation techniques. More standardised texts tend to be highly formulaic and are therefore easier to work with before the students move on to the more creative (dynamic) text types. In the context of language pairs such as English and Spanish, it is recommended that the course designers pursue their own research into text type, discourse patterns and genre conventions. This is necessary because, as Beeby (p. 122) explains:

> Translators into English are at an advantage in this respect, since so much more is known about the way texts function in English than in any other language. By contrast, very little work has been done on describing text types in Spanish, and the situation is made more difficult by the fact that many types of Spanish discourse are still in a state of flux.

Beeby outlines some of the problems encountered in this uncertain situation. Commercial, scientific and technical texts are heavily influenced by English, while political and administrative texts are constantly changing to accommodate the transformation into more democratic institutions. Even movements such as Plain Language can have an effect on how texts are evolving, particularly in the legal field. The need for in-depth research is most urgent in situations where certain text types had never existed before (a case in point is Catalan which, for a long time, was used only in domestic and literary contexts).

13.1.3   Discursive competence

Campbell (1997) adopts a 'translation **competence**' perspective in dealing with the issue of translating into the second language, and argues that an important aspect of such a competence is facility in the target language, particularly at the level of text and discourse (p. 56). This is often lacking in trainee and novice translators, a situation which poses serious problems in teaching as well as accreditation. As pointed out above, these problems become particularly acute in settings where translation into the major foreign languages is very much in demand, and where native speakers of these languages constitute a minority.

There are pedagogic implications for this complex set of issues. As Campbell observes, the main difficulty in translating into the native language is one of comprehending the source text, since it is much easier to handle one's first language's linguistic and textual resources. In translating into the foreign language, on the other hand, the real difficulty relates to composition, since coping with the source text poses little if any difficulty.

13.1.4   The inversa course: Scope and nature

With directionality and curriculum design in mind, McAlister (1992) discusses the feasibility of programmes preparing professional, non-literary translators for work into a foreign language. He suggests that this is possible provided that such courses are seen to be different in both scope and nature from training in the more usual track of translating into the mother tongue. A kind of training might be envisaged in which notions such as professionalism and level of expertise are not seen as absolutes. As McAlister suggests, once we leave the usual circuit of major languages (where purist criteria such as the insistence on translating only into the mother tongue obtain), we are in a situation which demands much more flexibility in the development and delivery of our training.

In terms of course content, McAlister proposes that training programmes in translation into the foreign language would be based on some form of needs analysis carefully negotiated with potential employers. Such a framework would accommodate the prescriptions of translation theory, while at the same time responding to market forces. In this way, the selection of texts would neither ignore nor lean too heavily towards routine tasks such as business correspondence and technical specifications. The needs for translation in fields such as administration, tourism, culture and entertainment would be explored, as this information is likely to yield the kind of texts which ensure variety and flexibility.

13.2   The nature of translation errors

13.2.1   Language teaching vs translation teaching?

The discussion of *directionality* inevitably raises the question of whether the focus of what is taught in a translation-training programme is on translation proper or simply on translation-related language skills. Also, if both domains must be involved, how should they be catered for, that is, how should language teaching relate to translation teaching? One way of dealing with this problem has been to insist that 'translation proper' should only be taught in specialised schools where the highest levels of linguistic competence could be assumed. However, for a variety of practical, social and political reasons, this would most certainly be unacceptable in many a department where translation is traditionally taught. In the context of Spain, Pym (1992a: 281) sums up the argument as follows:

> The power structures . . . are such that translation is and will continue to be used as a way of learning foreign languages, [and, to insist on] a perfect command of foreign languages before learning about translation . . . would mean teaching translation to virtually empty classes.

The relationship between language teaching and translation teaching has thus been problematical. Pym sees the two activities together and not separately. He deals directly with the subject of translation errors and, in the process, raises the important issue of what is and what is not a 'translation'. (See Koller, 1995 on this distinction.)

Concept 13.2   **Translation competence**

In dealing with the distinction translation vs non-translation, the notion of translation competence is invoked and defined as a combination of two skills (Pym, 1992a: 281):

1. The ability to generate a series of target texts (target text 1, target text 2, target text *n*) from a source text.
2. The ability to select only one from this array of texts and to propose it as a target text for a specified purpose and reader.

By this definition, *translation* **competence** is seen as distinct from *linguistic competence*. Knowledge of grammar, rhetoric, terminology, and even commercial considerations, do feature, but translation is taken strictly to be a process of generating and selecting between alternative texts.

13.2.2   Binary vs non-binary errors

This notion of '**competence**' is useful in any attempt to distinguish between translation and non-translation in terms of the debate alluded to above. Competence also looms large in the practical exercise of defining what constitutes a 'translation error'. The confusion in this sphere of translation teaching has a great deal to do with the tendency to consider as an error any performance which falls short of the ideal (i.e. the 'correct'). However, errors may be ascribed to a diverse variety of causes, ranging from lack of comprehension to misuse of register – factors which may be located on a variety of levels (language, **pragmatics**, culture). Taxonomic classifications of errors and examples to illustrate them cannot therefore be the answer, Pym argues, and what is urgently needed is a scheme which does away with such error typologies.

Concept 13.3   **An error typology**

In developing a scheme for the analysis of errors, Pym builds on the assumption implied by his definition of translation competence: a translation error must be *non-binary*. Non-binariness implies that a wrong answer is not opposed to a right answer but that the choice made is seen also alongside at least one further choice which could also have been taken up but was not, and alongside an endless number of possible wrong answers. As Pym (1992a: 282) puts it, 'for binarism, there is only right and wrong; for non-binarism there are at least two right answers and then the wrong ones'.

The distinction between binary and non-binary errors (Concept 13.3) has important implications for translation teaching. If the question of choosing between alternatives is not relevant (often because there are none), then what is involved will be language work and not translation. But does the correction of so-called binary errors lie totally outside the remit of the translation teacher altogether? In theory, teaching translation should set itself the ultimate goal of achieving translation competence, or 'the sum of communication acts by which translational non-binary errors are produced and converted into their opposite, namely translational knowledge' (p. 283). However, while 'all translational errors are non-binary, almost by definition' (Pym, p. 283), it does not follow that all non-binary errors are automatically translational. Pym supports this view and suggests that non-binarism is common in teaching anything beyond the simple basic level, and that any level of teaching language or translation will have binary as well as non-binary errors to account for and remedy.

Nevertheless, the distinction binary vs non-binary, and the way it is related to language teaching vs translation teaching, is valid insofar as it also concerns 'not where these errors occur, but how we should proceed with their correction' (Pym, 1992a). The claim that binary error correction is the task of the language teacher, while non-binary errors come within the remit of the translation teacher, is thus questionable. That is, no translation classroom could sensibly be envisaged to have remedied all binary errors, nor would there be a language classroom having to deal with binary errors only.

13.2.3   Research potential

The discussion of binary and non-binary errors and the scheme outlined by Pym (1992a) have generated a number of hypotheses for future research to explore (p. 286). It is suggested that one way of identifying tendencies characteristic of the learning process is to examine:

- the ratio of binary to non-binary errors in a particular translation or a series of translations, and to plot variation in terms of the nature of the text(s) translated, the purpose of translation, etc.;
- the rate of progress from binary to non-binary errors, since the accelerated reduction in binary errors and a proportional increase in non-binary errors is an excellent indicator of overall progress.

This kind of investigation is underpinned by an important assumption: Regardless of whether it is language or translation that is being taught, the successful completion of a learning period should be associated with a point at which errors become more or less almost exclusively non-binary.

13.3   Text typologies as a didactic instrument

The need to select from a variety of texts with which translators normally work is widely recognised in writings on translation pedagogy. However, the kind of framework within which text classification can most effectively be carried out and subsequently used in genuine translation teaching contexts has long been the subject of debate. Emery (1991) assesses the pedagogic scene within translator training and concludes that neither the notion of **text type** nor that of **text function** can provide an adequate basis for the classification and analysis of texts.

13.3.1   Current text classification schemes

Emery (1991: 567–8) identifies two kinds of problem with current text typologies. First, the notion of text type is of such a wide *scope* that it can subsume a huge array of text-form variants. For example, Zyadatiss's (1983) text-type **instruction** includes text forms as varied as Acts of Parliament, technical instructions, political speeches, sermons and advertisements. The second problem with existing typologies is related to the issue of *hybridisation*, since a particular text normally exhibits features of different text types (e.g. an instruction manual may be expository and descriptive as well as instructional at one and the same time).

The notion of text type is thus judged to be of little practical help. According to Emery (1991: 568), this is mainly due to 'the difficulty of linking particular text samples with particular text types in a plausible and systematic way'. An alternative, Emery suggests, might be sought in text function (e.g. **expressive texts**) as a basis for classification, but this too has its problems: 'the criterion is at once too "inclusive" and too "includable" to constitute a cogent framework for text classification' (p. 568). That is, the notion of function is both least delicate and so delicate that several functions can be discerned in the same text and all can be at variance with the macro-function.

An alternative to text type might be the notion of 'province' – a major situational dimension constituted of 'those variables in an extra-linguistic context which are defined with reference to the kind of occupational or professional activity being engaged in' (Emery 1991: 71).

Interestingly, this was proposed by Crystal and Davy as far back as the late 1960s to counteract the problems inherent in earlier approaches to register which had all but failed to distinguish between **field** (subject matter) and context proper.

Like 'function', however, the notion 'province' is not unproblematic. According to Emery (p. 569), there is first the difficulty of 'where to draw the upper bound of generality of the notional categories and where to draw the lower limit of specificity'. The following list worked out by Mason (1982: 23) is cited as a case in point: scientific/technical, administrative, political, religious, literary, journalistic, legal, sales. The list is in turn subdivided into a large number of 'sub-domains'. For example, a journalistic text may have a political subject, a religious text may be literary or historical, etc.

In addition to the issue of scope, another problem with 'province' concerns the theoretical 'status' of the category as a basis for text classification. Province has what Crystal and Davy implicitly recognise as a 'procedural priority' over the other dimensions which deal with 'attitude', 'status' and 'individuality', rendering such potentially useful categories inappropriate as classification criteria. A potential weakness thus emerges: being essentially 'situation-based', province 'may not give enough weight to [the] pragmatic dimension', an omission which cannot augur well for translation (Emery, 1991: 570).

Emery deals with these issues in terms of 'the criterion of **domain** or "social context" as the determining factor' to be viewed within 'an integrated approach encompassing insights from a number of linguistic theories' (p. 567). In this approach, 'text analysis' subsumes the 'ways in which trainee translators' sensitivities to this aspect [of context] can be heightened' (ibid.). This is illustrated from English and Arabic, but the scheme is said to be essentially 'language-pair independent' and utilisable in a variety of contexts across linguistic and cultural boundaries.

While translation theory under the 'linguistics' regime has focused on the issue of 'transfer', text-linguistic insights coming into translation studies have ensured that text analysis is reinstated as an aspect of crucial importance in the work of the translator. According to Emery, however, sensitising the student to the intricacies of text has to be undertaken within an approach less exclusively committed to such notions as text 'type' or 'function': the translator-trainee needs to be made aware of as comprehensive a range of approaches to linguistic analysis as possible (p. 571).

With this in mind, Emery argues in favour of what he calls the 'integrated approach'. What does the integrated approach consist of?

Macro-dimensions
1. Situational Dimensions
   - Variety of language
   - Medium (simple / complex)   .
   - Formality
        addresser / addressee role relation / profiles
        style: frozen-intimate
   - Domain / form-specific features

2. Text pragmatics
   - Function(s) of text / text-type(s) / purpose(s) of text-producer
   - Speech acts / illocutionary force
   - Text structure (coherence / cohesion)
   - Text tone

3. Text semiotics
   - Culture-located signs
   - Intertextuality

Micro-means
Semantic
Grammatical
Lexical
Textual

Figure 13.1   An integrated approach (adapted from Emery, 1991: 573)

What kind of methodology is proposed? What status does text analysis enjoy in this new scheme? These are questions which will be addressed in the following discussion of text type in translation curriculum design. Figure 13.1 sets out the various elements of the model.

The macro-dimensions characterise the text as a whole: alongside situational (social context) and pragmatic (communicative purpose) categories, a semiotic dimension is included, 'since, semiotically, a text can figure as a whole (e.g. Herbert's poem "Easter Wings" which visually/ graphically symbolises the "wings" in the title)' (Emery, 1991: 573).

The micro-means, on the other hand, function as instruments which facilitate the realisation of the major dimensions (pragmatics, etc.). To the usual grammatical and lexical means are added textual and semantic means. The latter are intended to deal with

> information selection which may vary between source and target text according to the perceived 'needs' of the readership, in contrast to lexical means which focus on the type of vocabulary . . . and types of collocational patterning.

(p. 574)

13.3.2   Emery's scheme assessed

At this point, it might be pertinent to point out that the scene portrayed by Emery in his appraisal is not in fact even 'current' at the time the article was published, but belonged to the late 1960s and early 1970s at best. The notions of 'text type', 'function' or 'province' outlined are so outmoded that they do not accurately reflect what is happening in text-type research today. Particularly in the last two or three decades, text typologies have developed in a number of interesting directions, and most of the shortcomings cited by Emery above have already been adequately addressed. The issue of hybridisation, for example, is now fully recognised as a 'fact of texts' (Hatim and Mason, 1990) and is dealt with through such refinements as the inclusion of a discourse as well as a genre dimension (as the present book has demonstrated in great detail).

With regard to the specific issue of *text type* and *text function*, it has to be noted that Emery's criticism would be better directed at those text-type schemes which apply what might be called 'single set criteria' informed by traditional register analysis. That is, what was rejected should have been those models of text types which tend to adopt register's field, tenor and mode defined in terms of such stark and meaningless oppositions as 'technical' vs 'non-technical' or 'formal' vs 'informal'. As will be explained shortly, text type classifications such as Reiss's function-based typology or Hatim and Mason's rhetoric-based typology have come a long way from what Emery was describing and are sufficiently comprehensive to resist such binary and narrow categorisations. As the discussion of Hatim's *Practical Guide* (1997 and successive editions) will demonstrate shortly, textual register is now more exhaustively seen in terms of the ideational, interpersonal and textual resources at the disposal of the text user and the translator. Textual pragmatics has also extended in a number of meaningful ways beyond speech-act analysis and utterance-based notions of 'implicature', and is now dealing with the 'text act' and 'text politeness' in translation (Hatim, in Hickey, 1998). Finally, the way text types evolve is now more adequately captured not only by such semiotic mechanisms as 'intertextuality' but also by 'interdiscursivity' (Fairclough, 1992; Candlin and Maley, 1997) (see Concept 9.5). This body of theoretical insights is gradually finding its way into translation classrooms around the globe within such pedagogic frameworks as Problem-Based Learning (Concept 13.4 below).

13.3.3   Curriculum design in translator training

One way of demonstrating how text typologies have been used as effective analytic tools in applied translation research is to take a closer look at the development of translator-training materials and to review briefly some of the earlier attempts in the area of curriculum design. There is a discernible pattern of a move away from a grammar-based towards a culture-based syllabus and, eventually, towards text-based course materials (Chau, 1984).

D.Y. Loh (1958)

To depict 'how things were', the following is an extract from the Foreword (in Chinese) to D.Y. Loh's *Translation: Its Principles and Techniques* (1958):

> The contents of this book are as follows: Chapter 1 discusses the basic principles of translating. Each section in that chapter focuses on one particular aspect. Its purpose is to inform the beginner of the *correct* concepts of translation work, so that he would not be led to think that translating is a minor skill which can be acquired without proper training. The eight chapters that follow develop these principles, *highlighting the similarities and differences of lexicon and sentence patterns between English and Chinese*, and pointing out the *standard* ways of translating. . . .
>
> The division of these eight chapters is not based on *the* eight parts of speech. Rather, it is based on the needs and convenience of translation work. For example, there is a chapter on 'nouns', another on 'personal pronouns', and another on 'pronouns, adjectives and adverbs'. Since there are no 'articles' in Chinese, there is a special chapter on articles. Numerals are also tricky for the translator; so one chapter is devoted to them.
>
> The contents of these chapters are mostly based on practical experience. *They are chiefly contrasts of English and Chinese grammars.* Differences and similarities of the parts of speech are pointed out. Emphases are laid on the differences. *Sample* translations are provided to demonstrate the practical use of translation methods, so that the learner *can learn to express the same thinking in two different languages.*
>
> Translated by Simon Chau and cited in Chau (1984)

Chau (1984)

Such attitudes and assumptions regarding what constitutes the essence of translator training were rejected by mainstream applied translation studies as far back as the early 1980s. Consider, for example, the following blueprint of what an intercultural syllabus might look like. In an 'idealized curriculum for translation teaching', the intercultural stage of training features among its aims (Chau, 1984):

- Enabling the students to be aware of, and to train them to be sensitive to, the cultural differences between societies, and their implications for translating . . .
- Providing the students with relevant information concerning the gaps, as well as the various means of bridging them . . .

The teaching content consists of the following:

1. Introduction to the study of culture – definition, scope, methods, history
2. Language and culture
    2.1 Language as a manifestation of culture
    2.2 Language as determined by culture
3. Area study of L1 culture
    3.1 History
    3.2 Socio-economic-political systems, past and present
    3.3 Philosophical-religious thinking
    3.4 Literature and the arts
4. (Same as 3 for L2 culture)
5. (Same as 3 for L3 culture)
6. Cultural distance and overlap: Comparison of L1 and L2 cultures
    6.1 History and ecology
    6.2 Socio-economic-political systems
    6.3 Philosophical-religious thinking
    6.4 Everyday life and customs
    6.5 Literature and the arts
7. Cultural distance and overlap: Comparison of L1 and L3 cultures (Same as 6)
8. Translation as an element of introducing a foreign (L2, L3) culture to SL Society
9. Thought and language
    9.1 The Sapir–Whorf hypothesis and translating
    9.2 The cultural limits of translatability
    9.3 Case Study 1 – sets of colour terms
    9.4 Case Study 2 – sets of kinship terms
10. Techniques of assessing cultural distance
    10.1 Componential analysis
    10.2 Hierarchical analysis
    10.3 Chain analysis
11. Techniques of familiarising students with TL cultural elements
    11.1 Folk taxonomies
    11.2 Role playing

12. Types of cultural correspondence in translating
    12.1 Linguistic translation and cultural equivalence
    12.2 Formal vs dynamic equivalence
    12.3 Case studies of D-E translating
13. Cultural metaphors and their translation

As can be seen from the above catalogue of teaching points, there are still problems with such important translation didactic notions as source and target register, intentionality, intertextuality and, perhaps more significantly, with the notion of 'culture'. Culture continues to be defined as one-sided almost exclusively in terms of 'socio-cultural objects' and 'area studies' and, within 'cultural linguistics', in terms of such themes as 'metaphor' and the Sapir–Whorf hypotheses. The scheme suggested above glosses over what might be called 'socio-textual practices' and the 'mentifacts' (perspectives) which underpin them, a failing that stayed with us in translator training materials until well into this century.

Adab (1996)

In the introduction to a textbook envisaged along similar lines to the kind of materials described above, the authors outline the merits of what they describe as 'a contextual approach to translation teaching':

> The aim of this collection is to encourage the translator to strive for accurate interpretation of the ST message, based on logical analysis of sign function and meaning, drawing on linguistic and sociocultural competence in the SL culture. This is then complemented by a pragmatic approach to the conceptual construction of the TT.
>
> (p. 30)

As the textbook unfolds, however, the approach turns out to be largely topic-based and predominantly register oriented:

Part I: Source Texts
Part II: Target Texts
Part III: Annotations

Initial practice
Welcome to Ouistreham

1000 words
1. The Pedigree of Plain English
2. Bless The Burgess, Thou Art Translated

3. Preaching Community
4. Defining a European Immigration Policy
5. Jobs and Competitiveness: The UK Approach
6. Law & Disorder
7. Doctor on Screen
8. The Inhumanity of Medicine
9. Black Death
10. Our Children's Education – The Updated Parent's Charter

(. . .)

[The main headings of an example annotation]

Sentence structure
Syntax
Other verbs
Other syntax
Lexis:
    Titles
    Collocations
    Terminology
    Loan words
    Other
Stylistic devices:
    Inversion
    Alliteration
    Imagery
    Repetition
    Cultural references
    Names of historical personages
    Acronyms
Punctuation:
    Inverted commas
    Use of colon

Apart from the topic bias, both grammar and lexis seem to be treated in a largely decontextualised fashion and not as areas of textual 'lexico-grammar'. However, lexical and grammatical features are best understood and practised only when considered in terms of their textural function. When seen as lexico-grammatical elements of texture, such areas as sentence structure or word order would be explained and eventually translated in the light of their contribution to the cohesion and coherence of entire texts, genres and discourses. An adequate lexico-grammatical description would thus be concerned with such aspects of functional language use as

- how a **cleft sentence** is employed to signal a conclusion to a counter-argument, to uphold the 'letter to the editor' as a genre and to convey racist discourse;
- how this array of textual values may optimally be preserved in the target text.

Hervey and Higgins (1992)

An approach which is based on more solid theoretical foundations, using more comprehensive models of register, pragmatics and genre, is that adopted in the Routledge series *Thinking Translation* (Hervey and Higgins, 1992: 2):

> The course has a progressive overall structure and thematic organization. After beginning with the fundamental issues, options and alternatives of which the translator must be aware, it examines a series of layers that are of textual importance in translation (from the generalities of culture and intertextuality to the nuts and bolts of phonic and graphic details). It then moves, via a number of semantic and stylistic topics (literal meaning, connotation and language variety), to a consideration of textual genres and the demands of translating texts in a range of different genres.

Discourse and genre criteria are fully integrated and text types are no longer seen in terms of purely formal intersentential relations and surface cohesion alone. Negotiating translator strategy in the light of factors such as textual practices features prominently.

Concept 13.4   Problem-Based Learning

Quite understandably, translation teaching has always lagged slightly behind theoretical developments in the field of Translation Studies. Translation teaching is, after all, an application of principles and strategies worked out in theory first. What is more difficult to explain, however, is why translation teaching and translation studies should also lag, often by longer than a decade or more (Chau 1984), behind developments either in Applied Linguistics or in Linguistics (or indeed any other parent discipline espoused by a given brand of translation didactics). To hazard a guess, this time lag may have something to do with the fairly low status accorded to translation teaching as a practical pursuit and to translation studies as a discipline in its own right. To this day, in many universities around the world, courses in translation do not 'make the grade' to be included as 'humanities' options and are instead given as 'free electives' on undergraduate degree courses.

To illustrate the time lag issue and the implications it might have for the way translation didactics has evolved, let us consider the case of Problem-Based Learning (PBL). In such practical pursuits as Teaching English to Speakers of Other Languages (TESOL), it has for some time now been almost axiomatic that students should be made active participants in their learning processes. This has translated into practical methods of instruction such as Problem-Based Learning (PBL), a process which encourages students to 'learn-how-to-learn'. Except sporadically and in a piecemeal fashion, such developments have hardly made a significant impact on translation didactics to date and, as the above catalogue of available course materials has shown, a great deal of translation teaching remains to this day far from being genuinely trainee-centred. It is only recently that solutions to real-world problems have begun to feature in the design of translation teaching curricula. Few and far between, such syllabi have started to include problem-solving skills necessary to meet the challenges posed by the profession (e.g. terminology, localisation).

As the name suggests, 'problem-based learning' is a learner-centred pedagogy which focuses on the solution of realistic problems. Learners should be in a position to identify:

1. The stage they are at in the learning process.
2. What they need to know to attain optimal competence spelt out explicitly in a set of well-defined objectives or unambiguously stated problems.
3. How and where to access new information that may lead to a satisfactory attainment of a given objective or the resolution of a given problem.

In all of this the role of the trainer would be one of facilitating the process of learning by providing adequate support at every step of the way from formulating appropriate questions, providing appropriate resources, guiding the process and assessing outcomes.

Informed by an essentially problem-based pedagogy, this survey of translation teaching materials, syllabi, textbooks, has shown how poorly translation teaching and learning performs in terms of the extent to which these activities have been sufficiently conducive to:

• confronting learners with challenging problems that are intrinsically open-ended, even ill-defined and ill-structured;
• engaging the learners to develop in their own minds, by themselves, schemes and models that facilitate the acquisition and construction of the knowledge required to work through specific problems.

The *Practical Guide*, to be discussed next, claims to have addressed some of these issues and may thus be taken as a step in the right direction towards true Problem-Based Learning in practice.

13.3.4   English–Arabic–English translation: A practical guide

In an important departure from the syllabuses based on grammar, culture and even register and genre that have been in use over nearly half a century of translator training materials, one of the earliest attempts to develop teaching materials along avowedly text-type lines was Hatim's *Practical Guide* (1997b and successive editions). The syllabus is designed to cater for the needs of the advanced translator trainee, and the major issue addressed is simply: How can a typology of texts be used as a basis for the delivery of more effective translator training?

Central to the text typology adopted in the approach underpinning the *Practical Guide* is the view that texts vary along a continuum, from those that can be 'extremely detached and non-evaluative' to those that are 'extremely involved and highly evaluative' (Concept 13.5). Language use is thus seen in terms of **rhetorical purpose** (e.g. argumentation, exposition), yielding finer categories (e.g. counter-argumentation, conceptual exposition), and a variety of text forms and text samples, right down to utterances serving particular language macro-functions such as the *ideational, interpersonal* and *textual*. This variation is identified on the basis of such factors as register membership (e.g. technical/non-technical, subjective/objective, spoken/written), including subject matter and formality considerations.

In all of this, the *Practical Guide* is informed by a basic assumption adopted from critical linguistics: to be distinctive, text forms must possess linguistic features that can be considered typical of the form in question (Fowler, 1986). From the perspective of translation theory, text types are also seen to be closely related to the actual process of translation, with different types placing different demands on the translator (Reiss, 1971).

Concept 13.5   **The text typology espoused**

Text type is a cover term for the way **text structure** and **texture** respond to, and in turn create, register membership, pragmatic intentionality and cultural semiotics. In the process, a particular contextual focus emerges. Three basic text types are distinguished:

1. *Exposition*, in which objects, events or concepts, are presented in a largely non-evaluative manner. Three basic forms of exposition are distinguished:

   • Description, focusing on objects viewed spatially;
   • Narration, focusing on events viewed temporally;
   • Conceptual exposition, focusing on the detached analysis or synthesis of concepts.

2. *Argumentation*, in which concepts and/or beliefs are evaluated, with the aim of forming future behaviour (with option). Two basic variants of argumentation are distinguished:

   • Counter-argumentation, in which a thesis is cited, then opposed;
   • Through-argumentation, in which a thesis is cited, then extensively defended.

3. *Instruction*, in which the focus is on the formation of future behaviour, but with no option (e.g. Treaties, Resolutions, Contracts, etc.).

Hatim and Mason (1990)

The *Practical Guide* under review is divided into three main parts: Translating Legal Texts (as an example of the instructional text-type), Translating Exposition and Translating Argumentation. Each part consists of a number of units (e.g. the Legal Preamble as a genre), and each unit typically starts with original texts aimed at sensitising the student to the text type in question, followed by texts 'for translation'. Each text presented is supported by text-in-context, translation-process notes and glossaries.

To clarify what is involved in the process of text selection, one type of text – exposition – is examined in greater detail. The text forms dealt with in this part of the textbook are listed below. Note how the arrangement reflects a gradation from least to most evaluative.

1. The Abstract
2. The Synopsis
3. The Summary
4. The Entity-oriented News Report (reporting the aims of a new organisation)
5. The Event-oriented/Non-evaluative News Report (reporting a sequence of events in a detached fashion)
6. The Event-oriented/Evaluative News Report (reporting a sequence of events in an emotive, even biased, manner)
7. The Person-oriented News Report (reporting a briefing given by a spokesman)

8. The Formulaic Report (a financial auditors' report)
9. The Executive Report (CEO's statement to the shareholders)
10. The Personalised Report (memoirs)

In this textbook, similar procedures are adopted for the presentation of the various forms of argumentation within genres such as the editorial, the letter to the editor and so on.

Throughout, texture is analysed in terms of how the use of such textual devices as cohesion and **theme–rheme** progression respond systematically to contextual requirements. Aspects such as the predominance or scarcity of emotive diction, metaphoric expression and subtle uses of **modality** (or the sparing use of such devices) are related to such contextual factors as register membership. These determine not only the unit of translation, but also the overall translation strategy.

Text structure (the compositional plan) and how this enhances **coherence** do not exist in a vacuum, but are embedded in more wide-ranging discursive practices. A structural format or a cohesive pattern can be assessed properly only in terms of its appropriateness to a given genre or discursive attitude.

The *Practical Guide*, in its published form, is at this stage at present. However, as Hatim and Mason (1997) point out, a further stage in the analysis and presentation of materials could be envisaged and further refinements introduced. This would ensure that the text types yielded are authentic, reflecting properly negotiated

- rhetorical purposes;
- discursive strategies;
- genre conventional structures.

The additional set of materials would also ensure that text 'impurity' is fully captured and hybridisation accounted for both within a single text and across textual boundaries. That is, additional training is provided in dealing with situations in which forms or entire text formats happen to be marked or unmarked, expectation defying or fulfilling.

To conclude, while some of the problems which Emery and other critics have identified in existing typologies must be recognised and should be taken up in future research, the general feeling among teachers and learners seems to be that classifying and analysing texts along typological lines is an attractive option and one which lends itself to the kind of teaching that is both stimulating and durable. Alternative text typologies are best seen as supplementing, and not cancelling each other.

The single most important issue in this kind of work is text hybridisation. But, as recent research into text types has shown, the issue of multifunctionality should not turn into a kind of 'anything goes' philosophy. For example, unless there is a good reason for doing otherwise, metaphors would best be rendered metaphorically in expressive texts, while they may have to be modified or even jettisoned in informative texts (Reiss, 1971: 62). Of course, it is wrong to postulate these tendencies too stringently, but it is quite appropriate to work with them as general guidelines.

Ideally, programmes such as the one outlined in the preceding discussion should be cyclical. Within a given unit of the course, Stage 2 would seamlessly build on and extend Stage 1, and Stage 3 would build on and extend Stages 1 and 2. Other forms of dealing with the various stages in a more integrated manner might be contemplated. It would be helpful, for example, to see the 'executive report' unit gradually shift the focus of the 'Chairman's annual statement' from the text *format*, to negotiating a *particular ideological position*, and finally to how the annual statement genre can be used for *effect* by a comedian, for example, or a poet. In the present *Guide*, this is not fully recognised and further research is needed to develop this aspect of curriculum design.

13.3.5   *The Practical Guide* assessed

Hatim's (1997) *Practical Guide* may thus be taken as an example of a training manual that has gone some way towards rectifying some of the more glaring omissions of previous attempts. The *Guide* embodies the crucial assumption that, whereas content knowledge is certainly important, communication strategies, problem-solving skills and self-directed learning are absolutely indispensable in any translation teaching activity. The trainee translator should be encouraged to become not only a 'descriptive linguist', describing text types in terms of lexico-grammatical features characteristic of the text type in question (through so-called 'sensitiser' texts), but also a 'critical analyst', reflectively identifying where he or she stands in terms of current performance, and in what ways the gap may best be bridged between current performance and optimal competence. To put this in terms of Problem-Based Learning terminology, trainee translators are taught how to:

- discover the nature of a problem;
- understand the constraints and options of problem resolution;
- understand the different viewpoints involved in resolving a given problem;

- negotiate the complex nature of the problem (psychological, socio-logical, ideological);
- resolve how competing solutions may inform decision-making.

Problem-Based Learning is thus about the need to position trainees in a simulated real-world working and professional context which can ultimately involve policy, process and ethical problems. These and related themes are issues for future research to explore, understand and resolve if training is to be holistic and comprehensive.

Further reading

- On the theory and translation dimension of text types, see Werlich (1976), Reiss in Chesterman (ed.) (1989), Hatim and Mason (1990), House (2009).

- On text type research in general and translation didactics in particular, see Hatim and Mason (1997, especially Chapter 10 on text-level errors), Kiraly (2005).

- On directionality, translation competence and related issues, see Campbell (1997).

III Developing practitioner research

Chapter 14

Action and reflection in practitioner research

This chapter will . . .

- present a conceptual map for doing practitioner research in translation studies, with such areas as **register**, **text**, **genre** and **discourse** analysis occupying centre stage;
- suggest topics and research questions, as well as types of data and analytic procedure, for translators and translator trainees intending to embark on research in translation studies.

Concept 14.1   **Discourse enabled by texts and genres**

Within the textual strand of the linguistics-oriented paradigm, current research into the diverse range of translation phenomena has been informed mainly by a register model of textual practices. Genre theory and the study of cross-cultural factors governing textual norms have also emerged as important sources of ideas for translation research. Finally, dealing with such important themes as ideology has necessitated that translation research focus on discourse or the use of language as a vehicle for the expression of cultural values and belief systems (racism, cultural hegemony, etc.) within and across languages. This multi-faceted research output in translation studies is set out in Concept Map VI.

The original triangle (Concept Map II, p. 49) is re-arranged here to highlight the new emphasis on the need in translation to communicate not only content but also values. The left-hand side now reflects a concern with 'text', subsuming the various aspects originally dealt with under 'register' (use, user, cohesion, etc.). This is seen in conjunction with the

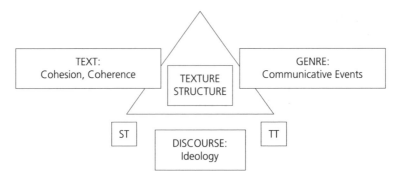

Concept Map VI   Text coherence and cultural norms

right-hand side of the triangle, which now reflects a concern with cultural norms and constraints, including those which specifically govern 'genre' as an aspect of language use. The base line of the triangle reflects contextual factors such as ideological perspective and socio-cultural attitudes dealt with under 'discourse'.

14.1   Textual practices and practitioner research

What has so far been referred to as the range of 'textual practices' in which communities of language users normally engage subsumes the various ways in which language is used as a means, not only of communicating information but also of doing things with words, thus affecting, even changing, reality. This multifaceted activity includes:

- performing a variety of rhetorical acts through *texts*;
- upholding the norms and conventions which ensure that language is used appropriately within the constraints of given communicative events or *genres*;
- expressing values, attitudes and assumptions through *discourse*.

The study of texts, genre and discourse has emerged as an important domain in translation research. As we have already seen, dealing with such practical matters as translation errors, syllabus design or whether translators should be trained to work into the foreign language has necessarily involved theoreticians and practitioners alike in a thorough re-examination of language use seen specifically as textual practices at work (e.g. discourse errors, **text structure**, **texture** and readability).

In Part III of this book, the focus will thus be on research projects which could serve as models for the kinds of investigations practitioners themselves might want to carry out. These projects will be presented in contexts already set by the theoretical positions outlined in Part I, by the research models documented in Part II and by the case studies presented throughout, especially in Chapter 15. Research aims, methodology and conclusions of suggested projects are emphasised throughout.

The framework within which the various research projects are envisaged is informed by an eclectic research methodology which, on the one hand, selectively uses quantitative and qualitative criteria and, on the other hand, fuses what has come to be known as **action research** with notions promoted under 'reflective practice' in applied linguistics (see 1.2; 1.3). This is an approach which essentially allows fuller involvement with the process of discovering the real nature of a problem and of taking action to address it.

Action research (i.e. practitioner reflective research) thus operates in the context of practical problems which affect all those involved. In the present context, problem solving will be aimed at as a means of upgrading the general quality of performance among novice and professional translators, and among learners and teachers of translation. This is basically achieved by linking knowledge and expertise available 'out there' with the practical experience which researchers bring to the task (see Concept 13.4 on Problem-Based Learning).

The process of doing action/practitioner research is a learning experience in its own right. Apart from the confidence-boosting value which this kind of research has when action begins to be seen as possible even on problems once thought to be virtually unsolvable, action/practitioner research provides practitioners with an orderly way of acquiring the knowledge and skills necessary to effect change. To appreciate more clearly what is involved in action research, let us consider the exploratory schema shown in Figure 14.1.

Thus, to engage in an effective programme of action/practitioner research, one would normally:

- *Identify a problem*. For example, you might want to look into when the use of a particular feature or set of features (a **cleft sentence**, repetition, a particular text form, a genre) is functional (i.e. purposeful) and when it is not? Some prior discussion or brainstorming is always useful at this stage of identifying the nature of the problem.

- *Investigate the problem*. Here, you would need to look into such factors as the symptoms, extent, incidence, location and effects of a problem.

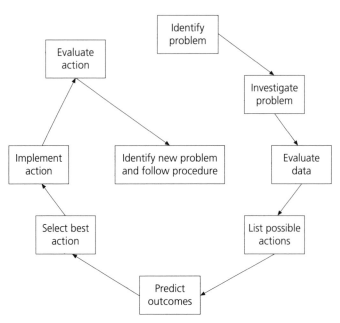

Figure 14.1   Schematic representation of the action/practitioner research cycle

You can do this by, for example, collecting a sample of translations and observing, recording, classifying and analysing how the 'problem' manifests itself as data. Part of this effort will be directed towards compiling a working bibliography of useful references which you might want to look up and eventually use.

- *Evaluate, organise and consolidate the data.* This is part of **managing** the sample you have chosen to analyse, weeding out irrelevant information and concentrating on aspects crucial to a fuller understanding of the process of how a 'problem' has come about.

- *List possible causes and likely courses of action to eliminate the problem.* For example, is the problem to do with negative transfer from the mother tongue, is it intrinsic to **competence** or performance in the target language, or is it ascribable simply to poor reading or writing, inadequate training or general lack of awareness which has resulted in particular accidental tendencies among learners? If any of these scenarios strikes you as plausible, how can you be sure? Assuming that the cause of a problem can generally be identified more or less certainly, what possible courses of action can be envisaged to solve the problem, albeit tentatively at this stage?

- *Predict outcomes.* This is one way of answering the most important question posed so far: how can you be sure that a particular phenomenon or set of phenomena is the cause of the problem? Of course, in a field such as translating and interpreting, one can never be definite about the cause of any of the problems one is likely to consider. Nevertheless, plausible scenarios tend to present you with a set of hypotheses which can be tested. This should enable you to predict 'what would happen if you were to take this or that course of action, as good a start as any on the arduous path of investigating a problem.

- *Select action and implement.* That is, put the plan into action. Test two groups of learners exposed to two different modes of learning or work with two different types of text, genre or discourse, for example.

- *Evaluate action.* Establish if the problem was correctly identified in the first place, see if the situation has improved, and ascertain if further research is necessary.

14.2   Researching text, genre, and discourse

Research Context 1: The translation of ideology

The triad text–genre–discourse is central to the study of ideology both *in* and *of* translation. This is illustrated in Hatim and Mason (1997) (see Chapter 9) where, among a number of other texts, a speech by Ayatollah Khomeini of Iran and its published translation are analysed. The study shows that factors such as cultural specificity and the striking mix of genres characteristic of political discourse are crucial factors in the work of translators and analysts of translation.

In the **socio-cultural** domain (i.e. the realm of cultural 'objects and artifacts', to be distinguished from **socio-textual** practices), features examined might include the sustained use in the speech by Khomeini of the 'blood' metaphor to serve a religious theme; for example, 'crimson and blood-stained commitment'. The incessant recurrence of an image and the concatenation of terms in each instance are devices which merit further investigation. If **motivated** (i.e. non-incidental), such devices can be vital to the construction of a text-world specific to given texts.

Socio-textual considerations (i.e. the realm of cultural 'perspectives' or 'mentifacts'), on the other hand, focus on how rhetorical acts are ordered within the wider framework of **text, discourse** and **genre**.

Textual conventions are seen as important and the use of certain lexical, grammatical as well as text development modes and devices can be particularly interesting: textual norms and the range of text structures available are issues which call for further cross-cultural research.

From this textual perspective, *discourse* is also implicated and cohesive features such as 'repetition' or 'parallelism', **interpersonal** features relating to 'power' or 'solidarity', as well as **ideational** features involving the expression or suppression of 'agency', for example, may all be seen in terms of how they tend to facilitate the expression of ideological attitudes and perspectives. For example, the function of 'full reiteration' vs 'partial recurrence' as kinds of 'repetition' within the textual mechanism of 'cohesion' have not been thoroughly researched to date. This is particularly the case in instances of language use where 'cohesion' (surface formal continuity) is deliberately disturbed to achieve a variety of rhetorical purposes. Further research is needed into how such cohesive devices can be used to reinforce points of view and display commitment in discourse.

Finally, translator mediation, seen this time from the vantage point of genre, may also provide us with interesting research opportunities. Although the translator's scope for modifying genres in translation is fairly limited, possibilities nevertheless exist at the level of genre-upholding lexical selection (collocations, imagery, etc.).

Research Project 1: Socio-textual practices

Aims

- To research issues of **texture** (cohesive devices such as recurrence).

- To analyse how the occurrence of such cohesive patterns relates to (even correlates more strongly with) textual norms and conventions and to the requirements of given genres and discourses.

Procedures

1. Select a corpus of texts belonging to the same genre, period, etc., and serving similar discoursal attitudes (e.g. a collection of political speeches by Third World leaders given at a summit conference on non-alignment, together with the translations of these texts).

2. Begin with the analysis of the source texts by scanning the corpus for instances of repetition (reiteration or recurrence), parallelism or any features which might strike you as somewhat 'non-ordinary'

(i.e. which depart from lexical, grammatical or textual 'norms' and where language use is thus somehow 'marked').

3. Reflect on and try to capture the **motivatedness** behind (i.e. the non-incidental nature of) the use of such devices, and distinguish this from the unmotivated (incidental) use. For example, the deployment of seemingly marked structures might turn out to be obligatory choices dictated by the linguistic **system** and, therefore, 'uninteresting' from a translation perspective. (On the incidental vs non-incidental use of language, see 'pitfalls in researching ideology', 9.2.3).

4. Once such haphazard instances are excluded from the data, consider more carefully the type of effect produced by the use of marked forms such as 'recurrence': Basically, why are they used, and what would have happened had they not been used in the way they were used?

   • Are they used to generate evaluativeness and thus serve the overall rhetorical purpose of the text (e.g. ensuring that a counter-argument is coherent)?

   • Are they used to highlight a particular discoursal attitude (e.g. expressing commitment to a cause)?

   • Are they used to uphold norms operative within given communicative events (e.g. keeping within what is appropriate for the 'sermon' as a **genre**)?

With insights yielded by the above kind of source text analysis, you now need to move on to the target texts. Scrutinise these texts to ascertain whether the translator has heeded the 'motivation' in the use of language (i.e. not necessarily through the use of the same or even similar ST **communicative clues**, but by somehow conveying the overall intention to serve given rhetorical purposes, ideological predilections or genre requirements).

Evaluation

Factors such as discourse or genre are part of 'socio-textual practices'. These are differentiated from the catalogue of features which merely serve a socio-cultural function (e.g. terms to do with ecology, material culture, institutions, etc.). Socio-cultural values are no less worthy of investigation, but only if the cultural insights yielded can be shown to serve higher-order text functions. That is, **socio-cultural** objects (e.g. what *honour* means to an Englishman or an Argentinian) tend to be fairly 'static', unless supplemented by socio-textual values of the kind referred to above (e.g. patriotism, racism).

A related hypothesis worth considering at this point relates to whether the translation shifts affected by the translator are themselves **motivated**. That is, the reason for not preserving a given marked feature might have to do with target language norms or the translator's own objective or subjective calculation of reader response. For example, recurrence in English is usually perceived as a highly marked structure and may thus be used only when the rhetorical purpose in the source text in question justifies the use of recurrence and when the overall effect is both transparent and acceptable to the reader of the English target text.

In the interest of text **coherence**, the use of textual phenomena such as recurrence needs to be justified. If the justification is related to such discoursal values as 'racism' or 'feminism', for example, and if, in the translator's judgement, these values are not likely to be appreciated by a target reader in whose society racism or feminism may perhaps be unheard of, then deciding against preserving this kind of recurrence would be a sensible course of action to take.

Where this is not the case (or where, according to a given translation **brief**, source text values are considered overriding), the conclusion must be that shifts of the kind described above are unwarranted. Through the kind of analysis proposed above, a set of constraints may be worked out and used as catalysts for further research. For example, whether the translation brief and the **audience design** involved justify a 'covert' or an 'overt' translation strategy (see 7.4) is a matter which can only be resolved by empirical research into what is possible or not possible to preserve in the authoritative translation of such samples of writing as a Dickens's novel or a press release.

Suggestions for further research

It would be useful to build on the kind of analysis described above in Project 1 by comparing the 'hortatory' genre (or text type), which has commitment to a cause as its discourse, with a more 'analytical' genre (or text type) such as a UN development agency annual report. In the latter kind of detached discourse, almost all instances of recurrence, etc. are likely to be 'functionless', that is, they are there merely as cohesive devices and not to persuade or manipulate. This is a hypothesis worth testing, with implications for translation quality assessment that merit further exploration.

14.3   Text matters

Research Context 2: Contrastive textology

In his critique of text typologies, Emery (1991) proposed an 'integrated approach' to texts and translation: **macro**-contextual categories such as 'communicative purpose' are seen in terms of how they are realised in **actual** texts through the use of a variety of micro-textual means, lexical and grammatical (on **macro**- and micro-levels of analysis, see 5.1.2). One area of this text-in-context interaction is singled out: **domain**. Domain-specific features have to do with professional or occupational activity. These characteristics can be further investigated and language-pairs can be compared in this respect, providing the teacher/researcher with a valuable text-contrastive base for the classification and subsequent analysis of texts.

Research Project 2: Domain analysis

Aim

- To conduct a contrastive analysis of contextual values related to 'domain' and of the lexico-grammatical means in use across different languages for realising such contextual values.

Procedures

1. Using a similar text-analytic methodology to that outlined in Project 1 on socio-textual practices, choose a literary or a non-literary sample of source texts from a language known not yet to have developed a sophisticated array of **registers** in certain areas (e.g. science, technology, business).
2. Focusing on the registers in which this particular source language is impoverished, analyse the translations of these texts into a language where registers are differentiated in a more sophisticated manner. In areas where language use is, for example, characteristically 'technical', English or any of the major European languages is likely to be an ideal choice in this regard.
3. Compare the source with the target versions and identify how the target language (e.g. English) tends to impose its own register configurations on a fairly undifferentiated (virtually mono-register) use of language in the source texts. There will be new items of vocabulary,

new syntactic formulations and even new text formats, which depart from source text formulations in striking ways and which, in the hands of a translator not familiar with register variation, would most probably be rendered non-technically and therefore unidiomatically.

Evaluation

This kind of research should yield some interesting insights into the way different languages and cultures tend to structure texts, convey discourse values and define genre appropriateness. Conclusions reached through such investigations can help with a variety of issues including language planning and education. They define areas of terminological deficit in the source or target language and suggest solutions accordingly. At first, the new vocabulary, grammatical reformulations or novel text formats might be resented or even rejected by native speakers. But new modes of thought or fashions of speaking will have been created in the process, with translation acting as a means of enriching an otherwise incomplete repertoire of **registers**. For speakers of that language to deal with these areas more efficiently, they would need to acquire new and more precise ways of talking in and about the new subject matter.

Suggestions for further research

1. This fairly simple research design can be extended to include a translation of relevant extracts from the resultant target texts (e.g. English) back into the source language. In this exercise, you will most likely encounter some serious difficulties since the terminology might not be available. But you will also discover how new terminology, different syntactic formulations and novel text formats can evolve under the constraints of the translation process. For example, there might have been no need in Arabic to talk technically and precisely about 'fast-food chains' and 'outlets', with words such as 'restaurants' and 'shops' proving adequate. This need can now be created by translation: sharper distinctions within areas of social reality are made, and the translator has to respond appropriately. There will be a new word or an existing word re-deployed for new purposes not previously recognised.

2. Many Muslim countries operate two kinds of courts: 'secular' courts and what is known as 'Islamic Law' courts (*shari'a courts*). The latter use proceedings and documentation unique to them in terms of genre, discourse and texts. More important from a translation perspective is the area of terminology, which confronts translators into most

European languages with an interesting challenge: to coin terms that can both sound legal and be accurate in reflecting source text meaning. With much demand by foreign embassies, for example, for authentic translations of documents issued by such courts (marriage, divorce, custody, etc.), this is fast becoming a thriving area of professional practice, and special training in this domain is important. Further research into the translation of texts coming out of *shari'a* courts is thus crucial. See Hatim, Shunnaq and Watterson (1996) *The Legal Translator at Work*, a manual dealing with this specific kind of texts.

Research Context 3: Pragmatic failure or success

The way different langua*ges and culture*s perceive reality has also been approached from the standpoint of **cross-cultural pragmatics**. In section 7.4 'overt' and 'covert' translation strategies are defined in terms of whether or not a translation carries traces of being visibly a translation. These translation strategies (the 'covert' in particular) are seen to be closely tied to cultural and linguistic norms which, to analyse properly, require an intercultural perspective. The way pragmatic intentions such as 'evasiveness' or 'forcefulness' are realised in language, and the extent to which such communicative purposes may be preserved in translation, are thus important areas for further research both in *text* analysis and in translation assessment. In the context of English and German, for example, House (1997) points out that communicative preferences actually exist across cultures, and variation may be detected along five basic dimensions: directness, self-reference, focus on content, explicitness and reliance on communicative routines. Other language pairs may usefully be examined from such a cross-cultural perspective.

Research Project 3: Cross-cultural pragmatics

Aims

- To investigate cross-cultural differences from the perspective of pragmatics.

- To use insights yielded by this kind of research as parameters for the assessment of translations.

Procedures

1. Choose a sample of texts (e.g. technical manuals, functional texts such as instructions for technical equipment or pharmaceutical products)

which you feel do not rely for their relevance solely on (i.e. are not closely bound up with) aspects of the source language and culture such as traditions, societal mores.

2. Choose another sample of texts from the same language which you feel do rely for their relevance specifically on addressing receivers in the source language and are thus intimately linked to familiar settings in the source culture (e.g. Winston Churchill's war speeches).

3. Analyse these texts in terms of textual practices such as 'evasiveness' or 'forcefulness', and 'communicative preferences' such as self-reference, explicitness (see Blum-Kulka et al., 1986 for useful analytic frameworks).

4. Set two groups of translators (professional and novice) the task of translating relevant extracts. Divide the professional group into those who will be given seminars in relevant translation theory (including such notions as 'genre' and 'discourse') before they embark on the translation, and those who will not receive such input. Do the same with the novice trainees.

5. Certain groups may be given an explicit translation **brief**, others will be asked to imagine a brief.

6. Assess the translations in the light of the following two hypotheses:

   • *To be optimally effective, texts of the first kind (e.g. the technical manuals) are normally translated using a* **covert translation** *strategy: the translation should have immediate relevance for the target reader.*

   • *To be optimally effective, texts of the second kind (e.g. Churchill's speeches) are normally translated using the overt strategy: the translation would aim for equivalence relations narrowly defined, with the target reader deliberately sidelined.*

Evaluation

In terms of the extent to which these strategies are followed, it is not unreasonable to expect that something like the following rank order will emerge, with the groups at the top performing better than those placed towards the bottom:

• Professional translators (who attended the 'theory' class and received a translation **brief**).

• Professional translators (who did not attend the theory class and were working to no brief).

• Novice trainees (who attended the theory class and received a translation brief).

- Novice trainees (who did not attend the theory class and were not working to any brief).

The task would still be relevant even if a comparison were not introduced between professional and novice translators. However, the group membership factor should lead to some interesting conclusions regarding the kind of shifts opted for and why.

Should this not be the case and the above hypotheses not borne out, the results would be just as interesting. Some form of introspection (using TAP, Immediate Retrospection, or the interview technique) would also be revealing in finding out how the texts were perceived, the problem areas were identified and the solutions were worked out.

Researching pragmatic intentions and communicative preferences within a cross-cultural framework is valuable. A complex network of constraints regarding what may or may not work in a given target culture is in evidence and must be recognised in any translation assessment.

Suggestions for further research

The translation of metaphors in business texts is an interesting area to explore. This issue has been approached from two different angles in translation practice: ST metaphoric expressions such as *prices soar*, *plummet*, etc. should be preserved in the TT; alternatively these are treated as clichéd expressions that can be ignored. Research could look into the function which such expressions are intended to serve in a given, say, TV business bulletin. The hypothesis to test is: on the one hand, in those texts or parts of texts that are intended to serve a predominantly 'informative' function, metaphors serve as a mere 'cosmetic' function (i.e. clichéd) and may therefore be jettisoned; on the other hand, in those texts or parts of texts intended to serve a predominantly **'persuasive'** functions, metaphors of this kind take on an element of 'functionality' that is crucial to preserve.

Research Context 4: A 'relevance' angle

On the basis of a general view of translation informed by Relevance Theory, Gutt (1991) discusses the issue of 'covert' translation and focuses on an English translation of a German tourist booklet, originally analysed by House (1977) (see 7.4.3).

Gutt poses the interesting question of how the translator can be so sure that source text 'implicitness', for example, is intended to produce effects such as 'flattering' the average source language reader and that this effect is part of some overall strategy.

Research Project 4: Relevance in translation

Aims

- To examine empirically thorny issues such as 'writing with intention' and 'reading for intention'.
- To ascertain whether notions such as 'effort' and 'reward', and 'interpretive' vs 'descriptive' use of language, proposed by Relevance Theory (see 3.3 and 8.1), can shed new light on what goes on in the translation process.

Procedures

1. Take a sample of popularised versions of classics such as *Wuthering Heights*, the Bible for children, the Qur'an for non-Arabs with fairly modest levels of literacy, or recent popularised scholarly studies of the kind which regularly appear in such professional magazines as *Nature* and *Scientific American*.
2. Take the non-popularised (original) versions of these texts.
3. Compare the two types of text (the original versions and the popularisations) with regard to factors such as degree of
   - technicality, with the focus on both content and **ideational** 'agency' emanating from the linguistic system of 'transitivity' (**field** of discourse);
   - formality in relation to power, solidarity and other **interpersonal** relationships emanating from '**mood**' and '**modality**' (**tenor of discourse**);
   - explicitness or implicitness as a function of 'distance' between addresser and addressee, seen in terms of how language is ultimately 'textualised' (**mode of discourse**).

Halliday's work (e.g. 1978) is useful in any study of these aspects of **register** membership, where **field**, **tenor** and **mode** are related to **ideational**, **interpersonal** and **textual** resources of meaning, respectively.

Insights yielded by this kind of text analysis may now be used as a basis for introducing a translation angle and for specifically looking into how translators react to the subtle shifts in register, pragmatics, etc. (see Project 1: Socio-textual practices).

The analysis may be further extended by comparing:

- several abridged versions of the same work, designed for different audiences (e.g. students in the case of *Study Notes* vs the kind of readers envisaged by *Great Novels Abridged*);
- different translations made from the abridged or the original versions, carried out in the light of different translation briefs and for different purposes, by the same translator or different translators.

Evaluation

It has been suggested that effects such as those examined by House and Gutt above (e.g. flattering the reader by resorting to withholding certain cultural information) are not measurable and cannot be quantified. Research of the kind outlined above should introduce a degree of rigour to the analysis of this unwieldy aspect of the process of reading, writing or translating.

Another problem area tackled by the research design outlined above relates to Gutt's point that, whether in translating or assessing translations, a reading of the source text is not sufficient by itself, since meaning is not a static entity that can be recovered mechanistically. Furthermore, Gutt maintains that **compensation** is not entirely unproblematic as long as the main aim remains one of seeking to establish **functional equivalence** and using this as a basis for translator decisions.

Suggestions for further research

With magazines and journals such as *Scientific American* or *National Geographic* increasingly venturing into the bilingual market, examining the language of popularised vs original versions of scholarly articles, for example, is becoming crucial from a translation point of view. Research which identifies how **ideational**, **interpersonal** or **textual** resources are deployed and translated is vital.

Research Context 5: Text type

Text-based models of translation (e.g. Reiss, 1971; Hatim and Mason, 1990, 1997) promote the view that, like most other dichotomies, the covert–overt distinction or the kind of receiver positions which Pym describes in terms of 'excluded', 'observational' and 'participative' roles (see 7.3) can be accounted for equally adequately within current text typologies. In the example used by Pym, what is intended by the English text of the 'invitation to tender' and the kind of participative position envisaged for its reader would be seen as part of the text-type profile determined for the sample in question.

Research Project 5: The text-type factor

Aims

- To assess the value of text-type awareness.
- To examine how this sensitivity to text in context can provide us with a reasonable basis on which to proceed in reconstructing context in general and working out audience designs in particular.
- To assess the role which an appreciation of text type can play in the process of translation.

Procedures

1. Set a group of trainees not yet exposed to a theory of text types and related pragmatics and **register** issues the task of translating a text belonging to an evaluative type (e.g. an argumentative editorial).
2. At more or less the same time, set the same group the task of translating a text belonging to a non-evaluative type (e.g. a detached news report).
3. Give the group a series of seminars in text analysis and draw your illustrations from the texts given as an assignment and from the kind of problems they have faced.
4. Find two texts comparable to the above and, after some intervening period, set the same group the task of translating these texts. The timing may be important, and leaving a gap between the first test and the second test could be revealing.
5. Analyse the data with a focus on elements that show awareness (or lack of awareness) of the text-type criteria at work (e.g. emotive diction and marked syntactic structures as the hallmarks of argumentation).

This analysis may be supplemented by specially designed interviews to assess how conscious or unconscious were some of the right or wrong decisions taken.

Evaluation

This fairly simple experimental design can be extended in a number of ways along lines adopted in the various designs outlined above. The analytic categories used (e.g. those relating to **ideational** or **interpersonal** resources) may also be employed in the description of translator behaviour (e.g. additions, deletions, modifications) vis-à-vis text type.

Suggestions for further research

1. Insights yielded by this kind of research would be helpful in designing translation courses, writing training manuals, and teaching translation.

2. A text-type framework would also be useful in researching discourse pragmatics regarding such questions as:

   • How do concepts such as **politeness**, relevance, clarity and truthfulness affect text production in different languages and different cultures, and which system is to be reflected in the translation? (Fawcett, 1997).

   • What are some of the constraints within which compensation may be made more explicit? This is particularly helpful to trainee translators who need to be systematically shown the means by which effects of the source text can be catered for in the target text (Harvey, 1995).

14.4   Discourse practices

Alongside such factors as the **register** membership of a text discussed in the previous section, the importance of 'discourse practices' in the expression of power and ideology in and through translation is now generally recognised. Such an extremely valuable source of ideas remains largely untapped, particularly in the teaching of translation. Yet, the pedagogic potential of this body of theorising is both rich and varied, as shown by researchers working from perspectives as disparate as Cultural Studies (e.g. Bruce, 1994) and Applied Linguistics (e.g. Campbell, 1998).

Research Context 6: The discourse of the dissenting voices

Bruce's (1994) analysis comprehensively discusses the role in translation of a heightened awareness of text and context and how they constantly interact with each other in the production of meaning. In the specific case of anarchist discourse in nineteenth-century France, these text-in-context interrelationships constitute the linguistic dimension of such 'subcultures' as that of the Commune, which is crucial to an appreciation of the cultural politics that was instrumental in marginalising the French writer Valles and his work, for example.

Bruce states that 'conscious theorisation of the problematic embodied in a particular source-text is a useful and . . . necessary step in achieving a "satisfactory" translation' (p. 47). Translating the culture of the Commune, for example, would first require an appreciation of the cultural politics underpinning this culture. Further studies may show whether and how such an appreciation is important in translation.

Literary and cultural theory have thus been particularly helpful in laying the foundations for conceptually more valid translation methodologies – a trend which, according to Bruce (p. 47) can only be enhanced by enlisting discourse analysis.

Research Project 6: Researching marginalisation

Aims

- To investigate the way in which discourse analysis can help the translator.

- To examine how a discourse perspective can enable the translator to cope more specifically with the range of complex issues encountered in the kind of situations exemplified by Valles's Commune writing.

- To discover whether a discourse approach can shed light on the reasons why marginalised writers are excluded from translation publishing.

Procedures

1. Choose a writer in your own language and culture whom you think has been undeservedly debarred from the international translation market, or a writer who has only been admitted after the passage of decades and with few published translations to his or her name. (See 10.3.3 for an example from the Arab literary scene.)

2. Adopting a framework similar to that proposed by Bruce (see 10.3.2 for a detailed account):

   - establish the cultural/political context which has surrounded the sample of writing you wish to analyse;

- apply discourse analytic techniques to investigate aspects of the texts, such as:
  - the **narrative** flow, and whether it is marked in some way (e.g. deliberately fragmented), and if so, why?
  - tense consistency and whether any shifts are in evidence (e.g. are tense shifts unexpected), and if so, what for?
  - **word play** (and its significance in the work);
  - figurative expression and the way this is deployed;
  - metaphoric expression (and the various functions served);
  - cultural references (and the intertextual allusions evoked);
  - shifts in perspective and positionality (and the rationale behind them).

3. Choose a translation of this author's work into one of the major European languages. Show how the features analysed above have been preserved in the translation or, alternatively, have been smoothed out to make the translation more 'readable' and the text generally more 'fluent'. You are more likely to find that, within a translation tradition such as the Anglo-American, it is the latter **domesticating** strategy that is adopted. However, there are always exceptions and, despite the tradition, you might find that the translator has opted for a **resistant** strategy. If resistance is the norm adopted, the enquiry should turn to why this strategy is opted for and, perhaps more significantly, how it is implemented.

Evaluation

These are important research questions which need to be answered with reference to numerous writers marginalised for one reason or another in various parts of the world and within a variety of cultural milieux.

The issue of what is 'worthy of translation' (i.e. how and why certain writers achieve world recognition and reach the international market, while others remain marginalised) can be investigated usefully by using discourse analysis.

Factors at work in reading and translating marginalised writers such as Valles have to do with what, in the case of the Commune, Bruce describes as 'the formal and functional specificity of the discourse of the Commune . . . that is, the qualities which render them "subversive"' (1994: 57). This 'historical specificity' resides not only within the cultural politics enveloping the text but also in the **actual** minutiae of language **texture**.

Where this formal and functional specificity resides, and how it is expressed, are matters which research designs of the kind outlined above are most suited to clarify.

Suggestions for further research

Image-making is an important issue. But we know very little about the strategies (linguistic, literary, rhetorical) which translators use in attempting to enhance the image of a foreign writer. For example, the Egyptian Naguib Mahfouz, who in 1988 won the Nobel Prize for literature, has been taken to task by critics for the 'popular fiction' (even 'low market journalistic') elements in some of his novels. Important research questions are:

- Is there textual evidence for this kind of accusations?
- If so, have such elements been 'neutralised' (i.e. upgraded to 'serious' fiction) by the translators who the critics say have done a great deal of image enhancement for the author to be considered for the Nobel Prize? And if so, how?
- What other image-enhancing strategies have the translators used with Mahfouz?
- Can such a framework be applied to other writers, from other languages and cultures, whose work you think has undergone image-enhancement?

Research Context 7: Resistant translation

Translations which resist hegemonic cultural norms have been of special interest in cultural studies. This has prompted a shift of focus away from merely dealing with the 'ideology in translation', and towards the 'ideology of translation' (see Chapter 10). In practice, resistance is managed through such techniques as opting for unidiomatic usage and other linguistically and culturally alienating features in the translated text, which together recreate the impression of foreignness.

Research Project 7: The ideology of translation

Aims

- To show through an assessment of translations how 'resistance' is managed in translation practices which set out to 'foreignise' and thus resist certain translation 'ethics' imposed by the more 'prestigious' traditions.

- To examine the issue of the delicate balance which resistant translation must achieve between the foreign text's strategic construction and domestic response.

Resistant translation aims to disrupt, but domestic literary and linguistic values and the domestic readership must feature in the translator's own strategic design: How are these conflicting constraints reconciled?

Procedures

Continuing with the theme tackled in Research Project 6 of why, while many authors remain unnoticed, some foreign or Western writers become attractive to the translation market in the West or in non-Western cultures, you may now want to look more closely at the issue of 'image' in translation.

1. Choose a writer in your own language and culture who you think probably does not deserve the international recognition he or she has garnered, and whose reputation you believe has been made possible by the elegant translations (both **literal** and free) which his or her work has seen.
2. Select an original from the works of this writer, along with its published translation.
3. Focus initially on the target text (consult with native speakers of the language if this is not your mother tongue).
4. Adopting a discourse analysis scheme such as that outlined in Research Context 6 (the discourse of dissenting voices):
   - underline features which attract your attention as being particularly 'fluent' or, for whatever reason, as standing out and displaying a more creative use of language;
   - reflect on whether the credit for this elegance should go to the translator as someone who has so skilfully *adapted* a source text that is essentially poor, or to the translator as someone who has set about the task of faithfully *rendering* a source text that is already worthy in its own right.
5. Next, compare the features identified so far with their equivalents in the source text.

Evaluation

This research methodology should reveal the degree of latitude which the translator has taken with the source text. Two kinds of conclusion present themselves:

- The translator will be shown to have displayed his or her skills as an image promoter, deploying all linguistic resources to make the translation read like an elegant original in the target language.
- Alternatively, credit would have to go to the writer of the original, with the translator minimally interfering with what is already most elegant.

Suggestions for further research

An important aspect of thorough domestication is the discourse and genre shifts that emerge as a result, stripping source texts of key characteristics. For example, smoothing source text discourse by introducing all kinds of discourse markers and by organising the text in particular ways alien to source text language and culture could turn a literary text into a clinical lab report, for example. You could focus on discourse markers (**connectivity**, transitional phrases, etc.) and examine the pragmatic effect which introducing such organising principles can have on the reader.

Research Context 8: Beyond transfer of information

In their analysis of translation as **re-writing** and manipulation, Bassnett and Lefevere (1990a: 12) conclude that 'translation has been a major shaping force in the development of world culture'. Within this framework, which is largely **semiotic** (i.e. which recognises the function of 'signs' in the way cultures express them), the issue of 'power' plays an important role in how languages respond (often subtly) to different variants of translation ethics. For example, translation can be 'faithful', merely involving 'an exchange of **signifieds**', with the focus on the transfer of information and with little or no regard for the cultural context in which **signifiers** are normally embedded. Alternatively, as Lefevere (1990: 17) urges translators to do, translation may go beyond the mere exchange of signifieds perceived in a kind of intellectual and emotional vacuum to capture instead the cultural, ideological and poetological overtones of the text.

Research Project 8: Cultures in contact

Aims

- To investigate how cultural context and linguistic expression become intertwined.

- To explain the way in which translations can become impoverished if the texts to be translated are stripped of intellectual or emotional overtones.
- To examine the complex issue of language and identity when this impinges on the process of translation.

Procedures

1. Take a sample of ideologically loaded writing, such as feature articles from a magazine such as *Reader's Digest*. Certainly when it was first launched, this particular magazine had a mission – namely, to articulate systematically a coherent ideological message relating to the American Dream. Furthermore, some articles from the magazine are translated into most of the world's languages, which makes it an ideal translation sample to analyse.
2. Find articles intended specifically to serve distinct ideological themes (e.g. the New World Order).
3. Adopting any of a number of frameworks available (see 'evaluation' below on Venuti, 1995; Bruce, 1994; Hatim and Mason, 1997, etc.):
   - assess the source text and compile a catalogue of features (e.g. the discourse of superiority and power), together with their linguistic realisations;
   - analyse the translation in the light of the translation shifts affected.

Evaluation

An example of this kind of study is Hatim (1999), which reaches the following conclusions. In the years immediately following the Second World War, the strategy adopted by the translators of *Reader's Digest* into Arabic systematically:

- domesticated (i.e. Arabicised) **socio-cultural** objects (e.g. ST 'society' became 'tribe', 'a glass of wine' became 'a cup of tea');
- foreignised (i.e. did not tamper with) ST socio-textual practices and kept intact what was in effect alien to the Arabic language and culture.

Such **macro**-textual structures include:

- discourse values (e.g. racism, 'bomb thine enemy');
- genre structures (e.g. An Open Letter to the President);
- text formats (e.g. the rebuttal 'Certainly . . . However').

It is safe to assume that, at the time, the average Arab reader would not be fully conversant with such textual values and structures. Nevertheless, these vehicles of attitudinal meaning were felt to be crucial to the message which *Reader's Digest* intended to convey.

Has the receiving language, Arabic, stood to gain from this socio-textual globalisation, or was this merely an 'onslaught' on indigenous values in a manner that was detrimental to the Arabic language and culture? This question can now be empirically answered and the various hypotheses tested for Arabic and across a number of other languages.

Text in context and issues such as language and identity can thus be examined not by relying exclusively on fairly static models such as 'to translate is to prove one's national identity', but by invoking a variety of perspectives (cultural and linguistic), reconciled with the aim of shedding light on what it is in language that gives true expression to identity.

Suggestions for further research

Frameworks suitable for this kind of analysis could be developed by fusing cultural analysis (e.g. foreignisation vs domestication) with discourse analysis – as Bruce (1994) has done – and with **critical linguistics** – for example, Fairclough's 'language and power' model (1989), and Fowler's 'language and ideology' model (1996). From the perspective of translation studies, such a joint effort may be exemplified by the work of translation theorists such as Hatim and Mason (1990). Here, culture is seen in terms of the way it manifests itself through semiotic **macro**-structures (e.g. discourse, genre).

Research Context 9: Mimicking target discourse

Mahasweta Singupta's (1990a) study of the Bengali poet Tagore's auto-translation (see 10.2.2) also addresses the issue of language and identity and focuses on the pitfalls of a translation in which faithfulness is exclusively shown towards the target language and culture.

Research Project 9: Politics and poetics

Aims

- To examine how – by changing not only the style of the original lyric, for example, but also the imagery and tone – the translator can bring into being an entirely different register which tends to match as closely as possible the dominant **poetics** in the target language.
- To reflect on the wider implications of such transformations.

Procedures

1. Acquire a sample of Tagore's 'autotranslations' into English.
2. Identify concrete manifestations of the way Tagore is said to have mimicked the dominant discourse of English. Changes involving embellishments such as imagery and tone would be particularly interesting.
3. Acquire translation of Tagore made from the poet's native language or from English into a language with which you are familiar.
4. Compare those translations made from Tagore's native language with those translated from Tagore's English versions.
5. Assess whether the translator from English has in fact noted the subtle changes introduced by Tagore to cater for an English readership.

Evaluation

This kind of analysis may be carried out on autotranslations done by other writers who have met a similar fate to Tagore (forgotten as quickly as he was made famous by the West). Cultural studies has provided us with insights into the process of the likely distortions that might occur. One particular weakness of the model, however, lies in the minimal reliance on textual evidence and on the analysis of extensive data (see 9.2.3).

An approach to cultural issues which draws on **critical linguistics** would be ideal for identifying, describing and explaining a variety of features which writers such as Singupta in the study outlined in 10.2.2 has incisively observed.

Suggestions for further research

The analytic apparatus used in this kind of project can be extended to include research into non-literary texts. Many writers and journalists are known to display masterly bilingual skills, producing materials in two languages simultaneously. The process by which this is achieved is well worth investigating.

Research Context 10: Appropriating the original

Piotr Kuhiwczak (1990) discusses a form of manipulation which involves an appropriation of the original, resulting from the translator's and publisher's untested assumptions about the source culture, and about the ability of the target reader to decode complex cultural messages.

Research Project 10: Manipulating discourse

Aims

- To examine how translations can manipulate structure and **texture** (and consequently shift register and overall pragmatic effects).
- To examine how such manipulation can, sometimes heavily, impinge on discursive practices which drive entire ideologies.

Procedures

1. Working within a similar framework to that adopted by Bruce (1994) or by analysts subscribing to the critical linguistic model (e.g. Hatim and Mason, 1997), analyse the first English translation of Milan Kundera's *The Joke* (1969). Focus on features to which the author objected in the translation (e.g. how digressions and repetitions have been smoothed).

2. Acquire the later English translation (the one which Kundera is said to have finally approved).

3. Compare the two versions and identify the various points of difference and similarity.

4. Choose relevant passages from the later version (i.e. the one where digressions and the like are preserved in translation to the satisfaction of the author).

5. Set novice translators – for example, those on a literary translation course – the task of translating these passages, and see if they can discern the seemingly insignificant **deviations** from the norm, how the various features are dealt with, etc.

6. Discuss *The Joke*'s case with the students who have taken the test, and document the debate in as much detail as possible, using examples from the novel as illustrations.

7. Run the test again, setting the same trainee translators the task of translating relevant passages.

Evaluation

The textual manifestations likely to be confronted in this kind of analysis may be uncovered by analytic procedures informed by models such as cultural studies or critical discourse analysis. The emphasis on culture promoted by these models of translation should enable the analyst to determine gross misrepresentations. What is perfectly acceptable in one culture can easily be seen by translators operating within different cultures as a bewildering array of irrelevancies which have to be tidied up.

In addition to these textual aspects, we need to learn more about the various agents of power that put pressure on the act of translation, and how these pressures are exercised (Fawcett, 1995). For example, ads can be studied as complex social events and as 'meanings' minus the experience of the commodities in question (McLuhan, 1970: 2). This domain of creating meaning has rarely been seen from a cross-cultural perspective on research into power in discourse.

In a similar vein, cultural perceptions are mobile and the effect of the way cultural media tend to interpenetrate must not be forgotten. For example, urgently in need of further investigation is the cross-cultural impacts of such magazines as *Cosmopolitan* or *Elle* (in English or in their various foreign language editions) in forcing the pace of socio-ideological change already driven by forces such as television and cinema (Paizis, 1998).

Suggestions for further research

It is interesting to note that written texts are more susceptible to distortive pressures than are visual texts. Films, for example, are clearly more resistant to substantial editing than books, but does it follow that dubbing and, more radically, **subtitling** can ever be innocent activities (Paizis 1998)? Further research into the discourse of the media might shed light on these issues.

14.5   Genre norms

Research Context 11: Genre in translation

Re-writing and manipulation have also been examined from the vantage point of genre theory. The examples which Maria Tymoczko (1990) cites in her study of *Hamlet* in West Africa (see 11.1.2) deal with the theme of resistance to faithful translation and bring 'orality' into the equation, all as aspects of 'genre'. Particular generic practices (e.g. plot sequences, rhetorical and linguistic structures) were shown to resist transfer (p. 49).

Research Project 11: Genre and related textual values in translation

Aims

- To examine the translation problems involved in rendering source text **macro**-structures such as the plot and rhetorical sequences.
- To show that certain socio-cultural features (e.g. 'fatalism') can become dynamic but only when seen in terms of the contribution they make to enhance the effectiveness of structures such as genre.

Procedures

For a comparable sample to the non-fictional text drawn from *Reader's Digest* in Research Project 8, you may now want to try out your analytic procedures on a sample from a well-known semi-literary genre in English: Mills & Boon novels. Familiarise yourself with this genre and with popular fiction writing in general (see Carter and Nash, 1990).

1. Acquire a Mills & Boon sample, together with the translation into a language you are familiar with. (From experience, it is always easier to find a translation first and then search for the original, since the originals are more readily available in British libraries or online, and are kept for many years after publication.)
2. Analyse the source and target texts, using a catalogue of features such as the following (outlined in Carter and Nash, 1990):
   - The use of 'non-core' verbs (e.g. 'dash', 'scuttle' vs the core verbs 'run', 'run').
   - The use of adjectives of sensory perception ('glittering'), descriptive of **texture** ('rough'), tactile sensation ('cool') and dimension ('broad').
   - The avoidance of symbolism, extended metaphor or extensive patterns of imagery.
   - The persistent use of a kind of metaphoric cliché.
3. Analyse the translation shifts (omissions, additions, etc.) and attempt to explain them in terms of such constraints as 'linguistic', 'literary-poetic' and 'ideological' (social, religious, etc.).

Evaluation

So-called cultural gaps, and even grammatical or lexical errors encountered in translation, may be textual in essence and can therefore be explained more adequately in terms of a failure to appreciate the conventions governing such **macro**-structures as genre.

Suggestions for further research

The analysis of genre in translation has so far leaned too heavily on literary and historical texts. However, day-to-day textual output in such fields as commercial publicity material, tourist brochures and bureaucratic memos are no less interesting or less amenable to analysis within the framework proposed above.

Research Context 12: Is 'faithfulness' enough?

In her study of *Peter Pan* in Bulgaria (see 11.1.2), Palma Zlateva (1990) addresses the issue of faithfulness and suggests that if 'characters' such as Peter Pan or Winnie the Pooh are to attract the interest and win the admiration of the foreign reader/spectator, the heroes must first become part of the target **universe of discourse**.

Research Project 12: Cultural acceptance

Aims

- To assess how the receiving culture plays the important role of 'client', taking over and assigning different functions to the translation of different texts.
- To assess how cultural assumptions can act as indicators of the way the work is likely to fare in the target culture.

Procedures

1. Using tourist brochures as a sample (or any comparable corpus of texts available in bilingual versions), focus on the target text and analyse this independently of the source.
2. Identify the kind of assumptions which emerge from reading the translation. These assumptions are likely to be 'cultural' (e.g. the use or avoidance of certain metaphors) and/or 'linguistic' (e.g. the use or avoidance of the active voice).
3. Develop a scheme in which the above observations (supported by textual evidence) add up to a world-view regarding what the target culture finds more acceptable (both culturally and linguistically). Norms of behaviour and linguistic usage will emerge. For instance, there is a tendency in Arabic to 'personalise' descriptions in tourist brochures by inviting the 'visitor' to become an active agent 'doing things' in

the tour in question ('on the right hand side, the visitor is able to see three wild cats in their natural habitat'), as opposed to the more impersonal style in English: 'on the right hand side, three wild cats are/may be seen in their natural habitat', which objectifies experience.

4. Adopt a similar analytic procedure in dealing with the source text sample. New categories may emerge. Make sure that these are checked against the target text sample analysed in the beginning.

A semblance of a 'world-view' (in stylistic as well as ideological terms) will emerge. This will define not only dominant patterns of linguistic expression across different languages but also the translation tradition within which the target text is produced.

Evaluation

The findings of such studies will be highly significant both from the perspective of translation criticism and didactics and from the wider perspective of studying cultures in contact. What these studies reveal has little if anything to do with the question of translation quality. The complexity which seems to be inherent in the process of cultures coming together through translation puts a different slant on 'faithfulness'. It is no longer possible to account for the notion in terms of mere equivalence of words or texts. Rather, faithfulness may now be seen as an attempt to make the target text function in particular ways, and translators can be said to be faithful when they deliver what a particular readership finds more acceptable.

Suggestions for further research

In the same way as we calque expressions (e.g. *peak hour*, *skyscraper*, etc. calqued in many languages), can genres be calqued? Which genres get calqued? How, and for what purpose? These are intriguing questions for further research.

Research Context 13: A training perspective on genre in translation

Shifting the focus slightly to non-literary matters and to the translation of so-called 'pragmatic' (i.e. instrumental) texts, James (1989) looks at the specific issue of genre in translation and suggests that the role of contextual specifications is often neglected in the training of translators, with the focus being invariably placed on the 'words on the page'. This difficulty is compounded by the fact that languages vary enormously in terms of the repertoire of genres and other **macro**-structures possessed. For example, the genre 'abstract' (e.g. of an academic article) is approached in significantly different ways by different languages.

Research Project 13: Genre awareness

Aims

- To assess how awareness on the part of the translator of larger discourse structures and genre specificities can help in avoiding the kind of errors often made in dealing with levels of language use beyond the sentence.
- To examine how shifts, often haphazardly introduced in the translation, can dislocate the text from its intended genre and thus distort the rhetorical structure of the original.

Procedures

1. Select a bilingual corpus of abstracts (or any clearly identifiable genre), with the source being a language in which the genre in question is felt to be handled differently from (e.g. in a less regimented way than) what is customary and **appropriate** for academic abstracts in a language such as English. (See the discussion of register in Research Project 2.)

2. Assess how the translator has coped with the genre requirements in the target language: what kind of modifications, omissions or additions has been affected to bring source text abstracts in line with what the target language reader might expect?

3. In cases where translations are not available, set a group of translator trainees the task of translating these abstracts. This study could take the pre/post-test format, with a workshop-style discussion of key features following the pre-test and just before a post-test is administered. This should demonstrate the value of genre awareness in the work of the translator.

Evaluation

In carrying out studies of this kind, a crucial assumption would be that, in the translation of **informative** texts (see Concept 6.5), transparency is a requirement that goes beyond gratuitous discussion of issues of linguistic imperialism or the pernicious effects of thorough domestication in translation. One way of dealing with 'genre violation' is to provide the translator with genre-based experience which, while no doubt grounded in source language preferences, is ultimately oriented towards target language expectations. The latter must be seen as overriding.

Suggestions for further research

An area which merits further research into genre is how genres evolve, lose some of their conventional characteristics and acquire new ones. For example, Mills & Boon (the English classic popular fiction genre) seems to be losing some of its 'old-fashioned romance' and moving into areas that at times border on the 'immodest' if not the all-out 'licentious'. How do translators cope with these kinds of shifts, particularly in translating into cultures in which so-called 'selectional **politeness**' (observing cultural taboos, moral decorum, etc.) (Sell, 1992) is still very strong.

For another example, you might want to look at the genre 'job advertisement' and how, in certain countries (e.g. Spain, Greece), this particular textual genre has undergone a drastic transformation in response to democratic changes which state institutions have witnessed in those particular countries in recent years. In such contexts, genre style seems to be shifting from power-oriented employer–employee relationship to one characterised by more 'solidarity'.

Research Context 14: Translation as genre

In Chapter 11 it was suggested that the act of translation itself might be seen as a genre in its own right. A translation might be seen in terms of the extent to which source text genres are preserved and the kind of translation shifts effected. In and by itself, however, a given translation might be seen as a valid instance of what all translated material should look or sound like (as opposed to what we find in monolingual communication, for example).

Research using translation corpora (see 12.1) is informed by the basic assumption that the language of translated texts reflects more than knowledge of, and competence in, the languages concerned. Even-Zohar (1978a: 77), for example, notes that, in translation 'we can observe patterns which are *inexplicable* in terms of any of the repertoires involved', that is, those of the source and target languages. Can this form of translational behaviour point to the existence of 'universal' features of translation?

Research Project 14: Translation universals

Aims

- To test whether translated texts exhibit particular patterns of **texture**. Such a tendency may be studied in relation to dominant translation strategies (e.g. domestication) and in terms of pragmatic effects such as **focus** and **foregrounding**.

- To test whether translated texts are more 'explicit', the form this 'explicitation' takes, and whether there are any differences between the kind of explicitation resorted to by foreign language learners and that found in translation are some of the questions which future corpus research could address (Toury, 1991: 51). Within translation studies itself, some of the questions being asked are:

  – Do professional translators go about explicitation differently from non-professionals?

  – Does the mode of translation (oral vs written) have a bearing on the matter?

- To test whether translated texts exhibit a higher degree of dis-ambiguation and simplification. The various forms, which such shifts take, including aspects of source and target text variation such as punctuation, are now within reach given latest developments in corpus research techniques.

- To test whether translated texts flout certain conventions and over-use certain features recognised as characteristic of 'good' style in the target language. Here, an interesting research question would relate to the kind of variation (ideological, etc.), which such translator-supplied features can introduce into the translation. These interventions have been found to give rise to certain patterns of distribution in the use of certain features. More significantly, such features are identified almost uniquely as a property of translated texts.

Procedures

One useful methodological procedure for researching universal features of translation would be to scan a corpus of translated texts and note the occurrence of any of these features regardless of the source language. The frequencies identified would then be compared with a similar corpus of original writing in the target language specified. This kind of data may at a later stage be run against comparable data obtained when different target languages are used.

Evaluation

Some of the hypothesis testing that has been done so far has proved to be most revealing. Shamaa (1978: 168–71), for example, reports that common words such as 'say' occur with a significantly higher frequency in English texts translated from Arabic than they do in original English writing (in fact, more than twice as high). Along similar lines, Blum-Kulka (1986: 33) observes that interesting qualitative differences might be identified in the way cohesive patterns emerge in target language texts compared with normal cohesion exhibited by original writing in both source and target languages.

However, the classification of corpora into 'monolingual' and 'bilingual' or 'multilingual', which has so far been crudely based on nothing more than the range of languages involved, needs to be developed further (Baker, 1995). Similarly, a corpus of translated texts may be expanded, and software tools are becoming increasingly more sophisticated in their capacity to retrieve such information as writer/speaker, first/second language, nationality, and **gender**.

In this kind of comparative analysis, the question to address would be whether these features vary across cultures and, if they do not, whether this can tell us something about the process of translation. Another interesting question might be whether the emerging consistency holds across different text types, types of translation, etc., and, if it does not, whether this can tell us something about the constraints which the use of a particular text type, for example, introduces into the process. Given uniformity of socio-cultural and historical context (as well as other variables such as text type), we might want to enquire into whether the existence of certain universal features might shed light on how translation norms evolve.

Suggestions for further research

Apart from universal and norm-oriented features of translational behaviour, a number of other areas await further corpus research (Baker, 1995):

- Comparative information on how the end product of the translation process has evolved over time.
- The size and nature of the unit of translation and the types of equivalence achieved in practice.

- The role of text type specification, translation types, and the wide range of discourses and genres necessarily involved in all acts of communication.

Further reading

- Williams and Chesterman (2002), a how-to guide to doing research in translation studies.

Chapter 15

Setting a teaching and research agenda: The case of style translation

---

This chapter will . . .

- weave together the various strands that have emerged so far in dealing with the translation, not only of 'what' is said, but also 'how' something is said;

- review new thinking on the issue of the translation of 'style', and advocate the need for a broader definition of style;

- propose a framework for teaching and researching 'style in translation', and thus suggest what the future might hold in this area of professional practice.

> ### Quote 15.1
>
> We have seen how much of the theory of translation – if there is one as distinct from idealised recipes – pivots monotonously around undefined alternatives: letter or spirit, word or sense. The dichotomy is assumed to have analysable meaning. This is the central epistemological weakness and sleight of hand.
>
> George Steiner (1975: 290)

15.1   Literal translation: Limitations and possibilities

The conclusion that George Steiner reached in the 1970s still rings true, and is probably the kind of conclusion which any serious attempt to survey translation theories would reach today. As this book has shown, no matter how novel the labels may have been (covert vs overt, instrumental vs documental, etc.), the choice in practice is still roughly the same: free vs literal. But is the choice so straightforward? How 'free', where and when? Where and when might 'literal' translation prove inadequate? These and similar questions remain largely unanswered.

Word-for-word (or formal or literal) translation works well most of the time and constitutes the bulk of what translators do. This kind of translation has also been highly praised and recommended as a procedure by many a translation theorist. Newmark (1981: 39), for example, suggested:

> In communicative as in semantic translation, provided that equivalent effect is secured, the literal word-for-word translation is not only the best, it is the only valid method of translation.

But, with the 'reflective practitioner' in mind (see 1.2), we should be wary of such generalisations and perhaps ask and attempt to answer the question: What are the constraints under which 'literal' (or for that matter, 'free') translation might or might not be satisfactory? This book has contributed to this effort of constraining translation method, suggesting a number of ways in which the limitations and possibilities of literal or free translation may usefully be examined within the framework of both applied text linguistics and practitioner action research. Particularly regarding 'literal' translation (which too often is seen simply as the default option), it is also suggested that such translation method investigations would be more effective if guided by something like the following fundamental principle:

> Literal or free translation runs risks, and these risks need to be carefully managed by always drawing on the sociolinguistic, pragmatic, discursive, and ultimately cultural constraints holding in relation to the two text languages in question in the specific context in question.
>
> (Candlin, 2011, personal communication)

This book has sought to discuss and demonstrate in some detail how the diverse range of textual and contextual variables (subsumed by such basic categories as 'register', 'intentionality', 'intertextuality', 'interdiscursivity', 'genre' semiotics) may best be managed, yielding a set of constraints on what can and cannot be done with literal or free translation.

15.2   Style and textual dynamism

This concluding chapter pieces together the evidence for the need to constrain translation method, weaving the various strands into a texture, and calling on future researchers to take up some of the more salient unanswered questions regarding such issues as the translation of dynamic uses of language and the status of text type in this process. One of the outstanding issues is 'the translation of style' chosen here as an ideal site within which to examine literal translation or free, with all its limitations and possibilities.

Particularly in the area of style studies and translation, however, an important caveat must be entered: to carry out 'style' analysis more effectively in translation teaching or research, the notion of 'style' must first be redefined sufficiently broadly to include and account for the textual phenomenon of markedness. This is an all-pervasive phenomenon not restricted to a particular linguistic level (phonology, lexis, grammar) or to a particular kind of texts (e.g. canonic literary forms). Markedness involves any contextually motivated departure from some 'norm', be this linguistic, textual or rhetorical, fictional or non-fictional. Style thus becomes virtually synonymous with the pragmatic process of 'doing novel things with words' (Austin, 1962), and with the creative process of producing and manipulating 'signs' for particular effects. Words as signs are semiotic constructs which mean something (in this context, something novel, creative, etc.), to someone (text producer, receiver or translator as mediator), in some respect or capacity (to do with source or target 'universes of discourse') (Peirce, 1982).

The study of style, then, is closely bound up with norms and motivated deviations from such norms, wherever these happen to be found, whether in *Wuthering Heights* or in the instructions on a cereal packet. Approaching 'style' in this way will certainly show the translation of style to be one of the more promising areas of research and teaching to have emerged from fifty years or more of 'translation studies'. To ensure that such an orientation remains relevant and durable, it is certainly helpful to consider the notion of style as a departure from norms alongside at least two other kinds of 'departure' worth noting in any examination of translational activity:

- A departure from received wisdom, represented by the elitist view that translating style is the sole prerogative of 'literary' translators, that style is exclusively a property of the 'literary' text, and that literary translation is a 'unique' translational event unparalleled by any other.

- A departure represented in translation studies by a shift of focus not only 'from word to text' as commonly observed, but also, and perhaps more significantly, from a concern with what might be called 'static' texts, to a concern with the more dynamic kinds of texts. Static texts are mostly machine-translatable instances of language use that tend to be largely 'formulaic' and in a sense 'ordinary' (e.g. legal pre-ambles, executive summaries, laboratory reports). Dynamic texts, on the other hand, are texts or parts of texts which are characterised by varying degrees of what Beaugrande and Dressler (1981) call 'informativity' (stylistic novelty, creativity, non-ordinariness). It is here that literal translation can usefully be put to the test and the range of factors governing its success or failure laid out. (On 'dynamism', see Concept 3.4.)

15.3   Register theory enriched

Since it was first articulated in the early 1960s, 'register' theory has been a rich source of insights, providing both text linguists and translation theorists with a framework that is optimally suited to deal with the kinds of 'departure' outlined above (the motivated departure from lin-guistic norms, the departure from restrictive notions of 'literariness' and 'literary translation', and the departure from a misplaced focus on the translation of static, predictable texts). Register analysis is thus perhaps the single most important contribution that sociolinguistics has made to the study of style, in translation and beyond. But, like 'linguistics', the term 'register' has often been used in a rather indis-criminate fashion (cf. Emery, 1991), and it would therefore be useful at this point to review some of the more important developments that register theory has undergone in the last three decades or so.

The 1980s was an important phase in the development of register analysis. It was felt that basic register factors such as 'field', 'tenor' and 'mode' (Halliday et al., 1964) were not sufficiently differentiated to cap-ture and account for the intricacies of the communicative act (Halliday, 1985; Martin, 1991). Within the new slant, which has proved to be highly relevant to a practice-driven discipline such as translation studies (Hatim and Mason, 1990), 'field' was extended beyond 'subject matter' concerns, and started to be seen in terms of 'representing' the world from a particular perspective, talking 'about our experience of the world, including the worlds in our own minds, to describe events and states and the entities involved in them' (Thompson, 1999: 28). In actual texts, this Hallidayan 'ideational' macro-function is realised by choices from the linguistic system of 'transitivity' which, among other things, can clarify or camouflage who is affected by what (e.g. through such processes as passivisation and nominalisation). Consider, for example, how, through transitivity shifts, the overall thrust of the following source text sample drawn from Arabic historical writing is shifted to serve a noticeably different 'ideological' focus in the English published translation:

> Text 15.1a (back translation of the Arabic source text)
> Subsequently, <u>the British occupying power seized</u> the country's agricultural resources <u>and mercilessly plundered</u> these assets to such a great extent that the occupation increased taxes to three times the rate they were before.
>
> Text 15.1b (published translation)
> Subsequently, the country's agricultural **resources were seized and mercilessly plundered** – to such an extent that taxes **increased** threefold.
> (Dar Al Ma'moun)

Although 'subject matter' remains essentially the same, texts such as the 15.1b (the English target text), dominated by structures such as the **agentless passive** and, perhaps more deviously, the 'ergative' *increased* (in bold), would mark register as a text-in-context configuration with a distinct preference for a style that is dominated by what Hasan (1985) labels an '–ed' role in representing 'agency', as opposed to the –er roles which predominate in 15.1a (the underlined segments in the Arabic source text). Can this 'stylistic' shift in agency be justified by 'historical writing' as the genre into which the translator was working (a question of 'audience design'), or are there hidden ideological motives? (See the discussion of 'interdiscursivity' in Concept 9.5, and 'ideology *in* translation' as opposed to 'ideology *of* translation' in Chapter 10).

Along similar lines to the way 'field' was redefined, 'tenor' was also re-considered beyond the customary 'formal–informal' distinction to include the use of language to interact with other people, to establish and maintain relations of power or solidarity, and to influence or form future behaviour (Thomson, 1996). These 'interpersonal' choices pertain to the linguistic systems of 'mood' and 'modality'. The sparseness or proliferation of 'declarative' sentences or 'usuality' modals, for example, marks texts differently within one and the same register. In the area of 'mood' (type of sentence structure opted for – statement, command, question), text producer-receiver interaction is enhanced immeasurably when an academic writer, for instance, keeps wondering what might happen next, asks 'rhetorical' questions or engages the reader with 'pseudo' commands such as *consider, note here that, bear in mind that*, etc. Modality would also be highly interactive when such 'usuality modality' adjuncts such as *often, frequently, usually*, and 'caused modality' verbs such as *suggest, indicate*, are frequent. Consider the highly interactive tenor (the recurring question–answer pattern and the modality of tentativeness) in the following text excerpts by Oliver Sacks (a neuro-surgeon who, for ideological reasons and to serve his patients better, decided to write 'soulful' medical novellas instead of only 'case histories' about those afflicted with memory loss). Commenting on one of his patients, Sacks asks:

Text 15.2
<u>How could</u> he, on the one hand, mistake his wife for a hat and, on the other, function as a teacher at the Music School?
Sacks (1985, cited in Francis and Krahmer-Dahl, 1992: 63)

In Arabic, a literal translation has, by and large, ensured that almost all the 'interpersonal' values (the 'mood' and 'modality' underlined) are preserved. In a Think Aloud Protocol/Immediate Introspection investigation conducted with the translator trainees assigned the task of translating the text, however, it was revealed that the 'equivalence' achieved at the interpersonal level in this context was invariably hit-or-miss and accidental, and that the majority of the translator trainees tested were not particularly aware of what Sacks was pragmatically seeking to achieve through the kind of style adopted.

The interpersonal text example cited above also illustrates how the register element 'mode' (traditionally seen in terms of the spoken–written medium) can now deal with a much richer ideational and interpersonal input than that simply involving subject matter concerns or formality relationships. Mode now avails the language user of textual, discursive and genre-related resources for structuring texts in much more creative and non-ordinary (i.e. dynamic) ways when communicative needs arise, as in the following example:

Text 15.3a
Neurology and psychology, curiously, almost never talk of 'judgment' – ... <u>and yet it is precisely the downfall of judgment which</u> constitutes the essence of so many neuropsychological disorders.
Sacks (1985, cited in Francis and Krahmer-Dahl, 1992: 64)

Textural cohesion (e.g. the use of the additive-adversative *and yet*), linguistically marked structures such as the cleft *'it is ... which ...,'*, 'theme-rheme' organisation and, most significantly, text structure coherence (the counter-argumentative text format), now play more than a facilitative role (i.e. a simply 'enabling' role, as traditional register analysis advocated). Similarly, intertextuality (i.e. textual allusion) now gives way to deeper levels of what has come to be known as 'interdiscursivity' (Concept 9.5) by which texts become vehicles for the expression of ideology and power relations, conjuring up images of entire discourse, genre and text types in form (e.g. the 'counter-argumentative' structure above) and in substance (discourse thrust) (Fairclough, 2003; Candlin and Sarangi, 2004). This diverse range of features may now all be subsumed under what is being promoted here as 'style'.

Texts in an interactive mode, illustrated by 15.2 and 15.3 above, are likely to be highly evaluative. Consider 15.3a again, and see how **theme-rheme progression** is made more dynamic, with the rheme of the first sentence (in bold) deployed as theme of the subsequent sentence.

Text 15.3a
Neurology and psychology, curiously, almost never talk of **'judgment'**
– and yet **it is precisely the downfall of judgment** which constitutes the essence of so many neuropsychological disorders.

This pattern, which recurs systematically in Sacks' texts, may be illustrated as follows:

T1 *Neurology and psychology* > R1 *judgment*

T2 (R1) *the downfall of judgment* > R2 *which constitutes the essence*

The Arabic rendering by the translator trainees assigned the task of translating 15.3a was problematic: it preserved the counter-argumentative format (. . . *and yet* . . .) and even conveyed a semblance of theme-rheme progression, but completely ignored the **cleft sentence** structure, for example:

Text 15.3b
Neurology and psychology, curiously, almost never talk of **'judgment'**
– and yet **the downfall of judgment** precisely constituted the essence of so many neuropsychological disorders.

This has compromised both the source text 'function' of the counter-argument and the 'discourse thrust' of the polemic involved. There is a world of difference (in 'universe of discourse' terms) between the unmarked:

The downfall of judgment constituted the essence

and the highly marked

it is precisely the downfall of judgment which constituted the essence

Once again, the Immediate Introspection conducted immediately after the above translation was produced revealed that what the majority of the translator trainees assigned the task of translating this text generally got 'right' (the counter-argument, etc.) was incidental, and that what they did not get right (the cleft, preserving text function and discourse thrust), was something the majority were not even aware of.

15.4   The ubiquitous nature of style

One way of demonstrating that style is no longer the exclusive property of literary texts is to line up textual evidence from case studies analysing 'style' in a range of texts and their translations. To make the point that style is simply ubiquitous, the texts selected are drawn from fields as varied as literature and journalism. Admittedly, the majority of the case studies in this chapter report on the analysis and translation of literary texts. But this 'bias' in favour of literary discourse is in itself highly suggestive, and highlights a further point: literary translation has for far too long been seen as a separate, slightly 'elitist', activity engaged in only by the 'gifted' translators, and certainly not amenable to such analytic procedures as those made available by such disciplines as the 'scientific study of language' or linguistics. Such claims are no longer tenable, as this book has made amply clear, and as the following analyses will demonstrate.

Lead Case Study I: 'Dubai and Dunces', *New York Times*, Thomas L. Friedman

The general theme addressed in this case study is the irreparable harm which riding roughshod over linguistically 'marked' or textually 'evaluative' text features does to texts' overall organisation, discourse thrust and genre integrity. The specific aim of the study is to illustrate the subtle translation shifts which result from the translator's obliviousness to relevant 'communicative clues' (see Concepts 8.1 and 8.2), a serious omission which often distorts source and target texts' 'stylistic profiles'. This study uses the Arabic translation of excerpts from an op-ed article by Thomas Friedman, a writer well-known for his highly interactive interpersonal style and for his purposeful manipulation of other ideational and textual resources:

Text 15.4a (English source text)

'Dubai and Dunces', *New York Times, Thomas L. Friedman*

<u>When it came to the Dubai ports issue</u>, the facts <u>never really</u> had a chance <u>– not in this political season</u>. <u>Still,</u> it's hard to imagine a more ignorant, bogus, xenophobic, <u>reckless</u> debate than the one <u>indulged in by</u> both Republicans and Democrats around this question of whether <u>an Arab-owned company</u> might oversee loading and unloading services in some U.S. ports.

Text 15.4b (back translation of Arabic target text)

Dubai Deal: Why don't we admit we have been stupid?

The facts have not had a chance in the debate raging around the question of whether Dubai World might oversee loading and unloading services in some U.S. ports. It's hard to imagine a more ignorant, bogus, xenophobic debate than the one in which both Republicans and Democrats have taken part.

The change in the title of the Arabic translation is a successful inter-personal move, since keeping the source text title as it is would have not only mystified, but perhaps also dulled the senses of, the Arabic reader. But the success stops here.

- All the crucial 'interpersonal' clues (underlined in 15.4a), which cumulatively build up the source text's stylistic profile as an excellent example of reader-friendliness and persuasive argumentation, have been completely glossed over in the Arabic translation: the fronted adverbial and the idiom *it came to*, the use of *never really*, the 'dash' which as a punctuation mark plays an important pragmatic role, and the tongue-in-cheek tone in *not in this political season*. Yet, these lexicogrammatical features collaborate to create solidarity and a highly persuasive tone, and to serve as a 'straw man gambit' (as part of counter-argumentation) in the English source text.

- The 'straw man gambit' is a claim cited to be rebutted, intended to establish common ground with an 'opponent' and thus pave the way for a more credible rebuttal as part of the unfolding counter-argument (*When it came to . . . Still, it's hard . . .*). This is part of the 'textual' dimension of the English source text which, along with the 'interpersonal' dimension, is drastically compromised in this translation.

- On the 'ideational' front, the use of the 'by-agent passive' *indulged in by both Republicans and Democrats* (note the clever choice of *indulge*) is not unmotivated. Nor is the deliberately vague, ironical reference to *an Arab-owned company* (as opposed to using the precise *Dubai*

World). All these important 'stylistic' features are neutralised by a translation which, all in all, may well have done justice to 'what' was said (and even this is arguable), but certainly not to 'how' it was said.

The article is an excellent example of how ideational, interpersonal and textual resources are fully tapped in projecting a style that is 'very Friedman'. For lack of space, this case study will now only focus on those segments that involve 'counter-arguments'. The aim is to see how the translator has fared with this important rhetorical aspect which, although, strictly speaking, part of 'textualisation', is nevertheless not without serious implications for the other two dimensions of any style profile – the 'ideational' and the 'interpersonal'.

(Elements in bold have been preserved in the Arabic rendering. Underlined elements have not been preserved (i.e. omitted or erroneously rendered).)

Text 15.5 (English source text)
What is so crazy about the Dubai ports issue is that Dubai is precisely the sort of decent, **modernising model we** should be **trying to nurture in the Arab-Muslim world. But we've** never really **had an honest discussion about either the** real **problems out there or the** real **solutions,** have we?

Text 15.6 (English source text)
President Bush keeps talking **about Iraq and the Arab world as if democracy alone is the cure** and all we need to do is get rid of a few bad apples. **The problem is much deeper – we're dealing with a civilization that is still highly tribalised and is struggling with modernity. Mr. Bush was right in thinking it is important to help Iraq become a model where Arab Muslims could freely discuss their real problems, the ones identified by Dr. Sultan, and chart new courses. His crime was thinking it would be easy.**

Text 15.7 (English source text)
I don't know how Iraq will end, but I sure know that we aren't going to repeat the Iraq invasion elsewhere anytime soon. Yet the need for reform in this region still cries out. **Is there another way? Yes – nurturing internally generated Arab models for evolutionary reform, and one of the best is Dubai, the Arab Singapore.**

Text 15.8 (English source text)
Dubai is not a democracy, and it is not without warts. But it is a bridge of decency that leads away from the failing civilization described by Dr. Sultan to a much more optimistic, open and self-confident society. Dubaians are building a future based on butter not

guns, private property not caprice, services more than oil, and globally competitive companies, not terror networks. **Dubai is about nurturing Arab dignity through success not suicide. As a result, its people want to embrace the future,** not blow it up.

To conclude this case study, it is apparent that whereas the translator has coped very well with the counter-argumentative aspect of 'textualisation' (usually a blind spot for English and Foreign Language learners and translator trainees), there is a great deal to be desired in attending to the ideational aspect (passivisation, nominalisation, etc.), and, perhaps more seriously, to the interpersonal nuance. It is in the latter aspect of register, expressed through **mood** and **modality**, that argumentative style finds its fullest realisation.

15.5   Interdiscursivity, genre and translation

We have thus far broadly defined 'style' in terms of how the various 'non-ordinary', marked, expectation-defying features of ideational, interpersonal and textual meanings tend to contribute to the way genres, discourses or texts evolve (i.e. establish and assert their identity). To stay with the translation of 'style' as theme, but to focus this time on literary discourse, literary translation and the category 'genre', the following examples are drawn from mini-case studies that could be developed into full-fledged action research projects to be conducted within a framework of reflective practice. In these case studies, it will be apparent that germane to any translation quality assessment is an examination of the extent to which translators have been attentive to the complex web of ideational and interpersonal meanings and to how these become textualised within the norms and conventions of given genres and discourse types (see Concept 9.5 on interdiscursivity).

Three approaches to dealing with stylistic 'non-ordinaries' may be identified. First, there is the *default, non-interventionist approach* through which straightforward literal translation can in most cases account adequately for the intricacies of ST discourse. This is illustrated from the translation into English of an Arabic novella by the Egyptian writer Yahya Haqqi – *Qindil Umm Hashim* (and its English translation *The Saint's Lamp*). The second approach to translating non-ordinariness involves *a mix of interventionist and non-interventionist measures*. This is illustrated from a translation into Arabic of George Orwell's *Nineteen Eighty-Four* (and its Arabic translation *1984*). Finally, there is the *all-out interventionist approach* whereby source text ideational or interpersonal meanings are carefully 're-negotiated' for the target text rendering to be effective, efficient and appropriate textually, discoursally and/or from the viewpoint of genre. This will be illustrated from a translation into English of Albert Camus's *L'Étranger* (and its English translation *The Outsider*).

The three case studies draw on fictional works that have one thematic feature in common: the three novels are about 'outsiders' and about different forms of spiritual alienation and inner passivity. In modern and classical literature, in English and more recently in many languages around the globe, these themes have been elevated to a 'genre', with many and varied manifestations (from horror to absurdist drama). It might therefore be helpful to start with a working definition of 'genre' and with an example of the particular genre which is interdiscursively conjured up by the three case studies occupying us in this section – namely, the **Gothic** genre. This is illustrated from *Melmoth the Wanderer* by the pioneer Gothic writer Charles Maturin.

A standard definition of genre stipulates that three basic elements are usually involved in any generic structure:

- a communicative event or a social function;
- formal linguistic traits;
- textual organisation.

For example, cookery recipes serve a social function (i.e. they represent 'communicative events'). They are written in predictably conventional ways (e.g. the use of the 'imperative' sanctioned in English), and they are textually organised in particular, predictable ways (Bhatia, 2004). This genre identity reflects and is reflected by what we have been referring to generically as 'style' – an assortment of marked ideational, interpersonal and textual values. Consider the 'stylistic' features in the text sample (Lead Case Study II below) of what we readily recognise as an instance of the Gothic genre.

15.6   Case studies

This section will present a number of case studies which, each in its own way, attempt to answer the question raised earlier regarding non-ordinary (i.e. creative) language use: Should the outward form of textual manifestations be preserved in translation? Or, to rephrase the question slightly: Should non-ordinary use of language be translated always as non-ordinary? If 'relevant', of course it should, and literal translation is an obvious procedure. But what if, as regrettably all too often is the case, literal translations turn out to be an unsatisfactory option? What else could the translator do? What are the criteria for the success or failure of literal translation? How could it be best managed? These are all important questions which this chapter has attempted to answer, and to which the following case studies should further respond.

Style in both literary and non-literary contexts will continue to occupy centre stage. Non-fiction has already been covered in the lead Case Study I on Friedman's journalistic article, analysed in 15.4 above. Led by Case Study II on the Gothic genre, the three case studies reported in detail below deal with the theme of 'the misfit': Case Study 1 sees this non-conformist as an 'outsider' (Albert Camus's novel *L'Étranger* and its English translation *The Outsider*); Case Study 2 approaches the issue from the standpoint of 'powerlessness' (George Orwell's *Nineteen Eighty-Four* and its Arabic translation *1984*); Case Study 3 focuses on the theme of 'alienation' (Yahya Haqqi's *Qindil Umm Hashim* and its English translation *The Saint's Lamp*). But first, let us deal with a genre considered to be interdiscursively key to the way these three narratives are crafted – the Gothic.

15.6.1   Lead Case Study II: *Melmoth the Wanderer*, Charles Maturin

Text 15.9
As Melmoth <u>leaned</u> against the window, whose <u>dismantled frame, and pieced and shattered panes, shook</u> with every gust of wind, <u>his eye encountered</u> but that most cheerless of all prospects, a miser's garden, <u>walls broken down, grass-grown walks whose grass was not even green, dwarfish, doddered, leafless trees, and a luxurious crop of nettles, and weeds rearing their unlovely heads</u> where there had once been flowers, <u>all waving and bending</u> in capricious and unsightly forms, as the <u>wind sighed</u> over them

The discursive reality depicted by this kind of literary language use is generally one which immerses its protagonists in morbid feelings. In this text, this sense of 'alienating eeriness' is realised by a process of 'textualisation' which ensures that, whereas Melmoth himself remains inactive (a mere absorber of impressions), his surroundings are perceived as active and sentient (as living beings). The objects in Melmoth's environment engage in incessant activity realised by a proliferation of material processes, with an inanimate agent and an ergative verb (e.g. *frames shook*) (Fowler, 1986).

But, the *frames shook* is hardly a real action. This 'inactivity' has to be explained in terms of the Gothic experience (a genre aptly labelled in many languages as 'the literature of darkness') in which the human agent invariably performs no action that causes a change to any object, and thus does not control his or her environment, nor even interact with it. As indicated above, this is a pervasive stylistic feature in those novels which deal with themes such as 'alienation' (*The Saint's Lamp*), 'passivity' (*Nineteen Eighty-Four*) and 'depravity' (*The Outsider*).

Concept 15.1   **The experiential meaning of transitivity**

A basic property of language is that it enables its users to formulate a mental picture of reality and to make sense of and express what goes on around and inside them. The linguistic system of 'transitivity' has evolved to cater for the expression of this kind of 'experiential' meaning. By 'transitivity' is meant the different types of 'process' that are recognised in the language, and the structures by which they are expressed. Essentially, this system seeks to represent:

1. The process itself.
2. Participants in the process.
3. Circumstances associated with the process.

For example:

    Later my grandfather set up a grain shop in the Square.

Here, *set up* is a process, *my grandfather* and *a grain shop* are participants, and *later* and *in the Square* are circumstances.

In assessing the style of *The Outsider* for example, Material Processes (or processes of 'doing') enjoy a particular status. These processes of 'doing' may be subdivided as follows:

1. Action processes (actor animate)
   i Intention processes (actor performs the act voluntarily)
      I clenched my fist
   ii Supervention processes (process happens independently of volition)
      It rained
2. Event processes (actor inanimate)
     My grip closed

In *Nineteen Eighty-Four* (the case study which follows) transitivity will involve the following ideational resources, in addition to other interpersonal and textual devices:

1. Passivisation.

2. Nominalisation.

3. Depersonalisation.

In the analysis of *The Saint's Lamp*, the final case study, terminology more compatible with the nature of Arabic predicates will be adopted:

1. Transitive Action Predicates in which the actor is inanimate. For example:
   The destructive axe of the town-planning department demolished it together with other old landmarks of Cairo.

2. Intransitive Process Predicates in which, although people act or move, they do not act on things and they move only themselves. For example:
   He would pause and smile, thinking: if only those girls knew how empty-headed they were!

3. Intransitive Process Predicates with an inanimate actor, where not only is the action directed at no one, but it is also done by no-one animate. For example:
   Gradually the square fills anew with people.

15.6.2 Case Study 1: Depravity – *L'Étranger: The Outsider*, Albert Camus

To see ideational, interpersonal and textual processes at work in fictional discourse, we now turn to creative literature, and start with Albert Camus's novel *L'Étranger* and an English translation entitled *The Outsider*.

Text 15.10a
Tout mon être s'est tendu et j'ai crispé ma main sur le revolver. La gâchette a cédé, j'ai touché le ventre poli de la crosse et c'est là, dans le bruit à la fois sec et assourdissant, que tout a commencé. . . . Alors j'ai tiré encore quatre fois sur un corps inerte où les balles s'enfonçaient sans qu'il y parut. Et c'était comme quatre coups brefs que je frappais sur la porte du malheur.

[My whole being tensed and I clenched my hand on the revolver. The trigger yielded, I touched the polished belly of the butt and it is there, in the noise both sharp and deafening, that everything began. . . . Then I fired four more times on an inert body into which the bullets sank without there being a trace. And it was like four brief knocks that I was striking on the door of misfortune.]

Text 15.10b
Every nerve in my body was a steel spring and *my grip closed* on the revolver. *The Trigger gave*, and *the smooth underbelly of the butt jogged in my palm.* And so, with that crisp, whip-crack sound, *it all began.* . . . But *I fired* four shots more into the inert body, on which *they left no visible trace.* And *each successive shot was another loud, fateful rap* on the door of my undoing.

A note on the context and the co-text of the above extract may be helpful at the outset. *L'Étranger* ('The Stranger' or *The Outsider*) is a French novel by Albert Camus published in 1942. The novel is often cited as an example of existentialism, absurdism, even nihilism. The title character, Meursault (a Frenchman in Algeria), kills a local Arab cold-bloodedly. This is a moment in the novel captured poignantly by the above extract, and it is important to understand precisely what happened, since the scene depicted is crucial to an understanding of the translation problem that has arisen.

> Walking back along the Algiers beach alone and armed with a pistol, Meursault encounters the Arab. Meursault is now disoriented on the edge of heatstroke, and when the Arab flashes a knife at him, Meursault shoots. Despite killing the Arab with the first gunshot, Meursault shoots the cadaver four more times. He does not divulge to the reader any specific reason for his crime or the emotions, if any, he experienced at the time aside from the fact that he was bothered by the heat and bright sunlight.

> (Synopsis from Wikipedia)

In a critical translation analysis on which this case study heavily draws, Hatim and Mason (1997: 7–10) describe the ST ideational profile (15.10a) as follows: of the eight *material processes* in the source text, four may be classified as *Event Processes*, and four as *Intention Action Processes*. This transitivity pattern distribution reflects a balance which the novel seems to have struck between two states of mind which the main character might be said to exhibit: Meursault as 'acted upon' vs Meursault as 'acting', as 'driven' by events as opposed to being an active participant in these events.

This ambivalence seems to have been resolved by the translator by leaning heavily on 'passivity' as the key trait of the character, certainly throughout the phase of character development in which the 'shooting of the Arab' takes place. An interesting, if controversial, feature of the translation has to do with the way the translator decided to shift source text transitivity fairly drastically, turning three of the material processes (in which the actor seemingly acts voluntarily) into event processes (in which the actor is inanimate). With two more such processes already there in the source text, the English translation ends up with a total of five processes. The predominant transitivity pattern in the target text is thus one which projects the main character as ' morbidly passive'. All event processes with an inanimate agent are italicised in Text 15.10b, and presented in the following table:

ST *j'ai crispé* ma main	LIT. *I clenched* my hand	TT my grip *closed*
j'ai touché le ventre poli de la crosse	*I touched* the polished belly of the butt	the smooth underbelly of the butt *jogged* in my palm
La gachette *a cédé*	The trigger *yielded*	The trigger *gave*
Que tout *a commencé*	Everything *began*	*It all began*
je frappais sur la porte du malheur	*I was striking* on the door of misfortune	another loud, fateful *rap* on the door of my undoing

This is a bold move on the part of the translator who, to hazard a guess, must have operated with an interdiscourse that highlights being 'acted upon' rather than being an 'actor' as Meursault's key character trait. Interdiscursively, this 'passivity' (which in this context must be understood in the sense of 'mindless', 'unfeeling' passivity) conjures up images of 'depravity', 'bestiality' and 'irrationality'. These are all back-drop themes which the translator seems to have been at pains to exploit by means of what may plausibly be seen as the injecting of the text with a Gothic touch through a sustained shift of source text transitivity.

Thus, the approach to textual or contextual non-ordinariness exemplified by the translation of *The Outsider* represents what might be described as radical interventionism. This procedure aims to produce a target text in keeping with the requirements of an interdiscourse that a literal translation would simply fail to serve.

Concept 15.2   **Mind style**

In proposing the 'mind-style' hypothesis, Fowler (1986: 157) has this to say about the various distinctions within the transitivity system:

> [These] convey different pictures of what is going on in the world. It is easy to imagine the types of mind-styles associated with a dominance of one sort of pattern: predominant action predicates may go with strong physical activity, foregrounded mental processes with an introspective mind-style, and so on.

This hypothesis has had a considerable influence on a range of disciplines (including translation studies) which saw in 'linguistic stylistics' a model of analysis that does justice to the view that language is not neutral with respect to discourse and that, therefore, certain syntactic forms will necessarily correlate with certain interdiscourses. In his analysis of *The Inheritors*, for example, Halliday (1971) finds intransitive structures to be particularly productive in relaying an atmosphere of 'helplessness': 'people act but not on things; they move but only themselves'. In this kind of 'no-cause-no-effect' discourse, moreover, a high proportion of the subjects are not people; they are either parts of the body or inanimate objects. For example:

> *The bushes twitched again*

This and similar analyses demonstrate that what processes, participants and circumstances feature in a text are ultimately responsible for the text producer's attempt to relay feelings of cognitive limitation, of a diminished sense of causation, of an unexpectedly vigorous objective world or of course the opposite of such phenomena.

15.6.3   Case Study 2: Powerlessness – *Nineteen Eighty-Four: 1984*, George Orwell

Having examined the source and target text's ideational (and, by implication, interpersonal and textual) profile in Camus's *The Outsider* as an example of creative fiction, we will now assess the translation of 'style' in *Nineteen Eighty-Four*, a dystopian political fiction written by George Orwell in a fairly new genre – that of Social Science Fiction. The novel depicts a society ruled by a dictatorship – a world of perpetual war, pervasive government surveillance, and incessant public mind control. In the Ministry of Truth, protagonist Winston Smith is a civil servant responsible for perpetuating the Party's propaganda by revising historical records to render the Party omniscient and always correct, yet his meagre existence disillusions him to the point of causing him to rebel against Big Brother. Since its publication in 1949, many of the terms used in the novel (e.g. *Big Brother*, *doublethink*, *Newspeak*) have become part of everyday language. In addition, the novel has promoted *Orwellian* as an adjective which refers to lies and manipulation in the service of totalitarian agendas. It is interesting to note that, in 1998, *Nineteen Eighty-Four* ranked thirteenth on its list of the 100 best English-language novels of the twentieth century.

In this novel, the discursive reality is thus generally one of 'passivity', with Orwellese becoming the predominant interdiscourse. In the original novel, and to serve the theme of a perfectly 'pacified' world and its inhabitants, the ideational resources of transitivity and the interpersonal resources of mood and modality are exploited to the full. Consider how in the following short stretch of text no less than five ideational and interpersonal devices collaborate in serving such themes as 'distance', 'absence of intimacy' and general 'passivity'.

Text 15.11 (ideational profile)

He ... **had been stricken**	Perfect aspect
immediately by **an overwhelming**	Passive voice
desire to possess it. ... At the	Nominalisation
time he was **not conscious** of	Depersonalisation
wanting it for any particular	Negation
purpose.	

In this case study, which draws heavily on an excellent analysis by Daniel Kies (1992), four features are selected for closer scrutiny from a translation quality assessment point of view. The Arabic material scrutinised is taken from one of the published translations.

Text 15.12a (passive voice)
She described to him as if she had seen or felt it ... **Even when her arms were clasped tightly around him.**

(p. 110)

Text 15.12b (back translation from Arabic)
She described to him as if she had seen or felt it ... **Even when her arms were <u>embracing him.</u>**

In the source text, the process of 'clasping' is presented as an **agentless passive**, obviously to show helplessness and the almost total lack of agency. The Arabic target text does not capture the sense of being at the mercy of an outside force. However, the Arabic translation opts for an equally defamiliarising device: the use of an inanimate agent (a body part) causing the action. It is worth noting that this structure is rhetorically alien to the conventions of Arabic, opted for here to ensure that source text 'inaction' is foregrounded. Restoring human agency in the Arabic text is an option open to the translator and perhaps even one that is encouraged by the stylistics of Arabic. Yet, this option was not taken up, which can only point to the translator's critical skills.

Text 15.13a (depersonalisation)
His thin dark face had become animated; **his eyes lost** their mocking expression.

(p. 45)

Text 15.13b (back translation from Arabic)
His thin dark face had started radiating with vitality; **his eyes lost** their mocking expression to appear dreamy.

Overall passivity is compromised in the Arabic version by opting for 'vitality' for 'animated', and 'being dreamy' for eyes losing their 'mocking expression'. However, depersonalisation is ideationally achieved through presenting the action as performed by an inanimate agent (the 'face' and 'eyes') which, as suggested above, is a rhetorically defamiliarising, non-ordinary use in Arabic. It would have been easier and less risky for the translator to restore human agency to the Arabic text, a temptation which, obviously to his credit, was resisted by the translator.

Text 15.14a (Intransitives)
The hallway smelt of boiled cabbage and old rag mats.

(p. 5)

Text 15.14b (back translation from Arabic)
The hallway **from which came the smell** of boiled cabbage and old rag mats.

The source text's use of the intransitive 'smell' to thwart ordinary causation is highly effective, lending the text the passive, suppressed agency needed. This grammatical nuance is preserved in Arabic by a manipulation of word order through which 'the hallway' remained as the 'source of the smell'. It would have been tempting in Arabic (as it always is) to import a spurious agent to perform the action of 'smelling' (e.g. we/one smelt boiled cabbage in the hallway'), but the translator resisted this and in so doing preserved ST discursive thrust.

Text 15.15a (nominalisation)
The stuff was like nitric acid, and moreover, in swallowing it, one had the sensation of being hit on the back of the head with a rubber club.

(p. 8)

Text 15.15b (back translation from Arabic)
The stuff was like nitric acid, and moreover, in swallowing it, one felt as though one was hit on the back of the head with a rubber club.

The source text *sensation* is transformed into 'someone senses or feels'. The indefinite 'someone' goes some way towards creating the air of uncertainty conveyed in the source text. However, the use of the verb 'sensed' serves to compromise full suppression of agency slightly. This is part and parcel of using the indefinite 'one' in Arabic, but in this context it is unfortunate, and an alternative wording could have neutralised agency almost completely.

To sum up, what we have in the present case study is a translator who, overall, shows a remarkably high degree of sensitivity to ST discursive complexity. It might be claimed that all the translator did in dealing with the bulk of this text was just to be literal. This is a cynical view to take, since (1) intervention by the translator is in evidence on a number of occasions, and (2) even when literal translation is opted for, this is done critically since the translator did have at his disposal ample opportunity to adhere to the Arabic style guide and avail himself of options which, if taken up, would have compromised ST discursive thrust.

In this context, it is important to highlight the crucial role played by 'bold' translations of this kind which challenged the rhetorical and fictional canons of Arabic language and literature, in the process enriching the linguistic and literary repertoires with new genres (e.g. the Gothic), new discourses (e.g. passivity) and new text formats (e.g. passives, inanimate agents). Regardless of whether novels or plays such as *1984* or *Waiting for Godot* were translated into Arabic or only read in the original at the time such works appeared in English, one thing is certain: they have left their mark on the style of Arabic fiction and entire literary and linguistic 'models' were borrowed or even calqued by writers eager to experiment and innovate. The next novel to be analysed (*The Saint's Lamp*) is an excellent demonstration of this kind of influence.

Unlike the all-out interventionism of *The Outsider*, the approach to textual or contextual non-ordinariness adopted by the translator of *Nineteen Eighty-Four* represents what may be described as partial interventionism: the translator intervenes as and when the need arises, that is when literal translation simply does not work, or does not even approximate to, the requirements of ST or TT ideational, interpersonal and/or textual values.

15.6.4   Case Study 3: Alienation – *Qindil Umm Hashim: The Saint's Lamp,* Yahya Haqqi

Qindil Umm Hashim (*The Saint's Lamp* in the English translation) is an Arabic novella by the Egyptian writer Yahya Haqqi. In this case study, the novella is subjected to a text, genre and discourse stylistic analysis of the kind introduced above, focusing on the ideational, interpersonal and textual resources deployed. *The Saint's Lamp* is a narrative about a man named Ismail who leaves Egypt for Europe to become an optometrist. Upon his return, Ismail finds that the Cairo he has come back to no longer holds the same appeal for him as before. Ismail no longer finds any relevance in societal and religious customs and traditions. His sense of bitter resentment fuels an inner struggle, and it is this, and the concomitant sense of alienation, that interest us here. The struggle relates to an internal and external striving to find a balance between collectivism and individualism, to reconcile East with West and to come to terms with a struggle between faith vs science. Ultimately it is the 'lamp in the Square' that symbolically provides him with the understanding to reconcile these struggles.

The novella is regarded as one of the most successful examples of prose writing in modern Arabic fiction. In the preface to his English translation (which we shall use throughout to access the Arabic original and assess the translation), University of Cambridge professor, literary critic and translator M. Badawi (1973: ix) observes that the novella is particularly 'rich in sociological significance. . . . It traces the spiritual development of Ismail [the main character], and the development of his social, moral and mental attitudes.' Ismail's 'spiritual' journey is characterised by what may be described as 'alienation' experienced by an Egyptian young man who goes through a phase in which he feels that he simply does not 'belong' (another 'outsider'), a feeling heightened by his exposure to 'Western' models of life and learning. Eventually, Ismail comes to terms with an inescapable reality and becomes happy. But several years of despondency precede this, and it is this period of spiritual hunger and bankruptcy that forms the focal point of the novella.

To set the scene for the analysis of 'alienation' in *Qindil Umm Hashim*, let us consider the following extract from the translation of the novella:

Text 15.16
At these words *silence* fell on the house, *the oppressive silence of the tomb* – that house where dwelt only *the Koran recitations and echoes of the Muezzin announcing prayers*. It was as if *they* all awoke and grew attentive, then were crestfallen and finally put out. In their place reigned *darkness and awe – they* could not live in the same house with that strange spirit that came to them from across the seas.

(*The Saint's Lamp*, pp. 26–7, italics added)

In general, what seems to happen in highly creative literary communication (and without any doubt *Qindil Umm Hashim* falls into this category) is a deliberate and systematic effort to confront, challenge and at times dismantle well-established socio-conceptual structures and to imbue expression with the unexpected and the unfamiliar, turning the ordinary into the unusual and foregrounding the unforeseen. In the ST of the extract cited above and of all the other extracts selected for this case study, the feeling of powerlessness finds its own discourse. This is the world-view expressed through limiting the action to non-human agents and directing it at no one – inanimate non-doers producing only non-events: *silence fell, dwelt only the Koran, they all awoke . . . , reigned darkness . . . , they could not live, strange spirit that came.*

In translation quality terms, Text 15.16 (like all the other texts cited in this case study) is almost a replica not only of what the Arabic says but also of how it says it. This is not surprising since here we are translating for a writer who has already done his ideational, interpersonal and textual 'homework' so meticulously as to reflect with extreme accuracy and succinctness the minutiae of the morbid reality he is trying to depict. The translation has simply emulated this success, and literal translation has worked admirably.

Two important points are worth rising at this juncture. First, as noted above, this particular style (the Gothic-like), at the time of writing this novel (the 1940s), was a newcomer into the rhetorical repertoire of Arabic fiction. Using inanimate subjects as agents, for example, is a stylistic feature that had been shunned by both linguist and critic. The second point relates to whether or not the translator was aware of the intricacies of the discourse and was consciously attempting to preserve the range of features that serve the theme of 'alienation'. This remains a matter of conjecture. However, noting the evidence from the insightful Preface to the translation, the academic status of the sponsoring body which commissioned and published the translation (the well-respected *Journal of Semitic Studies*) and the credentials of the translator, there is absolutely no reason even to suspect that there is a hit-or-miss literal translation or equivalence 'by accident'. The translator refers to the 'alienation' theme and the discourse thrust of the novella in the following terms:

> The problem, therefore, is set in social terms. It is not the eternal silence of the infinite spaces that terrifies Ismail, but the silence of the people around him, the absence of communication with his own family, the discovery that he has become déraciné, an outsider among his kith and kin.
>
> (Badawi, 1973: x)

This sense of alienation includes the trials and tribulations of Ismail on his spiritual journey. With this as a backdrop, the Square becomes the vantage point from which to observe Ismail's inner-world unfolding.

Although the Square is presented to us initially as a haven of peace, human agency is conspicuous by its absence:

Text 15.17
Later my grandfather set up shop in the Square. Thus our family lived within the precincts of the Saint's mosque and under her protection. The Saint's feasts and calendar became ours and the calls of the Muezzin our only clock.

(TT, pp. 1–2)

Notice how, apart from the first clause, the subjects are not people and the predicates are not of the 'action' type: *lived* is an intransitive process, and *became* a copular intransitive process. It is also worth noting that both verbs are 'ellipted' when a second event comes along: *and lived under her protection; and the calls of the Muezzin became our only clock*. The ellipsis seems to further highlight the prevalent atmosphere of ineffectual activity.

In another passage, non-human agency also dominates, except for an initial clause with the intransitives *stroll* and *stand*. Uncannily reminiscent of Melmoth's *leaning against the window*, the phrases *strolling by the Nile and standing on a bridge* are hardly 'actions':

Text 15.18
His greatest pleasure was to stroll by the river, or stand on the bridge. At nightfall, when the heat of the sun had gone and the sharply-etched lines and reflected light changed to curves and vague shadows, the square came into its own, ridding itself of strangers and visitors.

(TT, p. 5)

But, this peace, fragile as it is, is also short-lived. The Square introduces the necessary element of doubt and foreboding and, through the 'reflexive', signals the ultimate in combining activity with powerlessness and displaying inner strife:

Text 15.19
Gradually the square fills anew with people, weary figures, pale of face and bleary-eyed. They are dressed in what clothes they can afford, or if you prefer it, in whatever they have been able to lay their hands on. There is a note of sadness in the cries of the street-hawkers.

(TT, p. 5)

Here, subjects are not people, even when 'they' are dressed; they are 'figures', with *they* conceptually referring to the 'weary figures'. Furthermore, none of the subjects is engaged in actions with consequences. In fact, nothing seems to be under the control of the principal subject, which is in any case inanimate: even the clothes those poor people in the Square wore amounted to nothing more than 'whatever they have been able to lay their hands on'.

In conclusion, in examining the language of a small section of the novella (and further research is needed into this fascinating novel and fascinating textual phenomenon), one particular feature stands out. This is the predominance of intransitive process predicates which reflects the limits on people's actions and their world view. In an intransitive structure, the roles of 'affected' and 'agent' are combined. This clearly indicates total absence of cause and effect: people do not act on things around them, they act within the limitations imposed by these things. The domination of the people by their environment is embodied in the syntax.

This pervasive reading may be contrasted with the world of 'cause and effect' outside the Square, post alienation, towards the end of the novella:

Text 15.20
Ismail set up a clinic in Al-Baghalla district, near the hills, in a house that was fit for anything but receiving eye patients. His fee never exceeded a piaster per consultation. Among his patients there were no elegant men and women, but they were all poor and bare-footed. Oddly enough, he became more famous in the villages surrounding Cairo . . .

He performed many difficult operations successfully using means which would make a European doctor gasp in amazement . . .

Ismail married Fatima and she bore him five sons and six daughters.

(p. 38)

As indicated above, all these textual (ideational and interpersonal), discoursal and genre-related values have been preserved by the translator through what we might refer to as the non-interventionist approach, with formal equivalence adopted throughout. But not all texts or languages avail the translator of such one-to-one fit. Passivity, alienation and so on may be dealt with differently in other languages, and to approximate 'other' styles interdiscursively in translating into English (e.g. Gothic), major textual surgery may be required, as Albert Camus's *L'Étranger* text and its translation has demonstrated.

As we near the end of this tour through translation studies' 'house of many rooms', we cannot help but notice how we are conceptually turning full circle back to where we started, to Catford, Nida and Koller, and to basic distinctions such as 'formal' as opposed to 'dynamic' or 'pragmatic' equivalence, all revolving around the age-old distinction 'free' as opposed to 'literal' translation. Obviously, a great deal has happened along the way and a number of translation theories, including polysystems and *skopos*, have posed a serious challenge to traditional concepts of equivalence. At no stage, however, has equivalence been abandoned or text classification altogether jettisoned. On the 'equivalence' front, Stecconi (1994/1999: 171) has perceptively argued that 'in most Western cultures today, equivalence is that unique intertextual relation that only translations, among all conceivable text types, are expected to show'. On text typologies, the consensus among all those involved with languages in contact seems to be that language users are text users and that for intercultural communication to run smoothly, there has to be an awareness of how texts are used by real people in real communication – a premise upon which we in translation studies seem to have agreed all along.

15.7   Exemplar research projects

Any of the works examined in the above case studies (Thomas L. Friedman's op-ed, *Melmoth*, *The Outsider*, *1984*, *The Saint's Lamp*) could be subjected to further analysis and closer and more systematic scrutiny, with such aims as:

1. Ascertaining whether extensive stretches of source text material will show different and more varied ideational, interpersonal and textual resources, depicting characters' inner worlds and deployed consistently to perform the functions claimed for them in the above case study reports.

2. Assessing translations into a diverse range of world languages, in terms of how translators have actually dealt with source text multilayered universes of discourse and genre structures, as well as the textual, interpersonal and ideational resources deployed.

To demonstrate how such research questions might best be pursued, the following are suggestions that might serve both as areas for further research and as general 'how-to' research guidelines. The research projects chosen and introduced briefly here can be developed into fuller studies, possibly to appear as publishable articles, conference presentations, end-of-term papers or dissertations.

15.7.1   Research Project 1: Golding's *The Inheritors*

Practitioner-led action research of the kind outlined in the above case studies will inevitably be interdisciplinary. It will involve:

1. Translation theories of equivalence, and of the status of formal equivalence vs literal translation along the lines proposed above.

2. Text linguistics (on textuality), genre theory (on genre norms and conventions) and Critical Discourse Analysis (CDA) on interdiscursivity, form vs function, ideational resources such as Transitivity (passivisation, etc.) and interpersonal resources relating to Mood and Modality.

3. Studies in Literary Criticism and Linguistic Stylistics.

To illustrate this element of interdisciplinarity, and particularly how insights from linguistic stylistics (which has brought together the two perspectives of CDA and literary criticism) can potentially provide researchers with the necessary theoretical underpinnings and analytical tools, it might be helpful to recall briefly the 'mind-style' hypothesis explained above. Essentially, this suggests that the predominant use of certain linguistic structures can serve as an important indicator of participants' mental states or inner worlds (Fowler, 1986: 157). A concrete example of mind-style studies, would be Halliday's pioneering analysis of transitivity in William Golding's *The Inheritors*. On the basis of a fairly extensive sample of this text, it is concluded that intransitive structures tend to relay an atmosphere of 'helplessness' in which the majority of 'subjects' are not people, but, for example, either parts of the body or inanimate objects.

Informed by this kind of insightful analysis and the mind-style hypothesis, you might now want to consult a translation or more than one translation done into your own language, a language of habitual use, or a language you know well, and systematically assess how the translators have coped with the style of such a novel:

- Is source text's ideational profile preserved and, if any shifts are in evidence, what are the reasons for such shifts? Are the reasons:
  - linguistic (to do with the non-availability of the formal means of expressing transitivity, for example)?
  - rhetorical (whether the use of available forms is sanctioned as inappropriate in such contexts)?
  - pragmatic (whether the use of available forms would not secure uptake and acceptability on the part of the target language user)?
  - interdiscursive (to do with the difficulty of securing target language discourse or genre equivalence due to the unavailability or inaccessibility of such macro-structures in the target language)?

- In cases in which source text discourses and genres could against the odds make their presence felt in the target text and thus break through barriers in the target language linguistic and rhetorical repertoires, what implications might such bold innovations have or actually have had on language use or literary competence in the receptor languages?

In connection with this, it may be useful to point out that, if published translations do not exist, valuable research could still be done by assigning relevant stretches of texts to groups of professional or novice translators (or both) to translate. A pre-test and a post-test research methodology might be used, with the two kinds of test separated by workshops that seek to raise discourse and genre awareness and thus enhance competence in these areas. The ultimate goal would be to assess differences in translation quality that are bound to emerge as a result of being exposed to theoretical input. Think Aloud Protocols or Immediate Introspections could consolidate this kind of research in translator decision making, as explained in Chapter 12 (12.2).

15.7.2   Research Project 2: Hemingway's *A Movable Feast*

The kind of practitioner-led action research advocated would thus primarily seek to demonstrate that the types of 'processes', 'participants' and 'circumstances' which predominantly feature in a text ultimately reflect the text producer's attempt to depict such feelings as 'cognitive limitation' and a 'diminished sense of causation', or indeed an unexpectedly vigorous 'objective world', for example. To stay with literature for one more example, and to illustrate further how the steps outlined above might be pursued in actual action research projects, consider the linguistic stylistics of another well-known novel – Ernest Hemingway's *A Movable Feast*. Dealing with this work would mark a shift of analytic focus from the literature of 'morbidity' and 'darkness' to the literature of 'light' and 'vitality', from passivity and the suppression of human agency to full and vigorous activity, from the Gothic and Orwellian to a style remarkable for its energy.

With Hemingway, both text and genre work in tandem to serve an overarching discourse and thus enable the full expression of a powerful theme: the American Dream and how it is the 'male' protagonist (not the 'Mrs' at home or the 'girl friend' sipping juice in a café) who is behind the fulfilment of the nation's hopes and aspirations (Fowler, 1986: 166). This blatantly 'sexist' attitude, which has gone largely unnoticed by translators for a long time, is camouflaged by a veneer of textualisation which ensures that sentences are remarkably short and pointedly sharp. Ideationally, women are mostly perceived in a 'patientive' role, leaving their male counterparts to enjoy extraordinary 'activity'.

> Text 15.21
> A girl **came** in the café and **sat** by herself at a table near the window. She **was** very pretty with a face fresh as . . . I looked at her and she disturbed me and made me very excited. I wished I could put her in the story, or anywhere, but she had **placed** herself so she could **watch** the street and the entry of the café and the entry and I knew she was **waiting** for someone. So I went on _writing_.
>
> (*A Moveable Feast*, p. 13)

By contrast with stories narrated from the point of view of an 'omniscient' narrator with a privileged access to the characters' inner states of mind, the narrators in Hemingway's works say little about the characters' thoughts and feelings: the narrative is 'objective' or 'external' (Fowler, 1986: 166). In this kind of storytelling, a particular view of 'causation' seems to be promoted. In ideational terms, there is one dominant transitivity structure: the majority of clauses would present the main protagonist as an agent of physical actions affecting material objects in some way:

> Nick dropped his pack
> He took the axe out
> He smoothed out the sandy soil

All the predicates designate 'manual' actions literally involving the character in using his hands, while objects affected are items of his kit. The effect is of a sharp focus on a neat sequence of precise activities. Other predicates are no less deliberate: *looked for*, *wanted to*, etc. All in all, intentions are conscious, with an almost total absence of mental states or mental process predicates. Introspection and evaluativeness are minimal.

In concrete terms, all sentences are declarative, with the elements Subject, Verb, Object occurring most often in the order SVO. Furthermore, all clauses are in active voice, with no passive structure to disturb the SVO order. Agency is human, the hallmark of a tough, action-packed style. This is in stark contrast to those contexts which narrate women's 'doings': the female is subject to actions realised by 'patientive' verbs of a kind which shows introspection and passivity. Given Hemingway's preoccupations and his own image (i.e. his own persona, his discourse), this labour sharing between men and women is not unmotivated.

The Arabic translation presents the girl in a much more 'active', 'forceful' light than was intended in English. In fact, the Arabic translation, if anything, projects an equally strong image for both male and female protagonists, a focus not intended in the source. In part, this may be explained in terms of the nature of Arabic narrativity which tends to be stylistically more formal than its English counterpart. But, if aware of the discourse and genre intricacy at work in this piece of writing, the translator could have found numerous ways of circumventing this problem and foregrounding the salience of activity vs inactivity. The end result may not have been well received by the Arabic critical establishment, but the translator would have been on record as having made a bold, innovative move, as we have seen in the case Orwell in Arabic.

The discussion conducted so far of the various translations has highlighted one important point – namely, that the single most pressing challenge facing literary translators, researchers, trainers and trainees alike, is the need to demystify the skills involved and make them more amenable to description and critical analysis. Ultimately, however, the analysis cannot be exclusively 'linguistic'. Other factors are heavily involved, including the literary traditions in both source and target cultures, stylistic preferences in the source and target languages and the purpose of the translation.

This brings us closer to the area of common ground and shared interest between the translation of fiction and non-fiction. Take 'alienation' or 'marginalisation' as an example of inner feelings, and consider how the expression of such feelings by a writer can have serious implications for linguistic realisation in terms of **transitivity**, **mood**, **modality**. Is this an exclusively 'literary' issue? As the huge body of literature on Critical Discourse Analysis makes abundantly clear, devices such as the suppression of agency, obfuscating nominalisations, impersonalisation intended to deflect attention from certain issues or shift responsibility for certain actions, are not unheard of in various non-fictional discourses and genres (Fairclough, 1989/2001, 1993). Politics, journalism and advertising are but a few examples of areas of language in social life that could be investigated for texts which promote certain world views and in the process demote others through manipulating **ideational**, **interpersonal** and textual meanings, as the above case studies show for fiction (Toolan, 1992).

Further reading

- On linguistic criticism, Critical Discourse Analysis (CDA), genre theory, text analysis and other areas of particular relevance to the student of stylistics, see Fowler (1996), Toolan (1992), Carter et al. (2001), Martin (1991).

- On literary translation and the ramifications surrounding the issue of style, mind style and literary translation in general, see Baker (2000, 2004), Boase-Beier (2003, 2006).

IV Links and resources

Chapter 16

Resources

16.1 Links and resources

16.1.1 Translators' professional organisations

ADTI (Aquarius Directory of Translators and Interpreters) (Vorontsoff, Wesseling and Partners, Amsterdam)

AIIC (Association Internationale des Interprètes de Conférence). An organisation established in 1953 to protect the interests of conference interpreters:
   http://www.aiic.net

AITC (Association Internationale des Traducteurs de Conférence). An organisation headquartered in Switzerland, which includes translators, précis-writers, editors and revisers:
   http://www.aitc.ch

AITI (Associazione Italiana Traduttori e Interpreti). An organisation with a highly informative site, including rates schedule and extensive list of links:
   http://www.mix.it/AITI/AITI.htm

ALTA (American Literary Translators' Association). Site includes mission statement, officers, membership information:
   http://www.pub.utdallas.edu/research/cts/alta.htm

Aslib, The Association for Information Management, and *The Translator's Handbook*:
   http://www.aslib.co.uk/

ATA (American Translators' Association). Accreditation, conferences, publications:
http://www.atanet.org

ATICOM (Association of Professional Freelance Translators and Interpreters, Germany):
http://www.aticom.de

ATTI (Associazione Italiana Traduttori e Interpreti) (Luigi Muzii, Rome)

ARISA (American Translation and Interpreting Studies Association)

BCLT (British Centre for Literary Translation (University of East Anglia, Norwich)

CSTS (Canadian Society for Translation Studies):
http://137.122.12.15/Docs/Societies/CATS

CTIC (Canadian Translators' and Interpreters' Council):
http://www.synapse.net/~ctic/

CTS (Center for Translation Studies (University of Texas at Dallas)

CIUTI (Conférence Internationale d'Instituts Universitaires de Traducteurs et Interprètes):
http://wwwbzs.tu-graz.ac.at/ciuti

EFSLI (European Forum of Sign Language Interpreters

ESIST (European Association for Studies in Screen Translation)

EST (European Society for Translation Studies):
http://est.utu.fi/

EUK (Europäisches Übersetzer-Kollegium) (Straelen)

ESTS (European Society for Translation Studies) (University of Turku, Finland)

FIT (Fédération Internationale des Traducteurs). An international association of translator organisations founded in Paris in 1953. *Babel*, which started in 1955, is the official journal of FIT:
http://fit.ml.org

IAPTI (International Association of Professional Translators and Interpreters)

IATIS (International Association of Translation & Intercultural Studies)

IL (Institute of Linguists) (London)

ITI (Institute of Translation and Interpreting) (London)

ITIA (Irish Translators' and Interpreters' Association) (Dublin)

ITA (Irish Translators' Association). Constitution (in English and Irish), etc.:
   http://homepage.tinet.ie/~translation

ITI (Institute of Translation and Interpreting) UK:
   http://www.iti.org.uk

JAIS (Japan Association for Interpretation Studies)

KSCI (Korean Society of Conference Interpretation)

LTAC/ATTLC (Literary Translators' Association of Canada). Model contract, links, etc.:
   http://www.geocities.com/Athens/Oracle/9070/

QTIAQ (Quebec Translators):
   http://www.otiaq.org/

SINTRA (Brazilian Translators' Association). Bi-monthly newsletter, events, market rates in Brazil:
   http://www.sintra.ong.org/

Translation Centre (University of Massachusetts, Amherst):
   http://www.umass.edu/transcen/

TTA (The Translators Association) (London)

UBS (United Bible Societies):
   http://www.ubs-translations.org/

WASLI (World Association of Sign Language Interpreters)

WATA (World Arab Translators' Association)

16.1.2 Translators' discussion groups

Babels

Beacon for Freedom of Expression Project

Bahtera (Indonesian Language Mailing List):
   majordomo@lists.singnet.com.sg

British Centre for Literary Translation

Brussels Tribunal
  Majordomo@lists.singnet.com.sg

BIBLIA (Italian Literary Translators' Mailing List):
  http://web.tiscalinet/it/Handa

ECOS (traductores e intérpretes por la solidaridad)

FLEFO (Foreign Language Forum of CompuServe). The largest meeting
point of translators in Cyberspace:
  http://world.compuserve.com

German U-Forum:
  Listserv@twh.msn.sub.org

Hebrew Translators' Mailing List:
  Bebtranslators-subscribe@makelist.com

Hungarian Translators' Mailing List:
  Mfefo@egroups.com

Ibérica Mailing List. Mailing list for translators into and from Portuguese
and/or Spanish:
  http://www.rediris.es/list/info/iberica.html

Katha: Language, Culture, Translation

Lantra-L Mailing List. This relays about 150 messages a day on a
variety of topics, including terminology and business practices:
  LISTSERVE@segate.sunet.se

Poets against the War

Spanish Translators' Mailing List. Although designed with Spanish–
English translators in mind, this site is evolving fast: members can
exchange glossaries, trade tips, discuss ethics and client issues, etc.:
  http://www.eGroups.com/list/sptranslators

The Lysistrata Project

Tlaxcala: the Network of Linguistic Diversity

Traductores sen Fronteiras (TsF)

Traduttori per la pace/Translators for Peace

Translation, Interpreting and Social Activism

Translations for Progress

The Translation Studies Portal

16.1.3 Translators' educational resources

Chris Rundle's Subtitling Project

CyberBabel

E-Arabic Learning Portal (Mourad Diouri, CASAW, University of Edinburgh)

Federico Zanettin's Teaching Resources

Institut für Übersetzer und Dolmetscherausbildung of Innsbruck University. This site provides useful links to translation resources (universities, terminology, mailing and discussion lists, translation aids):
    http://info.uibk.ac.at/c/c6/c613/tranlink.html

Inttranews

Literary Translation (British Council)

MuTra conferences (High Level Scientific Multidimensional Translation Conferences)

NextPage

PEN (Translation)

Robert Bononno's Home Page. List of schools that provide training in translation worldwide:
    http://pages.nyu.edu/~rb28/t-schools.html

SignedLanguage

The Edward Said Archive

Translate: Project on Cultural Translation

Translation Quality Blog

Translational English Corpus

Translog

University of Hull Directory of Stage Translators

Universität des Saarlands. The site offers one of the most complete lists of translators' resources on the Web:
http://www.uni-sb.de/philfak/fb8/fr86/deutsch/www.htm

Universität Stuttgart, Institut für mascinelle Sprachverarbeitung. The site provides information about computational lexicography and research in machine translation:
http://www.ims.uni-stuttgart.de

University of Tampere doctoral theses

Translation Directory.com

16.1.4   Corpora

British National Corpus:
http://info.ox.ac.uk/bnc/

Catalogue of Electronic Texts on the Internet:
http://www.lib.ncsu.edu/stacks/alex-index.html

COBUILD The Bank of English:
http://titania.cobuild.collins.co.uk/

English Language Corpora:
http://info.ox.ac.uk/bnc/corpora.html

English Server Fiction: Novels:
http://eserver.org/fiction/novel.nclk

E-Text Archives Gopher:
Gopher://gopher.etext.org/

Linguistic Data Consortium:
http://www.Idc.upenn.edu/

Project Gutenberg e-texts:
http://www.pjbsware.demon.co.uk/gtn/index.htm

Religious Texts:
Gopher://locust.cic.net/11/

16.1.5   Translators' publications

The Electric Editors. A UK-based Web resource for publishing professionals and linguists, with a macro library and other services, including three mailing lists dealing with publishing, languages and computers:
http://www.ikingston.demon.co.uk/ee/home.htm

Language International. A demo version of the well-known Language International (John Benjamins Publishers), presenting summaries of articles from current and back issues and other relevant information:
http://www.language-international.com/

Rancho Park Editors. A collection of links to translators' organisations, dictionaries, glossaries and other resources:
http://www.ranchopark.com/translatorlinks,html

16.1.6 Publishing houses

The following publishers have book series in Translation Studies.

John Benjamins, The Netherlands:
http://www.benjamins.nl/

Multilingual Matters, UK:
http://www.multi.demon.co.uk/index.html

Rodopi, The Netherlands:
http://www.rodopi.nl/home.html

Routledge, UK/USA:
http://www.routledge.com/routledge.html

Stauffenburg, Germany:
http://www.stauffenburg.de

St Jerome, UK:
http://www.mcc.ac.uk/stjerome

TEXTconTEXT: http://www.t-online.de/home/textcontext/

16.1.7 Translation research

CETRA (Centre d'Etudes sur la Traduction, la communication et les cultures, Leuven, Belgium):
http://www.arts.kuleuven.ac.be/CETRA/

Ring of Translation Research:
http://www.ul.ie/~neylonm/transresearch.html

This includes home pages by:

- Jean Delisle (including a list of publications and ongoing projects)
- Michele Neylon (particularly the translation of fictional dialogue – Spanish to English)

- Helga Niska (papers and links on community and conference interpreting, terminology and computer-aided translation)
- Anthony Pym (the history and sociology of translation, including a list of translation schools)
- Gideon Toury (information and useful links; the author's latest papers will soon be on-line)
- Federico Zanettin (of interest to translators and interpreters, on-line language teaching and learning, translation and technology, corpus linguistics, etc.)

16.1.8 Translation journals and periodicals

Babel

Intralinea

Meta

Target: International Journal of Translation Studies (John Benjamins, Amsterdam)

The Translator: Studies in Intercultural Communication (St Jerome, UK)

Translation Studies Abstracts (St Jerome, UK)

TRANSST. An international newsletter of translation studies, published by the M. Bernstein Chair of Translation Theory and the Porter Institute for Poetics and Semiotics, Tel Aviv university, and edited by Gideon Toury and Jose Lambert

Transcript, the European Internet Review of Books and Writing

Words Without Borders

16.1.9 Online translation journals

This is a list of peer-reviewed online Translation Studies journals. All are open access, though in some cases there is a firewall in place for recent issues. The journals are in alphabetical order.

1611: A Journal of Translation History

Babilónia. Revista Lusófona de Línguas, Culturas e Tradução

Cadernos de Tradução

Cultus

Confluências

Doletiana

Glottopol (sociolinguistics journal; sometimes carries useful translation articles)

Intralinea

I.U. Journal of Translation Studies (Istanbul University)

Journal of Specialised Translation

Journal of Translation (on Bible translation)

New Comparison, the journal of the British Comparative Literature Association, includes some translation articles:
  http://www.bcla.org/index.htm

New Voices in Translation Studies

Meta (recent issues are firewall-protected)

MonTI (issues online six months after publication)

Mutatis Mutandis

New Voices in Classical Reception Studies (includes articles on translation)

Palimpsestes (some issues online at the http://www.revues.org open-access journals site)

Quaderns: revista de traducció

Revista de Lingüística y Lenguas Aplicadas

Revista Electrónica de Didáctica de la Traducción y la Interpretación

Revista tradumàtica : traducció i tecnologies de la informació i la comunicació

Scientia Traductionis

SKASE Journal of Translation and Interpretation

Tradução em Revista

Trans

trans-kom

TranscUlturAl

Translation & Interpreting. The international journal of Translation and Interpreting Research

Translation Today

Transversal, published by the European Institute for Progressive Cultural Policy

TTR (recent issues are firewall-protected)

16.1.10   Online glossaries and dictionaries

Eurodicautom Online Dictionary. Terminology database of the European Community, and online dictionary for the languages of the EC:
  http://eurodic.ip.lu

Manon Bergeron's Index of Financial Glossaries. A comprehensive list of financial and business glossaries classified by subject matter:
  http://mabercom.com

Microsoft's Computer Glossaries. Downloadable computer-related glossaries in 29 languages:
  ftp://ftp.microsoft.com/developer/msdn/newsup/glossary/
  bab.la dictionary (Dictionaries in many languages)

Ready Reference Collection (The Internet Public Library, University of Michigan):

European mirror (Lund University, Sweden)

Study Web

Virtual Reference Desk (Bob Drudge, refdesk.com)

Acronyms and Abbreviations (University College Cork)

Biographical Dictionary

Brewer's Dictionary of Phrase and Fable (bibliomania.com)

CIA World Factbook

Internet Dictionary Project (Tyler Chambers)

Internet Encyclopedia of Philosophy (ed. James Fieser, University of Tennessee at Martin)

Language Dictionaries and Translators (Word2Word Language Resources, San Jose, CA)

LOGOS online multilingual dictionary (Modena, Italy)

The Online English Grammar (Anthony Hughes)

Oxford Companion to English Literature

The Quotations Page (Michael Moncur)

Roget's Internet Thesaurus (thesaurus.com)

WWWebster Dictionary (Merriam-Webster's Collegiate Dictionary)

WWWebster Thesaurus (Merriam-Webster)

16.1.11   Video resources – interviews

http://www.est-translationstudies.org/resources/videos.html

Interviewees on the page:

Alexander, Neville

Austermühl, Frank

Chesterman, Andrew

Cronin, Michael

Even-Zohar, Itamar

Feinauer, Ilse

Gambier, Yves

Gile, Daniel

Hermans, Theo

Hodgson, Robert

Hönig, Hans

Jettmarová, Zuzana

Kiraly, Don

Kurz, Ingrid

Lambert, José

Marais, Kobus

Mason, Ian

Melby, Alan

Mikkelson, Holly

Milton, John

Nord, Christiane

O'Brien, Sharon

Pöchhacker, Franz

Schäffner, Christina

Shlesinger, Miriam

Tabakowska, Elżbieta

Takeda, Kayoko

Toury, Gideon

Trivedi, Harish

Wolf, Michaela

Ye, Zinan 叶子南

Zeng, Liren

16.1.12   Translation Studies research groups

Advanced Translation Research Group (ATRC) (Saarbrücken)

Avances en traducción e interpretación (AVANTI) (Granada)

Center for Research and Innovation in Translation and Translation Technology (CRITT) (Copenhagen)

Corpus-based Translation Studies (Ghent)

Culture and Translation (Ghent)

Expertise and Environment in Translation (PETRA) (Las Palmas de Gran Canaria)

Frå språk til språk: forskingsgruppe i omsetjingsvitskap og kontrastiv lingvistikk (Oslo)

Hermeneutics in Translation Studies (Darmstadt, Cologne, Freiburg)

Historia de la traducción en Iberoamérica (Alicante)

Iberian-Slavonic Translation Studies (International Society for Iberian-Slavonic Studies)

Intercultural Studies Group (Tarragona)

Interpreting and Translation Research Group (Sydney)

Language and Translation Technology (Ghent)

Machine translation group (Dublin)

Meaning and Understanding across Cultures (Oslo)

Procés d'adquisició de la competència traductora i avaluació (PACTE) (Barcelona)

Reception Studies and Descriptive Translation Studies (Lisbon)

Research Centre for Translations (RCT) (Institute of Chinese Studies, The Chinese University of Hong Kong)

Statistical machine translation group (Edinburgh)

Textual genres for translation (Castelló, Spain)

Traducción e historia en las culturas hispánicas (Barcelona)

Traducción y paratraducción (Vigo)

Tradumatica: Translation and new technologies (Barcelona)

Translation and interpreting (Aarhus)

Translation and linguistics (Durham)

Translation and reception in Catalan literature (Barcelona)

Translation and transcultural contact (York, Canada)

Translation Studies research group (Salford)

Transmedia

Transmission, Translation, and Transformation in Medieval Cultures (McGill, Canada)

Seminario de investigación en la historia de la traducción e interpretación (Valparaíso)

Voice in Translation (Oslo)

16.1.13   Translation Studies bibliographies

BITRA: Free online bibliography with abstracts, managed by Javier Franco (Universitat d'Alacant)

TSB: Translation Studies Bibliography, commercialised by John Benjamins

EST Recent publications: A list of references of recent publications with summaries and/or reviews

16.1.14   Translator-Training Observatory

This list is maintained by the Intercultural Studies Group under the auspices of the European Society for Translation Studies and the Training and Qualification Committee of the Fédération Internationale des Traducteurs (FIT)

Further information can be found in this American list of Graduate Schools, in the ATS list, and in this list of programs in the US

16.1.15   Miscellaneous translators' resources

CyberBabel. An original site by Hazem Azmy (Egypt), with a rich network of links classified by type:
http://victorian.fortunecity.com/postmodern/242/cyberbabel.html

Eva Easton's Site. Aimed mostly at language teachers, this site is also useful to translators: English grammar, glossaries, etc. in many languages:
http://eleaston.com/

Financial Translators' Page. A site by Jarry Beek listing links to sites of interest to financial translators and translators in general, classified by subject matter:
http://www.euronet.nl/~jarryb

Glenn's Guide to Translation Agencies. In addition to agencies, this site contains useful advice to beginning translators, links to dictionaries and databases, reference resources and information on specific countries:
http://www.glennsguide.com/

The Human Language Page. A comprehensive website featuring translation and language-related links, classified into linguistic, commercial, educational, etc.:

http://www.june29.com/HLP/

Translate. An attractive site by Eduardo e Tamara Barile (São Paulo, Brazil), offering useful information on links classified by category:

http://www.translate.com.br/

The Translators' Home Companion. One of the more established translators' web resources, offering useful links, dictionary reviews, etc.:

http://www.rahul.net/lai/companion.html/

16.2   Glossary of text linguistics and translation terms

Terms in bold are defined or illustrated within the entries in which they occur. Terms in italics are defined elsewhere in the glossary and readers are urged to refer to the relevant entries for further details.

Acceptability A standard of *textuality* which all well-formed texts must meet, and which stipulates that the diverse range of purposes served by the text are accepted as 'intended'. This is counter-balanced by **intentionality**, a standard which stipulates that utterances must be designed in such a way as to reflect the purposes for which they are used. Both 'acceptability' and 'intentionality' are *pragmatic* constructs. Thus, a joke or a witty remark that does not elicit the desired effect in an audience is a case of something 'intended' but perhaps not communicated well enough to be 'accepted'.

Action In German functionalist theories of translation, translation action is conceived primarily in terms of a process of intercultural communication, the end product of which is a text capable of functioning appropriately in specific TL contexts of use (see *Skopos*).

Action Research In research methodology terms, 'action' is understood in the sense of the intention to bring about positive change. Action research is collaborative and practice-driven, seeking solutions to problems within a practice–theory–practice cycle.

Actual Language 'use', in contradistinction with language 'usage', the latter normally seen at a virtual, systemic level. The 'virtual' aspect relates to the language system before *context* is brought to bear on the process of text reception or production. For example, the Arabic concept 'jihad' is 'holy war' at a 'virtual' level (i.e. etymologically). In 'actual' language use, however, 'jihad' is often associated with 'concerted effort'.

Agent Deletion The omission in a passive sentence of the noun or noun phrase which follows *by*, e.g. *the reasons outlined* (by the writer). Such uses of the grammar can be ideologically motivated.

Agentless Passive See *Agent Deletion*

Analytical Knowledge Knowledge acquired or conveyed through a process of reasoning (e.g. in the field of translation, the trainee is constantly invited to reflect on why this word and why here). This is to be distinguished from 'craft knowledge' which is usually acquired through experience and conveyed intuitively.

Appropriateness This emanates from a trade-off between *efficiency* (largely *form*-based) and *effectiveness* (largely *content*-based). 'Shut up!' may well be **efficient** but it is certainly not **effective** as a sign, hence the 'appropriateness' of silence which is effective and efficient, as well as appropriate.

Audience Design Catering through texts for the communicative needs of an audience made up not only of hearers/text receivers but also of invisible sectors such as over-hearers, etc.

Back-transformation A kind of paraphrase in which surface structures are replaced by other, more basic structures (e.g. even nouns into verbal expressions).

Binary A division in terms of 'either/or' not 'more-or-less' (e.g. binary errors to do with the grammatical system, as opposed to non-binary errors located at the level of discourse).

Brief or **commission** Statement of the communicative purpose for which a translation is needed. This is usually seen in the light of clients' requirements.

Canon Texts considered part of the heritage of a particular community and thus mandatory reading in school and university curricula.

Cleft Sentence A sentence in two parts, each with its own verb, to emphasise a particular piece of information, e.g. *it was Mrs. Smith who gave Mary the dress.*

Closeness of Fit The degree of structural or lexical compatibility across different languages.

Code Switching A change by a speaker (or writer) from one language or language variety to another.

Cognitive Has to do with the organisation of language and mind in terms of such templates as *schemata, scripts, frames.*

Coherence See *Cohesion*

Cohesion A standard of *textuality* which all well-formed texts must meet and which stipulates that a sequence of sentences display a range of grammatical and/or lexical relationships, to ensure surface structure continuity. For example:

    A. *Where have you been?*
    B. *To the Empire.*

In this exchange, there is an 'ellipsis' linking *have been* in A's utterance with B's *to the Empire*. This accounts for 'cohesion'. **Coherence**, on the other hand, is a standard which caters for the conceptual relatedness of meanings at deeper levels, stipulating among other things that the grammatical and/or lexical relationships involve the conceptual meanings of the various elements of text and not only continuity of surface *forms*. Thus, the ellipsis in the above exchange could conceivably be seen as conveying 'marital tension', a function of 'coherence'.

Commission See *Brief*

Communicative See *Context*

Communicative Clues Grammatical and lexical features which indicate the purposes for which utterances are used (e.g. the use of parallel structures or alliteration to convey irony).

Compensation Manipulating a text to make up for the loss incurred by the act of translation.

Competence A person's ability at the *virtual* level to create and understand sentences, a sequence of sentences, etc., in contradistinction with **performance** involving *actual* language use. Thus, whereas 'competence' subsumes the knowledge we consciously and subconsciously possess about how to speak a language, 'performance' has to do with our real world linguistic output. Performance may accurately reflect competence, but it may also include speech errors due to slips of the tongue or external factors such as memory problems and limitations.

Competence See *Textual Competence*

Componential Analysis Breaking down lexical items into their basic elements of meaning.

Connectivity See *Cohesion*

Connotation, Connotative Meaning Additional meanings which a lexical item acquires beyond its primary, *referential* meaning, e.g. 'notorious' means 'famous' but with negative connotations.

Connotation The additional meanings that a word or phrase has beyond its central meaning.

Content See *Form*

Context This includes aspects of message construction involving the various standards of *textuality*. Three 'contextual' domains may be distinguished: *communicative*, including aspects of the message such as *register* membership; *pragmatic*, including *intentionality*; and *semiotic*, including *intertextuality*. These factors may also be seen in terms of **cotext**, the language which occurs immediately before or after a particular textual or linguistic unit, and which can influence the particular forms used.

Contrastive Textology Using parallel texts of various kinds (e.g. bilingual or texts drawn from the same language and serving similar functions as the basis of contrastive analysis within and across different languages).

Cotext See *Context*

Core Linguistics An approach to linguistics which stresses the importance of language as a system and which investigates the place that linguistic units such as sounds, words and sentences have within the system.

Covert Translation Term coined by Juliane House (1977). A translation which conceals anything that betrays the foreignness of a ST. Unlike *overt* translation, a covert translation approximates as far as possible to original writing.

Critical Linguistics The analysis of language use with the aim of discovering concealed ideological bias.

Cross-cultural Pragmatics The study of culturally different ways of using language, and of different expectations among different members of linguistic communities regarding how meaning is negotiated.

Cultural Objects Cultural *signs* which tend initially to lack dynamism and are thus normally catalogued in lists of the 'culturally quaint' (*kufiyya*, *'iqal* – 'an Arab's head gear'). These 'socio-cultural' entities are concepts related to such aspects of social life as material culture, institutions, ecology, etc. Cultural objects may be compared with textual practices which imply a dynamic process of signification in which signs are best viewed as 'acts' intended to perform some *function* in some *context*. Practices are socio-textual and cover both the *form* and the function of what we do with words when expressing an attitude or conveying a perspective or *discourse* (e.g. religious fundamentalism) or operating within the conventions of a *genre* (e.g. the fairy tale).

Deconstruction A method of reading a text by highlighting apparently peripheral elements in order to bring out concealed meanings of an ideological nature: no text has a fixed or stable meaning.

Defamiliarisation The effect produced by opting for *marked* (i.e. expectation-defying) structures (e.g. repetition, parallelism).

Deictic Deixis literally means 'pointing via language', with the deictic function normally performed by pronouns (*he*, *she*) or demonstratives (*this*, *that*).

Deviation A departure, which tends to be agreed upon usually implicitly, from a linguistic *norm*, convention or standard of acceptable *form*, content or rhetorical organisation. Deviations normally occur for a 'good reason' (i.e. both *marked* and *motivated*), mostly to do with pursuing a particular rhetorical aim. For example, a cleft sentence structure or a cataphora (linguistically *marked*) is invariably used for rhetorical effect (i.e. *functionally*).

Diction The choice of words to achieve particular effects.

Direct Translation In Vinay and Darbelnet's taxonomy, it is a translation method that encompasses calque, borrowing and literal translation. In *relevance* theory, direct translation is a kind of translation performed in situations where we need to translate not only what is said, but also how it is said. In machine translation, it is the replacement of an ST item by a TL item as a word-for-word translation.

Directionality A term which refers to whether translation occurs into or out of the translator's native language (or language of habitual use). See *inversa translation*

Discourse The use of language in speech or writing to relay attitudes and negotiate meaning in the light of social conventions. Discourses are modes of speaking and writing which involve participants in adopting a particular attitude towards areas of language in social life (e.g. racist discourse, bureaucratese). The minimal unit of discourse analysis is the discourse 'statement' (e.g. the racism of a remark).

Domain In register analysis, an area of professional activity in which one particular language variety or a combination of varieties is regularly used (e.g. legal English).

Domesticating Translation, Domestication A translation strategy, discussed by Venuti (1995), in which a transparent, fluent style is adopted in order to minimise the foreignness of an ST. See *Foreignising Translation*

Effective See *Appropriate*

Efficient See *Appropriate*

Evaluativeness See *Markedness*

Expressive Function Language used to express feelings, with formal properties being at least as important as their meanings.

Field of Discourse An element of *register*, basically covering subject matter, but may go beyond this to include aspects of perceiving the world from the perspective of social institutions and social processes at work. These are part of the *ideational* resources of meaning, serving an *ideational function*.

Firthian Linguistics A school of linguistics also known as functional linguistics, which examines features of language use with reference to their social functions in communication (J.R. Firth and M.A.K. Halliday being the main proponents).

Focus A phenomenon related to how information is distributed in sentences, and how certain parts of the sentence are marked as being more 'salient' than others (e.g. *it is the man sitting on the left who objected* vs *The man sitting on the left objected*).

Foregrounding See *Defamiliarisation*

Foreignising Translation, Foreignisation A translation which seeks to preserve 'alien' features of an ST in order to convey the 'foreignness' of the original. Discussed in Venuti (1995). See also *Domestication*

Form Elements of abstract linguistic systems, and features of language and internal relations between these features within the system, as distinct from such categories as *content* which deal with meanings; see *Core Linguistics*. Form may also be contrasted with **function**, a user-oriented notion indicating the 'meaning' that the text has for the receiver, and the use to which a text is put. Function also subsumes the 'purposes' for which utterances are used.

Formal Linguistics The study of abstract linguistic systems features of language and internal relations between these features within the system.

Frame One of various *cognitive* templates tapping 'knowledge of the real world'. Frames are pre-existing knowledge structures with fixed static patterns, e.g. a restaurant frame or *script*.

Free Translation A type of translation in which more attention is paid to producing a TT which reads naturally than one which adheres closely to ST wording.

Function See *form*

Functionalism A descriptive approach to translations and translation action, which takes the intended function of the target text to be over-riding in translator decision making.

Gender The term is used to designate the socio-cultural attitudes which go with biological sex, and the effects which these might have on linguistic expression.

Genre Conventional forms of text associated with particular types of communicative events (e.g. the news report, the editorial, the cooking recipe).

Gloss Translation The kind of translation which aims to reproduce as literally and meaningfully as possible the form and content of the original (as a study aid, for example).

Gothic A fictional genre which makes salient the characters' morbid feelings and general passivity.

Graphological Related to the writing system and spelling.

Hermeneutics A model which considers the act of translation in the wider context of human communication across barriers of language, culture, time and personality.

Hierarchy of Correspondences The order of priorities set up by the translator, who has to decide which ST features to preserve in TT, possibly at the expense of other features (Holmes 1971).

Hybridisation Texts are not purely this or that type, but a mixture, bearing traits of different types.

Iconicity A *semiotic* notion which refers to a natural resemblance between the form of a sign (*'signifier'*, be it a letter or sound, a word, a structure of words, or even the absence of a sign) and the object or concept (*'signified'*) it refers to in the world or rather in our perception of the world (e.g. onomatopoeia, 'cuckoo').

Ideational Function See *Field, Metafunctions*

Ideology A body of assumptions which reflect the beliefs and interests of an individual, a group of individuals or an institution.

Illocutionary Force See *Speech Act*

Imitation A type of interpretation in translation which involves, for example, the creation of a new poem, where only such aspects as the title or point of departure might be preserved from the ST.

Implicature When cooperative *maxims* are 'broken' or 'violated', there is no indirect, implied meaning (*or implicature*) to be detected. *Implicatures* only arise when the 'maxims' are 'flouted' (i.e. not adhered to for a good reason). For example, to say *the evil of the two lessers*, 'flouts' the cooperation maxim 'manner' by deliberating speaking unidiomatically, and in the process conveying the implied meaning (*implicature*) that 'we do not have much of a choice, say, between two candidates; neither of them is any good'). See *Maxims*

Indirect Translation A translation which responds to the urge to communicate as clearly as possible. See *Direct Translation*

Inference The text receiver's use of additional knowledge to make sense of what is not explicit in an utterance.

Informativity A standard of *textuality* which all well-formed texts must meet, and which determines the extent to which items of linguistic expression in a text are known/unknown, expected/unexpected. See *Deviation*

Intentionality See *Acceptability*

Interpersonal Function Language used to regulate the level of communicative intimacy between text producer and text receiver. See *Solidarity, Metafunctions*

Intertextuality A standard of *textuality* which all well-formed texts must meet, and which deals with the dependence of one text or part of text upon other previously encountered texts.

Invisibility A term adopted by cultural studies to describe translations which tend to be heavily domesticated (i.e. which read as an original).

Kernel The most basic syntactic representation of a sentence's deep structure.

Knowledge of the World A *pragmatic* concept denoting the acceptance of certain belief systems and the various *schemata, frames, scripts* involved.

Langue The abstract linguistic system which underlies language use.

Lexico-grammar An innovative, more *functional* approach to the study and description of the grammar and vocabulary of a language which emphasises continuity rather than discontinuity in grammatical and lexical descriptions through the study of collocations and idioms, or the analysis of syntactic function, for example.

Literal Translation A translation strategy in which a text (or part of a text) is subjected to translation at a low level of linguistic organisation (e.g. the level of the word).

Locutionary Force See *Speech Act*

Macro- The *micro*-level involves an orientation to the description of language use at lower levels of linguistic organisation (the sound, the word, the phrase as part of *texture*). This is in contradistinction with **macro**-level phenomena as clause relations and genres. See *Macro-structure*

Macro-structure The way a text is structured in outline form, and the patterns yielded at this level of coherence (e.g. the argumentative pattern Claim > Counter-claim).

Managing Whereas **monitoring** is a non-evaluative and detached treatment of a particular discourse topic, as in 'conceptual exposition' and some forms of 'narration' and 'description', managing is an evaluative approach to discourse, as in 'position-argumentation'. See *Markedness*

Markedness An aspect of language use where some linguistic features are highlighted when used in a non-ordinary (i.e. less 'basic' or less 'preferred' than stipulated by the >NORM). For example, *it was Mary who stole the purse* as a 'marked' variant of the 'unmarked' *Mary stole the purse*.

Maxims According to American language philosopher Paul Grice (1975: 45), 'cooperation' stipulates that language users make [their] conversational contribution such as is required, at the state at which it occurs, by the accepted purpose or direction of the talk exchange in which [they] are engaged.

To achieve this, language users tend to heed four maxims:

1. Quantity: Make your contribution as informative as (but not less or more informative than) is required.
2. Quality: Do not say what you believe to be false, or that for which you lack adequate evidence.
3. Relation: Be relevant.
4. Manner: Be such that the intentions you have for what you say are plainly served.

These are theoretical postulates which state ideal *norms* that, in practice, may be broken (inadvertently), violated (when a *deviation* from the *norm* of adhering to them is not communicated properly), or flouted intentionally, giving rise to *implicatures*.

Mentifacts A term used together with the related terms *sociofact* and artefact to describe how cultural traits, such as beliefs, values, ideas, take on a life of their own spanning over generations, and are conceivable as objects in themselves. See also *Cultural Objects*

Metafunctions As functional components of the semantic system, these are modes of meaning that are present in every use of language. Thus, the *ideational function*, which emanates from *field of discourse*, represents the speaker's meaning potential as an observer: language is about something (e.g. *Ten Blacks Shot By Police* vs *Police Shoot Ten Blacks* are two different ideational structures, catering for two different ideological perspectives). The *interpersonal* component, which emanates from *tenor of discourse*, represents the speaker's meaning potential as a social actor: language as a means of 'reaching out' or 'holding back' (e.g. different uses of *modality* relay different shades of *power* or *solidarity*). Finally, the *textual* component, which emanates from *mode of discourse*, represents the speaker's text-forming potential: how texts are made both relevant and operational (e.g. choices of what occupies the slot 'theme' in the sentences of a text is an orchestrating, textual consideration).

Micro See *Macro-*

Mind Style The use in a *defamiliarising* way of certain linguistic features which would then become characteristic of a particular text (e.g. passivisation in George Orwell's *1984*).

Modality The use of language to indicate attitudes of the speaker/writer towards the state or event expressed by the use of language in question.

Mode of Discourse See *Register*

Monitoring See *Managing*

Mood Type of sentence structure (is a sentence cast in the form of a question, a command or a simple, straightforward declarative 'statement'?).

Motivated The 'good reason' principle in using language to serve given rhetorical functions in a contextually determined manner, particularly when *violations* of *norms* are involved.

Narrative Voices Different perspectives from which characters in a narrative are portrayed.

Norms Linguistic conventions which subsume what is considered *appropriate* for a particular situation or purpose in speech or writing. These conventions may be seen in terms of implicitly agreed-upon standards of acceptable content and rhetorical organisation. But conventions can be deviated from for a 'good-reason' mostly to do with pursuing a particular rhetorical aim.

Overt Translation See *Covert Translation*

Paratextual Features Forms of glossing such as translator prefaces, footnotes.

Parole The actual use of language by an individual.

Patriarchal Language Established, refined and regulated language use traditionally taught and used. It is male-biased, excluding or denigrating references to women or women's activities.

Performance See *Competence*

Performative An utterance which performs an act (e.g. *Watch* out = 'warning').

Persuasive A text function (to be distinguished from the **informative** function), with 'persuasion' invariably admitting and encouraging *marked* use of language as an interest-arousing ploy, and more.

Poetics The linguistic study of norms governing literary norms.

Politeness A *pragmatic* phenomenon which involves rhetorical purposes such as 'deference' for the addressee, and 'showing awareness' of another person's public self-image. Politeness theory is centred on the notion of 'face' and the need to establish, maintain and save face during inter-action with others (e.g. We generally avoid asking personal questions of strangers). Two main factors regulate the degree of 'imposition' which is ideally kept to a minimum: *power* and *solidarity*. Any irregularity in handling these two constructs (e.g. being too soft or over-friendly) would result in failure to mitigate the degree of imposition in a wide range of what are known as Face Threatening Acts (FTAs).

Polysystem The term refers to a perspective or strategy in literary analysis informed by the fact that any literature comprises not only the traditional (canonic) genres but also many other popular forms ranging from sacred texts to soap operas. In dealing with translation within this approach (which has come to be replaced by the label Descriptive Translation Studies), more attention is given to the target text than to the source text, and to such *paratextual features* as the notes appended to translations.

Positivism A trend in the human sciences which emphasises the scientific, objective nature of enquiry.

Power In the analysis of *politeness*, *tenor* or, more specifically *interpersonal function*, two basic types of relationship may be distinguished: **power** and solidarity. 'Power' emanates from the text producer's ability or desire to impose his or her plans at the expense of the text receiver's plans. 'Solidarity', on the other hand, is the willingness on the part of the text producer seemingly or genuinely to relinquish power and work with his or her interlocutors in a spirit of cooperation.

Pragmatics The study of the purposes for which utterances are used. With *speech acts* as the minimal unit of analysis, pragmatics hinges on the notion of **intentionality**, which concerns the purposes for which utterances are used.

Propositional Related to the basic meaning which a sentence expresses.

Pseudotranslations Target-language texts regarded as translations, though no genuine source texts exist for them.

Re-writing *Metalinguistic* processes, including translation, which can be said to reinterpret, alter or generally manipulate text to serve a variety of ideological motives.

Redundancy Repetition in utterances to avoid a high information load.

Referential To do with the relationship between words and the things, actions, events and qualities they stand for. See *Denotation*

Register The set of features which distinguish one stretch of language from another in terms of formal variation to do with the language 'user' (geographical dialect, idiolect, etc.) and/or with language 'use' (*field* or subject matter, *tenor* or level of formality and *mode* or speaking vs writing).

Relevance In cognitive linguistics, the principle of relevance derives from the tendency on the part of communicators to expect maximal benefit for minimal effort and to increase the effort only if more benefit is in store.

Resistant Translation Involving unidiomatic usage and other linguistically and culturally alienating features in the translated text so as to create the impression of foreignness.

Rhetorical Purpose The function a text is intended or perceived to fulfil in use. See *Text Type*

Salience A process of rhetorically underscoring and specifying certain concepts. See *Markedness, Deviation*

Scale and Category Grammar See *Systemic Functional Grammar*

Schemata A *cognitive* template tapping knowledge of the 'real world'. Schemata are pre-existing knowledge structures based on experience with language use in given cultural settings (e.g. stories, descriptions).

Script A **cognitive** template tapping knowledge of the 'real world'. Scripts are sequences of events and actions and the way they relate to different situations viewed from a cross-cultural perspective (e.g. bargaining, protesting). For example, a text may be structured around the 'restaurant script' which represents our knowledge of how restaurants work: waitresses, cooks, and tables where customers sit, peruse menus, order their meals and pay the bill at the end.

Semantic The study of deeper layers of word meanings.

Semiotic Related to *signs* and their function in the use of language e.g. what the word-*sign honour* would mean to an Englishman, an Argentinian, and an Arab; see *Sign*

Semiotics A discipline for the study of *signs* in society, yielding insights into what might considered an important dimension of context which regulates the relationship of texts to each other as signs. Semiotics thus relies on the interaction not only between speaker and hearer but also between speaker/hearer and their texts, and between text and text. This *intertextuality* is governed by a variety of *socio-cultural* factors (e.g. *politeness*), and *rhetorical purpose* (e.g. the way news reporting is done in a given language). These factors and conventions are ultimately responsible for the way *socio-textual practices* develop within a given community of text users (see *genre, text, discourse*).

Short-term Memory That part of memory where information received is stored for short periods of time while it is being analysed and interpreted.

Sign A *semiotic* construct comprising two components, in which the linguistic form (the 'signifier') stands for a concrete object or concept (the 'signified'). When the notion of sign is extended to include anything which means something to somebody in some respect or capacity, signs could then be used to refer to all kinds of socio-cultural objects (e.g. the concept of *honour* (as a *micro*-sign) and what it would mean to an Englishman, to an Argentinean, to an Arab). At a higher level, signs become intertwined with global structures such as *text, genre* and *discourse* (*macro*-signs), and even to more global structures such as that of Myth.

Signified See *Signifier*

Signified See *Sign*

Signifier The sequence of sounds (or graphic signs) by which a speaker refers to a physical entity or abstract concept. The concrete object or abstract idea referred to by the signifier is known as the signified (e.g. the word *star* – a signifier – may be used to convey the idea of a 'luminous heavenly body' – its signified).

Situationality A standard of *textuality* which all well-formed texts must meet, and which captures the relatedness of utterances to the situation in which they occur.

Skopos A theory which holds that translation strategy is determined by the function of the translated text, which may not be the same as that of the source text.

Socio-cultural Concepts related to material culture such as institutions, ecology, etc. This is distinguished from *socio-textual practices* (e.g. *discourse, genre*).

Socio-textual Practices covering the *form* and *function* of what we do with words when expressing an attitude (Discourse) or operating within the conventions of *genre*. These are distinguished from the purely *socio-cultural*.

Socio-facts See *Mentifacts. Socio-cultural Objects*

Solidarity See *Politeness*

Speech Act An action performed by the use of an utterance in speech or writing, involving 'reference' and 'effect'. A distinction is made in speech act theory between a **locutionary** act (the act of saying something – e.g. it is hot in here), an **illocutionary** act (what is intended by the locutionary act – 'please open the window'), and a **perlocutionary** act (what the ultimate effect could be – demonstrating who is 'boss' around here).

Straw Man Gambit The thesis is set up to initiate a line of argumentation which involves opposition to the thesis cited.

Stress Accentuating a certain part of the utterance, giving it more prominence.

Structuralism Proponents of structuralism would argue that a specific domain of culture may be understood by means of a structure – modelled on language – that is distinct both from the organisations of reality and those of ideas in the mind. See *Transformational-Generative Grammar*

Subtitling A method of language transfer used in translating types of mass audio-visual communication such as film and television.

Syntactic Structures, Syntax The grammatical structures and arrangements of elements in a language or text.

System The abstract linguistic system which underlies language use.

System-oriented Related to factors such as linguistic *competence* which is an essentially abstract representation.

Systemic Functional Grammar .A systemic-functional theory of language advanced by M.A.K. Halliday in the latter part of the twentieth-century. Halliday focuses on language in use, as a communicative act, and describes three strands of functional meaning co-occurring in a text: *ideational, interpersonal* and *textual*.

Technical Rationality See *Analytical Knowledge*

Tenor of Discourse See *Register*

Text A set of mutually relevant communicative functions that hang together (*texture*) and are put together (*structure*) in such a way as to respond to a particular *context* and thus achieve an overall **rhetorical**

purpose. For example, in response to a Claim which the text producer thinks is flawed, he or she may attend to Counter-Claim as a rhetorical purpose, which entails the use of particular evaluative forms of linguistic expression with a particular structure format: Claim–Counter-claim–Substantiation. The minimal unit of text analysis is the text element (e.g. thesis cited to be opposed).

Text Linguistics A discipline (to be distinguished from *core linguistics*) dealing with modern interdisciplinary concerns relating to *text* in *context* and how these issues intimately relate to each other in highly diverse and systematic ways, and are closely bound up with language in social life.

Text Structure The compositional plan of a text. Different **text types** exhibit different structure formats. Some of these are formulaic as in the structure of the Preamble: 'X and Y, having met . . . , Considering, Re-emphasising, . . . have agreed . . .'. Other formats are less formulaic, though fairly predictable. For example, a *managing* Counter-argument has the following structure: 'Thesis Cited, Opposition, Substantiation, Conclusion'. A *managing* Through-argument simply has 'Thesis Cited, Thesis Extensively Defended'. *Monitoring* texts, on the other hand, displays the most open-ended of formats; for example, 'Scene Set, Aspects of the Scene Set'.

Text Type The way *text structure* and *texture* are made to respond to *context*, displaying a particular text-type focus. Three basic text-types may be distinguished: exposition, argumentation and instruction.

Textual Competence The ability not only to apply the lexical and grammatical rules of a language in order to produce well-formed sentences (linguistic *competence*) and to know when, where and with whom to use these sentences (sociolinguistic competence), but to know how to make an utterance play a role within a sequence of utterances that eventually becomes part of a well-formed *text*, *discourse* and *genre*.

Textual Function The use of language in the creation of well-formed texts.

Textuality Models of textuality essentially recognise seven primarily relational standards which all well-formed texts must meet in one way or another: *situationality, cohesion, coherence, intentionality, acceptability, intertextuality, informativity*.

Texture Aspects of text micro-organisation which contribute to the overall effect of texts hanging together internally, reflecting *coherence* and *cohesion* and responding to *context*. Texture includes aspects of the message such as *Theme-Rheme* organisation, as well as text idiom and *diction*.

Theme-Rheme Two terms which represent the way in which information is distributed in a sentence. Theme is given information serving as the point of departure of a message. Rheme is the remainder of the message in a clause in which Theme is developed. For example:

Theme	*Rheme*
The lion	beat the unicorn all round the town

Thick Translation, Glossing, Commentary A translation that seeks through annotations and accompanying glosses to situate the text in its rich cultural and linguistic context.

Transformational-Generative Grammar A theory of grammar proposed by the American linguist Noam Chomsky in 1957. Chomsky attempted to show how, with a system of internalised rules, native speakers of a language put their knowledge to use in forming grammatical sentences. He proposed a two-level structure for the sentence: the 'surface structure', which is the linguistic structure we see or hear, and the abstract 'deep structure' of basic elements that is used for *semantic* analysis.

Transitivity A *core-linguistic* category relating to the number and type of objects required by a verb phrase. Transitivity patterns can contribute to the development of a certain *mind style* which characterises the work of a particular author or text.

Type-Token Ratio A measure of the ratio of different words to the total number of words in a text, sometimes used as a measure of the difficulty of a text.

Universals of Translation Linguistic features which typically occur in translated rather than original texts and are thought to be independent of the influence of specific language pairs.

Universe of Discourse The entire domain, field, institutional framework and cultural context surrounding a text.

Vocative A kind of hortatory text. See *Text Type*

Word Play A stylistic device using alliteration or other forms of phonological manipulation to produce added meanings.

References

Adab, B.J. (1996) *Annotated Texts for Translation: English-French*. Clevedon: Multilingual Matters.

Ahlsvad, K.-J. (1978) Translating into the translator's non-primary language. In Horguelin, P. (ed.), pp. 183–8.

Amman, M. (1990) Anmerkungen zu einer Theorie der Ubersetzungskritik und ihrer oraktischen Anwendung, *TEXTconTEXT* 5: 209–50.

Anderman, G. and Rogers, M. (Eds) (1990) *Translation in Teaching and Teaching Translation Vol. II: Translation in Language Teaching and for Professional Purposes.* Surrey: University of Surrey Centre for Translation and Language Study.

Appiah, K.A. (1993) Thick translation. *Callaloo*, 16 (4): 808–19.

Argyris, C. and Schön, D. (1978) *Organization Learning: A Theory of Action Perspective.* Reading, Mass.: Addison Wesley.

Arrojo, R. (1994) Fidelity and the gendered translation. *Traduction, Terminologie, Rédaction*, 7 (2): 147–64.

Arrojo, R. (1995) Feminist, orgasmic theories of translation and their contradictions. *TradTerm*, 2: 67–75.

Arrojo, R. (1996) On perverse readings, deconstruction, and translation theory: A few comments on Anthony Pym's Doubts. *TradTerm*, 3: 9–21.

Arrojo, R. (1997) Asymmetrical Relations of Power and the Ethics of Translation. *TEXTconTEXT*, 11: 5–24.

Arrojo, R. (1998) The revision of the Traditional Gap between Theory and Practice and the Empowerment of Translation in Postmodern Times. *The Translator*, 4: 25–48.

Austin, J. (1962) *How to do Things with Words.* Oxford: Clarendon.

Badawi, M.M. (1973) *The Saint's Lamp*. Leiden: E.J. Brill.

Baker, M. (1992) *In Other Words: A Coursebook on Translation.* London and New York: Routledge.

Baker, M. (1993) Corpus Linguistics and Translation Studies: Implications and Applications. In Baker et al. (eds).

Baker, M. (1995) Corpora in Translation Studies: An Overview and Some Suggestions for Future Research. *Target*, 7 (2): 223–44.

Baker, M. (1996) Linguistics and Cultural Studies: Complementary or Competing Paradigms in Translation Studies? In Lauer et al. (eds), pp. 9–19.

Baker, M. (1997) Corpus-based translation studies: The challenges that lie ahead. In Somers, H. (ed.), pp. 175–86.

Baker, M. (2000) Towards a methodology for investigating the style of a literary translator, *Target* 12 (2): 241–66.

Baker, M. (2004) The status of equivalence in translation studies: An appraisal, in Jose Maria Bravo (ed.) *A New Spectrum of Translation Studies. Valladolid: Universidad de Valladolid.* Pp. 63–71.

Baker, M., Francis, G. and Tognini-Bonelli, E. (eds) (1993) *Text and Technology: In Honour of John Sinclair.* Amsterdam and Philadelphia: John Benjamins.

Baker, M. and Saldanha, G. (2009) (eds) *Routledge Encyclopedia of Translation Studies.* Routledge: London & New York.

Bassnett, S. (1980, 1991) *Translation Studies.* London: Routledge.

Bassnett-Maguire, S. (1980) *Translation Studies.* London: Methuen.

Bassnett, S. and Lefevere, A. (eds) (1990a) *Translation, History and Culture.* London and New York: Pinter.

Bassnett, S. and Lefevere, A. (1990b) Introduction: Proust's Grandmother and the Thousand and One Nights. The 'cultural turn' in translation studies. In Bassnett and Lefevere (eds), pp. 1–13.

Bassnett, S. and Lefevere, A. (1998) *Constructing Cultures: Essays on Literary Translation.* Clevedon: Multilingual Matters.

Bauer, H. (2003) Not a translation but a mutilation: the limits of translation and the discipline of sexology. *Yale Journal of Criticism*, 16 (2): 381–405.

Beaugrande, R. de (1978) *Factors in a Theory of Poetic Translation.* Assen: Van Gorcum.

Beaugrande, R. de (1980) *Text, Discourse, and Process: Toward a Multidisciplinary Science of Texts.* Norwood, NJ: Ablex.

Beaugrande, R. de (1989) Coincidence in translation: Glory and misery again. *Target*, 3, 17–53.

Beaugrande, R. de (1995) *A New Introduction to the Study of Text and Discourse.* London: Longman.

Beaugrande, R. de and Dressler, W. (1981) *Introduction to Text Linguistics.* London: Longman.

Beaugrande, R. de, Shunnaq, A. and Heliel, M. (1994) *Language, Discourse and Translation in the West and Middle East.* Amsterdam: John Benjamins.

Beeby, A. (1996) Course profile: Licenciature en traduction e interpretacion, Universitat Autonoma de Barcelona, Spain. *The Translator*, 1: 113–26.

Beeby, A. (2003) Genre literacy and contrastive rhetoric in teaching inverse translation. In Kelly, D. et al. (eds), pp. 155–66.

Bell, R.T. (1991) *Translation and Translating: Theory and Practice.* London: Longman.

Berman, A. (1985/2000) Translation and the trials of the foreign (trans. L. Venuti). In L. Venuti (ed.).

Bettelheim, B. (1983) *Freud and Man's Soul.* New York: Alfred Knopf.

Bhatia, V. (2004) *Worlds of Written Discourse: A Genre-Based View.* London; Continuum.

Bhatia, V. (2002) Legal Discourse across Multilingual, Multicultural, and Socio-political Contexts. University of Illinois, Urbana-Champaign, USA, 17–20 October.

Bhatia, V., Candlin, C., Engberg, J. and Trosborg, A. (eds) (2003) *Multilingual and Multicultural Contexts of Legislation.* Frankfurt am Main: Peter Lang.

Bhatia, V.K., Candlin, C. and Engberg, J. (2008) *Legal Discourse Across Cultures and Systems*. Hong Kong: Hong Kong University Press.

Blum-Kulka, S. (1986) Shifts of cohesion and coherence in translation. In House and Blum-Kulka (eds), pp. 17–35.

Boase-Beier, J. (2003) Mind style translated, *Style* 37 (3): 253–65.

Boase-Beier, J. (2006) *Stylistic Approaches to Translation*. Manchester: St Jerome.

Bolton, G. (2010) *Reflective Practice, Writing and Professional Development* (3rd edition). Ithaca, NY: Cornell University Press.

Boud, D., Keogh, R. and Walker, D. (1985) *Reflection, Turning Experience into Learning*. London & New York: Routledge.

Britton, J. (1963) Literature. In J. Britton (ed.), pp. 34–61.

Britton, J. (ed.) *The Art and Current Tendencies in Education*. London: Evans.

Broeck, R. van den (1978) The concept of equivalence in translation theory: Some critical reflections'. In J.S. Holmes, J. Lambert and R. van den Broeck (eds).

Bronowski, J. and Mazlish, B. (1974) *Western Intellectual Tradition from Leonardo to Hegel*. New York: Harper-Row.

Bruce, D. (1994) Translating the commune: Cultural politics and the historical specificity of the anarchist text. *Traduction, Terminologie, Rédaction*, 1: 47–76.

Bruce, D. and Butler, T. (1993) Towards the discourse of the commune: Characteristic phenomena in Jules Valles's *Jacques Vingtras*. *Texte* (13).

Bühler, K. (1934) *Sprachtheorie [Language Theory]*. Jena: Fischer.

Burns, A. (2010). *Doing Action Research in English Language Teaching: A Guide for Practitioners*. New York: Routledge.

Campbell, J. (1993) Culture and ideology in the translation of poetry. In Gambier and Tommola (eds).

Campbell, S. (1997) *Translation into the Second Language*. New York: Longman.

Camus, Albert (1988) *The Stranger* (trans. Matthew Ward).

Candlin, C.N. (1991) 'Preface' to Bell (1991).

Candlin, C.N. and Crichton, J. (eds) (2011) *Discourses of Deficit*. Basingstoke: Palgrave Macmillan.

Candlin, C.N. and Crichton, J. (eds) (forthcoming, 2012). *Discourses of Trust*. Basingstoke: Palgrave Macmillan.

Candlin, C.N. and Crichton, J. (eds) (in preparation). Discourse practices (Palgrave Advances in Linguistics). Basingstoke: Palgrave Macmillan.

Candlin, C.N. and Maley, Y. (1997) Intertextuality and interdiscursivity in the discourse of alternative dispute resolution. In Gunnarsson, B-L, Linnel, P., and Nordberg, B. (eds), pp. 201–22.

Candlin, C.N. and Sarangi, S. (2001) Motivational relevancies: some methodological reflections on sociolinguistic practice. In Coupland, Sirangi and Candlin (eds).

Candlin, C.N. and Sarangi, S. (2004) Making applied linguistics matter. *JAL*, 1 (1): 1–8.

Carr, W. and Kemmis, S. (1986) *Becoming Critical*. London: The Falmer Press.

Carter, R. and Nash, W. (1990) *Seeing Through Language*. Oxford: Basil Blackwell.

Carter, R., Goddard, A., Reah, D., Sanger, K., and Bowring, K. (2001) *Working with Texts: A Core Introduction to Language Analysis*. London & New York: Routledge.

Catford, J.C. (1965) *A Linguistic Theory of Translation*. London: OUP.

Chamberlain, L. (1988/2004) Gender and the metaphorics of translation, *Signs* 13: 45–72.

Chamberlain, L. (1992) Gender and the metaphorics of translation. In L. Venuti (ed.) pp. 61–2.

Chatman, S. (ed.) *Literary Style: A Symposium*. New York: Oxford University Press.

Chau, S. (1984) *Aspects of Translation Pedagogy: The Grammatical, Cultural and Interpretive Teaching Models*. PhD thesis, University of Edinburgh.

Chesterman, A. (ed.) (1989) *Readings in Translation*. Helsinki: Oy Finn Lectura Ab.

Chesterman, A. (1993) From 'is' to 'ought': Laws, norms and strategies in translation studies. *Target*, 5 (1): 1–20.

Chesterman, A. (1997) *Memes of Translation*. Amsterdam: John Benjamins.

Chomsky, N. (1957) *Syntactic Structures*. The Hague: Mouton.

Chomsky, N. (1965) *Aspects of the Theory of Syntax*. Cambridge, Mass.: MIT Press.

Chukovskii, K. (1984) *The Art of Translation* (trans. and ed. L.G. Leighton). Knoxville: University of Tennessee Press.

Coupland, N., Sarangi, S. and Candlin, C.N. (eds) (2001) *Sociolinguistics and Social Theory*. London: Pearson.

Crystal, D. (1981) *Directions in Applied Linguistics*. London: Academic Press.

Crystal, D. and Davy, D. (1969) *Investigating English Style*. London: Longman.

Davidson, D. and Harman, G. (eds) (1975) *The Logic of Grammar*. Encino, CA: Dickenson, pp. 64–75.

Davies, A. and Elder, C. (eds) (2004) *The Handbook of Applied Linguistics*. London: Blackwell.

Davies, M. and Ravelli, L. (1992) *Advances in Systemic Linguistics*. London: Frances Pinter.

Delisle, J. (1982) *L'analyse du discourscommeméthode de traduction*. Ottawa: University of Ottawa Press, Part I, trans. P. Logan and M. Creery (1988).

Delisle, J. (1988) *Translation: An Interpretive Approach*. Ottawa: University of Ottawa Press.

Delisle, J. (2002) *Portraits de traductrices*. Ottawa: Les Presses de l'Université d'Ottawa.

Derrida, J. (1981) *Positions*, trans. Alan Bass. Chicago: University of Chicago Press.

Devitt, A. (2004) *Writing Genres*. Carbondale: Southern Illinois University Press.

Diaz-Diocaretz, M. (1985) *Translating Poetic Discourse: Questions of Feminist Strategies in Adrienne Rich*. Amsterdam: John Benjamin.

Dijk, T. van (ed.) (1985) *Handbook of Discourse Analysis*, Vol. 4. London: Academic Press.

Dollerup, C. and Loddegaard, A. (Eds) (1992) *Teaching Translation and Interpreting 1: Training, Talent and Experience*. Amsterdam and Philadelphia: Benjamins.

Emery, P. (1991) Text classification and text analysis in advanced translation teaching. *Meta*, XXXVI (4): 567–77.

Enkvist, N.E., Spencer, J. and Gregory, M. (1964) *Linguistics and Style*. London: Oxford University Press.

Ericsson, K. and Simon, H. (1980) Verbal reports as data. *Psychological Review*, 87 (3): 215–51.

Ericsson, K. and Simon, H. (1984) *Protocol Analysis: Verbal Reports as Data*. Cambridge, Mass.: MIT Press.

Ericsson, K. and Simon, H. (1987) Verbal reports on thinking. In Faerch and Kasper (eds).

Even-Zohar, I. (1978a) *Papers in Historical Poetics*. Tel Aviv: Porter Institute for Poetics and Semiotics.

Even-Zohar, I. (1978b) The position of translated literature within the literary polysystem. In Holmes et al. (eds), pp. 117–27.

Faerch, K. and Kasper, G. (eds) (1987) *Introspection in Second Language Research*. Clevedon: Multilingual Matters.

Fairclough, N. (1989) *Language and Power*. London: Longman.

Fairclough, N. (1992) *Discourse and Social Change*. Cambridge: Polity Press.

Fairclough, N. (2003) *Analysing Discourse: Textual Analysis for Social Research*. London: Routledge.

Fawcett, P. (1995) Translation and power play. *The Translator*, 1 (2): 177–92.

Fawcett, P. (1997) *Translation and Language: Linguistic Theories Explained*. Manchester: St Jerome.

Fawcett, P. and Heathcote, O. (eds) (1990) *Translation in Performance: Papers on the Theory and Practice of Translation*. Bradford: University of Bradford.

Fawcett, P. and Munday, J. (2009) Ideology. In Baker and Saldanha (eds).

Fernandez Nistal, P. and Bravo Gonzalo, J.M. (eds) (1995) *Perspectivas de la tradución inglés-español*. Valladolid: Universidad de Valladolid.

Flotow, L. von (1991) Feminist translation: Contexts, practices, theories. *Traduction, Terminologie, Rédaction*, 4 (2): 69–84.

Flotow, L. von (1997) *Translation and Gender: Translating in the 'Era of Feminism'*. Manchester: St Jerome.

Foucault, M. (1977) What is an author? (trans. D. Bouchard and S. Simon). In Bouchard (ed.).

Fowler, R. (1985) Power. In van Dijk (ed.).

Fowler, R. (1986/1996) *Linguistic Criticism*. Oxford: Oxford University Press.

Fraser, J. (1993) Public accounts: Using verbal protocols to investigate community translation. *Applied Linguistics*, 14 (4): 325–43.

Fraser, J. (1994) Translating practice into theory: A practical study of quality in translator training. In Picken (ed.), pp. 130–42.

Fraser, J. (1996) The Translator Investigated: Learning from Translation Process Analysis. *The Translator*, 2 (1): 65–79.

Frow, J. (2006). *Genre*. London: Routledge.

Gaboriau, L. (1979) *A Clash of Symbols*. Toronto: The Coach House Press.

Gambier, Y. and Tommola, J. (Eds) (1993) *Translation and Knowledge: Proceedings of the 1992 Scandinavian Symposium on Translation Theory*. Turku: Tampere University Centre for Translation and Interpreting.

Gee, J. (1990) *Social Linguistics and Literacies: Ideology in Discourses*. London: Falmer Press.

Gellerstam, M. (1986) Translationese in Swedish novels translated from English. In Lars Wollin and Hans Lindquist (eds) *Translation Studies in Scandinavia: Proceedings from the Scandinavian Symposium on Translation Theory*. Lund: CWK Gleerup, pp. 88–95.

Gentile, A., Ozolins, U. and Vasilakakos, M. (eds) (1996) *Liaison Interpreting: A Handbook*. Melbourne: Melbourne University Press.

Gentzler, E. (1993) *Contemporary Translation Theories*. London and New York: Routledge.

Gerloff, P. (1988) *From French to English: A look at the translation process in students, bilinguals and professional translators*. Unpublished DEd thesis, Harvard University.

Ghadessy, M. (ed.) *Text and Context in Functional Linguistics*. Amsterdam/Philadelphia: Benjamins.

Gile, D. (1995) *Basic Concepts and Models for Interpreter and Translator Training*. Amsterdam and Philadelphia: John Benjamins.

Godard, B. (1984) Translating and sexual differences. *Resources for Feminist Research*, 13 (3): 13–16.

Godard, B. (1988) Preface. In *Lovhers*, by N. Brossard (trans. B. Godard). Montreal: Guernica Press.

Godard, B. (1990) Theorizing feminist theory/translation. In Bassnett and Lefevere (eds).

Goffman, E. (1981) *Forms of Talk*. Philadelphia: University of Pennsylvania Press.

Gollin, S. and Hall, D. (forthcoming) *Teaching and Researching Language for Specific Purposes*. London: Longman.

Grabe, W. and Stoller, F. (2002). *Teaching and Researching Reading*. Harlow, UK: Longman.

Graham, J.F. (ed.) (1985) *Difference in Translation*. Ithaca, NY: Cornell University Press.

Grice, H.P. (1975) Logic and Conversation. In D. Davidson and G. Harman (eds).

Gumperz, J. (1982) *Discourse Strategies*. Cambridge: Cambridge University Press.

Gunnarsson, B-L, Linnel, P., and Nordberg, B. (eds) *The Construction of Professional Discourse*. London: Longman.

Gutt, E. (1991) *Translation and Relevance: Cognition and Context*. Oxford: Blackwell.

Gutt, E. (1998) Pragmatic aspects of translation: Some Relevance-Theory observations. In Hickey (ed.), pp. 41–53.

Gutt, E.-A. (2000) Textual properties, communicative clues and the translator. In M. Pilar Navarro Errasti, Rosa Lores Sanz, Silvia Murillo Ornat and Carmina Buesa Gomez (eds) *Transcultural Communication: Pragmalinguistic Aspects*. Zaragoza: ANUBAR.

Gutt, E-A. (2005) On the significance of the cognitive core of translation, *The Translator* 11 (1): 25–49.

Hall and Kies (2012) *Language for Specific Purposes*. London: Palgrave Macmillan.

Halliday, M.A.K. (1971) Linguistic Function and Literary Style: An enquiry into the language of William Golding's 'The Inheritors'. In Seymour Chatman (ed.), pp. 362–400.

Halliday, M.A.K. (1978) *Language as Social Semiotic*. London: Arnold.

Halliday, M.A.K. (1985) *An Introduction to Functional Grammar* (1st edition). London: Arnold.

Halliday, M.A.K., McIntosh, A. and Strevens, P.D. (1964) *The Linguistic Sciences and Language Teaching*. London: Longman.

Harris, B. (1992) Natural translation: A reply to Hans P. Krings. *Target*, 4 (1): 97–103.

Hartmann, R.R.K. (2001) *Teaching and Researching Lexicography*. London: Longman.

Harvey, K. (1995) A descriptive framework for compensation. *The Translator*, 1 (1): 65–86.

Hasan, R. (1985) *Linguistics, Language & Verbal Art*. Deakin: Deakin University Press.

Hatim, B. (1988) The fuzzy nature of discourse in the translation process: Towards a text-based pedagogy of translation. In Anderman and Rogers (eds).

Hatim, B. (1997a) *Communication Across Cultures: Translation Theory and Contrastive Textlinguistics*. Exeter: Exeter University Press.

Hatim, B. (1997b) *English/Arabic/English Translation: A Practical Guide*. London: Saqi.

Hatim, B. (1998) Text Politeness: A semiotic regime for a more interactive pragmatics. In Hickey (ed.), pp. 72–102.

Hatim, B. and Mason, I. (1990) *Discourse and the Translator*. London: Longman.

Hatim, B. and Mason, I. (1992) Genre, discourse and text in the critique of translation. In Fawcett and Heathcote, pp. 1–13.

Hatim, B. and Mason, I. (1997) *The Translator as Communicator*. London and New York: Routledge.

Hatim, B., Shunnaq, A. and Watterson, G. (1996) *The Legal Translator at Work.* Amman: Al Hilal Publishing.

Henry, R. (1984) Points for inquiry into total translation: A review of J.C. Catford's *A Linguistic Theory of Translation. Meta*, 29 (2): 152–8.

Hermans, T. (1985a) Translation studies and a new paradigm. In Hermans (ed.), pp. 7–15.

Hermans, T. (ed.) (1985b) *The Manipulation of Literature: Studies in Literary Translation.* London: Croom Helm.

Hermans, T. (1991) Translational norms and correct translations. In Leuven-Zwart and Naaijkens (eds).

Hermans, T. (1995) Disciplinary objectives: The shifting grounds of translation studies. In Fernandez Nistal and Bravo Gonzalo (eds), pp. 9–26.

Hermans, T. (1999) *Translation in Systems: Descriptive and System-oriented Approaches Explained.* Manchester: St Jerome.

Hervey, S. and Higgins, I. (1992) *Thinking Translation: A Course in Translation Method: French to English.* London and New York: Routledge.

Hewson, L. and Martin, J. (1991) *Redefining Translation.* London and New York: Routledge.

Hewson, L. and Martin, J. (1995) From translation as product to translation as variation. In I. Mason and C. Pagnoulle (eds) *Crosswords: Issues and Debates in Literary and Non-literary Translating.* Liège: University of Liège.

Hickey, L. (ed.) (1998) *The Pragmatics of Translation.* Clevedon: Multilingual Matters.

Hjort, A.M. (1990) Translation and the consequences of scepticism. In Bassnett and Lefevere (eds), pp. 38–45.

Holmes, J.S. (1969) Forms of verse translation and the translation of verse form. *Babel* (Avignon), 15; reprinted in Holmes (1994), pp. 23–33.

Holmes, J.S. (1972a) The cross-temporal factor in verse translation. *Meta* (Montreal), 17; reprinted in Holmes (1994), pp. 35–44.

Holmes, J.S. (1972b) Rebuilding the Bridge at Bommel: Notes on the limits of translatability. *Dutch Quarterly Review of Anglo-American Letters* (Assen), 2; reprinted in Holmes (1994), pp. 45–52.

Holmes, J.S. (1978a) Describing literary translations: Models and methods. In James Holmes, Jose Lambert and Raymond van den Broeck (eds) *Literature and Translation: New Perspectives in Literary Studies*; reprinted in Holmes (1994), pp. 81–91.

Holmes, J.S. (1978b) The future of translation theory: A handful of theses. Paper presented at the International Symposium on Achievements in the Theory of Translation, 23–30 October (Moscow); reprinted in Holmes (1994), pp. 99–102.

Holmes, J.S. (1985) The state of two arts: Literary translation and translation studies in the West today. In Hildegund Bühler (ed.) *Translators and Their Position in Society* (Vienna: Braunmüller); reprinted in Holmes (1994), pp. 103–11.

Holmes, J.S. (1988a) Describing literary translations: Models and methods. In J.S. Holmes (ed.), pp. 80–91.

Holmes, J.S. (1988b) The Name and Nature of Translation Studies. In Holmes (ed.), pp. 67–80.

Holmes, J.S. (ed.) (1988) *Translated! Papers on Literary Translation and Translation Studies.* Amsterdam: Rodopi.

Holmes, J.S. (1994) *Translated.* Amsterdam & Atlanta: Rodopi.

Holmes, J.S., de Haan, F. and Popovic, A. (eds) (1970) *The Nature of Translation*. The Hague: Mouton.

Holmes, J.S., Lambert, J. and van den Broeck, R. (eds) (1978) *Literature and Translation: New Perspectives in Literary Studies with a Basic Bibliography of Books on Translation Studies*. Leuven: Acco.

Holz-Mänttäri, J. (1984) *Translatorisches Handeln: Theorie und Methode*. Helsinki: Suomalainen Tiedeakatemia.

Homel, D. and Simon, S. (1989) (eds) *Mapping Literature*. Montreal: Véhicule Press.

Horguelin, P. (ed.) *Translating, a Profession*. Proceedings of the Eighth World Congress of the International Federation of Translators. Paris: Fédération Internationale des Traducteurs. Ottawa: Conseil des Traducteurs et Interprètes du Canada.

Hörmann, H. (1976). Meinen und Verstehen. Frankfurt: Suhrkamp.

House, J. (1977) *A Model for Translation Quality Assessment* (2nd edition, 1981). Tübingen: Narr.

House, J. (1986) Acquiring translational competence in interaction. In House and Blum-Kulka (eds).

House, J. (1997) *Translation Quality Assessment: A Model Re-visited*. Tübingen: Narr.

House, J. (2007) Translation criticism: From linguistic description and explanation to social evaluation, in M.B. Papi, G. Cappelli and S. Masi (eds) *Lexical Complexity: Theoretical Assessment and Translational Perspectives*. Pisa: Pisa University Press, pp. 37–52.

House, J. (2009) *Translation*. Oxford: Oxford University Press.

House, J. and Blum-Kulka, S. (eds) (1986) *Interlingual and Intercultural Communication: Discourse and Cognition in Translation and Second Language Acquisition Studies*. Tübingen: Narr.

Jääskeläinen, R. (1989) Translation assignment in professional vs non-professional translation: A think-aloud protocol study. In Séguinot (ed.), pp. 87–98.

Jääskeläinen, R. (1993) Investigating translation strategies. In Sonja Tirkkonen-Condit and John Laffling (eds) *Recent Trends in Empirical Translation Research*. Studies in Languages, Joensuu, Finland.

Jakobson, R. (1959/2000) On linguistic aspects of translation. In L. Venuti (ed.) (2000), pp. 113–18.

James, C. (1980) *Contrastive Analysis*. London: Longman.

James, C. (1989) Genre analysis and the translator. *Target*, 1 (1): 29–41.

Johnson, B. (1985) Taking fidelity philosophically. In Graham (ed.).

Kade, O. (1968) *Zufall und Gesetzmassigkeit in der Übersetzung*. Leipzig: VEB Enzyklopadie.

Kelly, D., Martin, A., Nobs, M-L., Sanchez, D. and Way, C. (eds) (2003) *La direccionalidad en traduccion e interpretacion: perspectivas teoricas, profesionales y didacticas*. Granada: Atrio.

Kies, D. (1992) The Uses of Passivity: Suppressing Agency in Nineteen Eighty-Four, in M. Davies and L. Ravelli 1992, pp. 229–50.

Kiraly, D. (2005) Project-based learning: A case for situated translation, *Meta* 50 (4): 1098–111.

Kinloch, D. (2007) Lilies or skelfs: Translating queer melodrama, *The Translator* 13 (1): 83–103.

Koller, W. (1979) *Einführung in die Übersetzungwissenschaft. Heidelberg*: Quelle & Meyer.

Koller, W. (1989) Equivalence in translation theory (trans. A. Chesterman). In A. Chesterman (ed.), pp. 99–104.

Koller, W. (1995) The concept of equivalence and the object of translation studies. *Target*, 7 (2): 191–222.

Konigs, F.G. (1987) Was beim Übersetzen passiert? *Die neueren Sprachen*, 86 (2): 162–85.

Kress, G. (1985) *Linguistic Processes in Sociocultural Practice*. Victoria: Deakin University Press.

Krings, H.P. (1987) The use of introspective data in translation. In Faerch and Kasper (eds), pp. 159–76.

Kuhiwczak, P. (1990) Translation as appropriation: The case of Milan Kundera's *The Joke*. In Bassnett and Lefevere (eds), pp. 118–30.

Kundera, M. (1969) *The Joke* (trans. D. Hamblym and O. Stallybrass). London: Macdonald & Co.

Kundera, M. (1988) Key words, problem words, words I love. *The New York Times Book Review*, 6 March, 1, 24–6.

Ladmiral, J.-R. (1979) *Traduire: theorèmes pour la traduction*. Paris: Payot.

Lane-Mercier, C. (1997) Translating the untranslatable: The translator's aesthetic. Ideological and political responsibility. *Target*, 9 (1): 43–68.

Larose, R. (1989) *Theories contemporaines de la traduction* (2nd edition). Quebec: Presses de l'Universite du Quebec.

Lauer, A., Gerzymisch-Arbogast, H., Haller, J. and Steiner, E. (eds) (1996) *Übersetzungswissenschaft im Umbruch. Festschrift für Wilss zum 70. Geburtstag*. Tübingen: Narr.

Laviosa-Braithwaite, S. (1997) *The English Comparable Corpus (ECC): A resource and a methodology for the empirical study of translation*. PhD thesis, UMIST, Manchester.

Leech, G. (1983) *Principles of Pragmatics*. London: Longman.

Lefevere, A. (1985) Why waste our time on re-writes? The trouble with interpretation and the role of rewriting in an alternative paradigm. In Hermans (ed.).

Lefevere, A. (1990) Translation: Its genealogy in the West. In Bassnett and Lefevere (eds).

Lefevere, A. (1992) *Translation, Rewriting and the Manipulation of the Literary Frame*. London and New York: Routledge.

Leuven-Zwart, K.M. van (1989) Translation and original: Similarities and dissimilarities, I. In *Target*, 1 (2): 151–81.

Leuven-Zwart, K. van and Naaijkens, T. (eds) (1991) *Translation Studies: The State of the Art*. Amsterdam: Rodopi.

Levine, S.J. (1983) Translation as (sub) version: On translating Infante's *Inferno*. *SubStance*, 42: 85–94.

Levine, S.J. (1991) *The Subversive Scribe: Translating Latin American Fiction*. Minneapolis: Greywolf Press.

Levy, J. (1969) *Die Literarische Übersetzung: Theorie einer Kunstgattung*. Frankfurt am Main: Athenaum.

Lörscher, W. (1991a) *Translation Performance, Translation Process, and Translation Strategies: A Psycholinguistic Investigation*. Tübingen: Narr.

Lörscher, W. (1991b) Investigating the translation process. *Interface*, 6 (1): 3–22.

Lörscher, W. (1993) Translation process analysis. In Y. Gambier and J. Tommola (eds) *Translation and Knowledge: Proceedings of the 1992 Scandinavian Symposium on Translation Theory*. Turku: Centre for Translation and Interpreting, University of Turku.

Lotbinière-Harwood, S. de (1991) *Re-Belle est Infidèle. La Traduction comme pratique de réécriture au féminin (The Body Bilingual. Translation as a Rewriting in the Feminine).* Toronto and Montreal: The Women's Press.

Lotbinière-Harwood, S. de (1995) Geo-graphies of Why. In S. Simon (ed.) *Culture in Transit: Translating the Literature of Quebec.* Montreal: Véhicule Press.

McAlister, G. (1992) Teaching Translation into a Foreign Language – Status, Scope and Aims. In Dollerup and Loddegaard (eds), pp. 291–8.

McDonough, J. and McDonough, S. (1997) *Research Methods for English Language Teachers.* London: Arnold.

Maccura, V. (1990) Culture as Translation. In Bassnett and Lefevere (eds), pp. 64–70.

McLuhan, (1970) From *Cliché to Achetype.* New York: Viking Press.

Malmkjaer, K. (1992) Review of *Translation and Relevance* by E.A. Gutt. *Mind and Language,* 7 (3): 298–309.

Malmkjaer, K. (1993) Who Can Make *Nice* a Better Word than *Pretty?* Collocation, Translation and Psycholinguistics. In Baker et al. (eds).

Martin, J.R. (1991) Intrinsic functionality: implications for contextual theory. *Social Semiotics* 1 (1): 99–162.

Mason, I. (1982) The role of translation theory in the translation class. *Quinquereme,* 5 (1): 18–33.

Mason, I. (1994) Discourse, ideology and translation. In R. Beaugrande, A. Shunnaq and M. Heliel (eds), pp. 23–34.

Mason, I. and Pagnoulle, C. (eds) (1995) *Cross-words: Issues and Debates in Literary and Non-literary Translation.* Liege: English Department, University of Liege.

Massadier-Kenny, F. (1997) Towards a Redefinition of Feminist Translation Practice. *The Translator,* 1: 55–69.

Moore, A., Candlin C.N. and Plum, G. (2001) Making sense of viral load: one expert or two?, *Culture, Health & Sexuality,* 3 (4): 429–50.

Munday, J. (2001) *Introducing Translation Studies: Theories and Applications.* London & New York: Routledge.

Neubert, A. (1984) Text-bound Translation Teaching. In Wilss and Thome (eds), pp. 61–70.

Neubert, A. (1994) Competence in translation: A complex skill, how to study and how to teach it. In Snell-Hornby et al. (eds), pp. 411–20.

Neubert, A. and Shreve, G.M. (1992) *Translation as Text.* Kent, Ohio: The Kent State University Press.

Newmark, P. (1981) *Approaches to Translation.* Oxford: Pergamon.

Newmark, P. (1984/5) Literal Translation. *Paralleles,* 7.

Newmark, P. (1988) *A Textbook of Translation.* Hemel Hempstead: Prentice Hall.

Newmark, P. (1993) *Paragraphs on Translation.* Clevedon: Multilingual Matters.

Nida, E.A. (1964) *Towards a Science of Translating.* Leiden: Brill.

Nida, E.A. (1969/1989) Science of translation. In Chesterman (ed.), pp. 80–98.

Nida, E. (1979) A framework for the analysis and evaluation of theories of translation. In Richard W. Brislin (ed.) *Translation: Applications and Research.* New York: Gardner Press, pp. 47–91.

Nida, E.A. and Taber, C. (1969) *The Theory and Practice of Translation.* Leiden: Brill.

Niranjana, T. (1992) *Siting Translation: History, Post-structuralism, and the Colonial Context.* Berkeley, Calif.: University of California Press.

Nord, C. (1991a) *Text Analysis in Translation: Theory, Methodology, and Didactic Application of a Model for Translation-Oriented Text Analysis*. Amsterdam and Atlanta: Rodopi.

Nord, C. (1991b) Skopos, loyalty and translational conventions. *Target*, 3 (1): 91–109.

Nord, C. (1992) Text analysis in translator training. In Dollerup and Loddegaard (eds).

Nord, C. (1997) *Translating as a Purposeful Activity: Functionalist Approaches Explained*. Manchester: St Jerome.

Nunan, D. (1992) *Research Methods in Language Learning*. Cambridge: Cambridge University Press.

Nystrand, M. (ed.) (1982) *What Writers Know: The Language, Process and Structures of Written Discourse*. New York: Academic Press.

Paizis, G. (1998) Category romances – Translation, realism and myth. *The Translator*, 1: 1–24.

Pan, F.K. (1977) Towards a formal training program. In T.C. Lai (ed.) *The Art and Profession of Translation: Proceedings of the Asia Foundation Conference on Chinese-English Translation*. Hong Kong.

Peirce, C.S. (1982) *The Writings of Charles S. Peirce: A Chronological Edition*. Volumes 1–6. And 8. Eds. Peirce Edition Project. Bloomington, Ind.: Indiana University Press.

Picken, C. (1983) *The Translator's Handbook* (2nd edition, 1989). London: Aslib.

Picken, C. (ed.) (1994) *ITI Conference 7 Proceedings*. London: Institute of Translation and Interpreting.

Popovic, A. (1970) The concept 'shift of expression' in translation analysis. In Holmes et al. (eds), pp. 78–87.

Pym, A. (1992a) Translation error analysis and the interface with language teaching. In Dollerup and Loddegaard (eds), pp. 279–88.

Pym, A. (1992b) The relation between translation and material text transfer. *Target*, 4 (2): 171–89.

Pym, A. (1995a) European translation studies, *une science qui dérange*, and Why equivalence needn't be a dirty word. *Traduction, Terminologie, Rédaction*, 8 (1): 153–76.

Pym, A. (1995b) Doubts about deconstruction as a general theory of translation. *TradTerm*, 2: 11–18.

Pym, A. (1996) Review article: Venuti's visibility. *Target*, 8 (1): 165–77.

Pym, A. (1997) Koller's *Äquivalenz* Revisited. *The Translator*, 3 (1): 71–9.

Qian Hu (1992a) On the implausibility of equivalence response (Part I). *Meta* 37 (2): 289–301.

Qian Hu (1992b) On the implausibility of equivalence response (Part II). *Meta* 37 (3): 491–506.

Qian Hu (1993) On the implausibility of equivalence response (Part III). *Meta* 38 (2): 226–237.

Qian Hu (1994) On the implausibility of equivalence response (Part V). *Meta* 39 (3): 418–32.

Reiss, K. (1971) *Möglichkeiten und Grenzen der Übersetzungskritik: Kategorien und Kriterien für eine sachgerechte Beurteilung von Übersetzungen*. [*Possibilities and Limitations of Translation Criticism: Categories and Criteria for a Fair Evaluation of Translations*]. Munich: Hueber.

Reiss, K. (1989) Was heisst und warum betreibt man Übersetzungswissenschaft? *Lebende Sprachen*, 34 (3): 97–100.

Reiss, K. (1977/89) Text types, translation types and translation assessment (trans. A. Chesterman). In A. Chesterman (ed.), pp. 105–15.

Reiss, K. and Vermeer, H.J. (1984) *Grundlegung einer allgemeinen Translationstheorie.* [*Groundwork for a General Theory of Translation*]. Tübingen: Niemeyer.

Richards, I.A. (1953) Toward a Theory of Translating. In Wright (ed.), pp. 247–62.

Roberts, C. and Sarangi, S. (2003) Uptake of Discourse Research in Interprofessional Settings: Reporting from Medical Consultancy, *Applied Linguistics* 24 (3): 338–59.

Robinson, D. (1991) *The Translator's Turn.* Baltimore and London: The Johns Hopkins University Press.

Rorty, R. (1982) *Consequences of Pragmatism.* Minneapolis: University of Minnesota Press.

Sacks, O. (1970/1985) *The Man Who Mistook His Wife For A Hat and Other Clinical Tales.* New York: Simon & Schuster.

Santaemilia, Jose (2005) *Gender, Sex and Translation: The Manipulation of Identities.* Manchester: St Jerome.

Sarangi, S. and Candlin, C.N. (2001) Motivational relevancies: some methodological reflections on sociolinguistic practice. In N. Coupland, S. Sarangi and C.N. Candlin (eds).

Sarangi, S. and Candlin, C.N. (2003) Trading between reflexivity and relevance: new challenges for applied linguistics. Editorial. Special Issue of *Applied Linguistics* 24 (3): 271–85.

Sarangi, S. (2004) Mediated interpretation of hybrid textual environments. Editorial. *Text* 24 (3): 297–301.

Schäffner, C. (1999) (ed.) *Translation and Norms.* Clevedon: Multilingual Matters.

Schleiermacher, F. (1813/1992) On the different methods of translating. In R. Schulte and J. Biguenet (eds), pp. 36–54.

Séguinot, C. (1989a) The translation process: An experimental study. In Séguinot (ed.).

Séguinot, C. (ed.) (1989b) *The Translation Process.* Toronto: HG Publications.

Séguinot, C. (1991) A study of student translation strategies. In Tirkkonen-Condit (ed.).

Sengupta, M. (1990) Translation, colonialism and poetics: Rabindranath Tagore in two worlds. In Bassnett and Lefevere (eds), pp. 56–63.

Schön, D. (1983) *The Reflective Practitioner. How professionals think in action*, London: Temple Smith.

Shamaa, N. (1978) *A linguistics analysis of some problems of Arabic to English translation.* Unpublished PhD dissertation, Oxford University.

Sell, R.D. (1992) *Literary Pragmatics.* London and New York: Routledge.

Shlesinger, M. (1989) Extending the theory of translation to interpretation: Norms as a case in point. *Target*, 1 (1): 111–15.

Shlesinger, M. (1991) Interpreter latitude vs due process. Simultaneous and consecutive interpretation in multilingual trials. In Tirkkonen-Condit (ed.).

Shlesinger, M. (1995) Shifts in cohesion in simultaneous interpreting. *The Translator*, 1 (2): 193–214.

Shuttleworth, M. and Cowie, M. (1997) *Dictionary of Translation Studies.* Manchester: St Jerome.

Simon, S. (1996) *Gender in Translation: Cultural Identity and the Politics of Transmission.* London and New York: Routledge.

Simpson, P. (1993) *Ideology and Point of View.* London: Routledge.

Snell-Hornby, M. (1988) *Translation Studies: An Integrated Approach.* Amsterdam: John Benjamins.

Snell-Hornby, M., Pochhacker, F. and Kaindl, K. (eds) (1994) *Translation Studies: An Interdiscipline*. Amsterdam: John Benjamins.

Somers, H. (ed.) *Technology, LSP and Translation: Studies in Language Engineering, in Honour of Juan C. Sager*. Amsterdam and Philadelphia: John Benjamins Publishing Company.

Sperber, D. and Wilson, D. (1986) *Relevance: Communication and Cognition*. Oxford: Blackwell.

Spivak, G. (1993/2000) The politics of translation, in L. Venuti (ed.), pp. 397–416.

Stecconi, U. (1994/1999) Peirce's Semiotics for Translation Teaching, *Koine* (4): 161–80.

Steiner, G. (1975) *After Babel*. Oxford: Oxford University Press.

Swales, J.M. (1991) *Genre Analysis*. Cambridge: Cambridge University Press.

Swales, J.M. (2004). *Research Genres: Explorations and Applications*. Cambridge: Cambridge University Press.

Thompson, G. (1996) *Introducing Functional Grammar*. London: Arnold.

Thompson, G. (1999) Acting the part. Lexico-grammatical choices and contextual factors. In M. Ghadessy (ed.), pp. 101–24.

Tirkkonen-Condit, S. (1992) A theoretical account of translation – without translation theory. *Target*, 4 (2): 237–45.

Tirkkonen-Condit, S. (ed.) (1991) *Empirical Research in Translation and Intercultural Studies*. Tübingen: Gunter Narr.

Tirkkonen-Condit, S. and Laffling, J. (Eds) (1993) *Recent Trends in Empirical Translation Research*. Joensuu: University of Joensuu, Faculty of Arts.

Toolan, M. (1992) *Language Text and Context: Essays in Stylistics*. London and New York: Routledge.

Toury, G. (1980) *In Search of a Theory of Translation*. Tel Aviv: The Porter Institute for Poetics and Semiotics, Tel Aviv University.

Toury, G. (1982) The communication situation and the production of interference forms by L2 learners. *RELC Journal*, 13 (2): 62–77.

Toury, G. (1985) A rationale for descriptive translation studies. In Hermans (ed.), pp. 16–41.

Toury, G. (1991) What are descriptive studies into translation likely to yield apart from isolated descriptions? In Leuven-Zwart and Naaijkens (eds), pp. 179–92.

Toury, G. (1995) *Descriptive Translation Studies and Beyond*. Amsterdam and Philadelphia: John Benjamins.

Tymoczko, M. (1990) Translation in oral tradition as a touchstone for translation theory and practice. In Bassnett and Lefevere (eds), pp. 46–55.

Vanderauwera, R. (1985) *Dutch Novels Translated into English: The Transformation of a Minority Literature*. Amsterdam: Rodopi.

Venuti, L. (ed.) (1992) *Rethinking Translation: Discourse, Subjectivity, Ideology*. London and New York: Routledge.

Venuti, L. (1995) *The Translator's Invisibility: A History of Translation*. London and New York: Routledge.

Venuti, L. (1998) American Tradition. In M. Baker and K. Malmkjaer (eds) *Routledge Encyclopedia of Translation Studies*. London & New York: Routledge, pp. 305–16.

Venuti, L. (ed.) (2000) *The Translation Studies Reader*. New York and London: Routledge.

Vermeer, H. (1989) Skopos and commission in translational action (trans. A. Chesterman). In Chesterman (ed.), pp. 173–87.

Vermeer, H. (1989/1992) *Skopos und Translationsauftrag – Aufsätze*. Frankfurt am Main: IKO.

Vinay, J.P. and Darbelnet, J. (1958, 2nd edition 1977) *Stylistique comparée du français et de l'anglais: Méthode de traduction*, Paris: Didier, trans. and ed. J. Sager, and M.-J. Hamel (1995) as *Comparative Stylistics of French and English: A Methodology for Translation*. Amsterdam and Philadelphia: John Benjamins.

Walkerden, G. (2009) Researching and developing practice traditions using reflective practice experiments. *Qual Quant*, 43: 249–63.

Werlich, E. (1976) *A Text Grammar of English*. Heidelberg: Quelle & Meyer.

Widdowson, H. (1979) *Explorations in Applied Linguistics*. Oxford: Oxford University Press.

Wilkinson, R. (1990) Information structure variability: Translating into the foreign language. In Anderman and Rogers (eds).

Williams, J. and Chesterman, A. (2002) *The Map: A Beginner's Guide to Doing Research in Translation Studies*. Manchester: St. Jerome Publishing.

Wilson, A. (2004) When contextualization cues mislead: Misunderstanding, mutual knowledge, and non-verbal gestures. *California Linguistic Notes*, Volume XXIX No. 1 Summer, 2004.

Wilss, W. (1982) *The Science of Translation: Problems and Methods*. Tübingen: Narr.

Wilss, W. (1994) A framework for decision-making in translation. *Target*, 6 (2): 131–50.

Wilss, W. and Thome, G. (eds) (1984) *Translation Theory and Its Implementation in the Teaching of Translating & Interpreting*. Tübingen: Narr.

Wright, A.F. (ed.) (1953) *Studies in Chinese Thought*. Chicago: University of Chicago Press.

Zlateva, P. (1990) Translation: Text and pre-text. 'Adequacy' and 'acceptability' in crosscultural communication. In Bassnett and Lefevere (eds), pp. 29–37.

Zyadatiss, W. (1983) Text type oriented contrastive linguistics and its implications for translation pedagogy at university level. *IRAL*, 20 (3): 175–91.

Index